To Claudia —

Warm regards —

Also by Hugh Best

Spirit of a Century

Red Hot & Blue:
An X-Rated History of the American Revolution

Debrett's Texas Peerage

Thunderbird Country Club

ADVENTURES
IN THE
PEN TRADE

HUGH
BEST

GATEWAY PRESS, INC.
Baltimore, MD   1999

Please direct all correspondence and book orders to:

Hugh Best
502 Chestnut Lane
Wayne, PA 19087

ISBN 0-9668213-0-0

Library of Congress Catalog Card Number 98-75591

Published for the author by

Gateway Press, Inc.
1001 N. Calvert Street
Baltimore, Maryland 21202-3897

Printed in the United States of America

For our grandchildren...

Trey, John, Katie, Henry
and Joseph Hugh, all Best!

Contents

Illustrations

ADVENTURES
IN THE
PEN TRADE

IT BEGAN WITH CLARK GABLE

Until that summer of '35, when I met Clark Cable making MUTINY ON THE BOUNTY, the only celebrity I had seen in my 15 years growing up in Rome, Georgia was Buster Brown with his tiny bulldog, Tyge.

Buster was a breezy midget in a little boy's "best suit." He wore sort of a mini-Norfolk jacket combined with an Eton collar, flowing bow tie, Tam O'Shanter beret, knickerbockers, cotton stockings and, of course, Buster Brown Shoes, the product he and his little runny-nosed, flatulent, fangs-baring bulldog advertised. Buster and Tyge's picture inside each Buster Brown Shoe is what made them so special to boys and girls of that day. To see Buster in the flesh was a thrill.

Later, another "advertising" midget came to town wearing a bellboy costume, walking down Broad Street shouting (CALL FOR PHILIP MORRIS!!!). He also handed out samples of Philip Morris cigarettes. That was after I had traveled clear across the United States and Canada on The Georgia Caravans travel camp.

It was GRAPES OF WRATH-time, but we coed campers certainly didn't travel Okie-style through the Dust Bowl on our trek to California.

We were ensconced in ten custom-made buses, each carrying twenty passengers. Every bus had its own kitchen galley, complete with chef. Meals were passed down the aisle to us as we zoomed down the highways. We ate off trays that folded down from the backs of facing seats.

Our bus not only had its driver and chef, but a baggage boy to load and unload our special-designed tan-canvas luggage, folding cots-and sleeping bags.

We would usually camp out in the open under starry skies around a campfire, singing songs, roasting wieners and trying to "make time" with one of the beauties aboard. During the day, males and females were segregated to separate buses, and CERTAINLY during sleeping time. Even though our counselors stressed that "this is not a courting caravan," every night or so "an old buckaroo would oodle-oodle-oo as she lay sleeping." All innocent fun.

Since this was to be our "adventure of a lifetime," exploring Canada's Rockies, Grand Canyon, Yosemite, Glacier, Indian reservations, deserts, the West Coast and HOLLYwood, I decided to keep a journal. Didn't Admiral Byrd when he set off for the South Pole?

Little did I dream that I would encounter Admiral Richard Byrd himself during our two-week stint in Los Angeles, along with Clark Gable, Errol Flynn, Olivia de Haviland, Al Jolson and just about everybody-who-was-anybody in the movie capital that summer.

Master-mind of The Caravans was wheeler-dealer "Mr. Rose." This man would stop at nothing to have celebrities play host to us two hundred-plus "prominent" youth from the South. For instance, the mayor of Memphis, or Vancouver, would send out motorcycle escorts to meet us at the city limits to parade us through the main streets to the city park or college campus where we would pitch tent for the night. Being from Atlanta, naturally Coca Cola bottlers had been told to have "Coke parties" in our honor, inviting local "prominent" teenagers to come meet their peers from

Piedmont Driving Club territory.

When we heard that our leader Rose had lassoed President and Mrs. Herbert Hoover into inviting us for tea on their roof garden atop the President's Mansion at Stanford University in Palo Alto, everyone agreed that "Rose must have brass balls."

Then, when he engineered it so that movie stars would invite us for "sho-nuff Georgia watermelon cuttings" at their homes, we knew that Rose not only had brass balls, but gold-plated ones, at that.

However, a privileged four of us didn't need Mr. Rose when it came to meeting "stars." We had our families' friend, fellow Georgia native Nunnally Johnson, writer-producer extraordinaire at Twentieth Century Fox. Witty playwright, Saturday Evening Post regular, former newspaper man, Nunnally had made it big in the movies. His GRAPES OF WRATH and WORLD OF HENRY ORIENT are considered film classics. Nunnally could command any studio to open the gates to us four, and he did. His daughter Marjorie was our age so she and her pals partied us all the way from her daddy's Del Mar Club on the beach at Santa Monica to the St. Catherine Hotel on Catalina island. Here, Clark Gable was on location filming MUTINY ON THE BOUNTY. We arrived late, just as Clark was finishing for the day.

"You missed the action!" he greeted, flashing a bemused smile. "We were expecting you earlier." Then, pointing to the patch of beach where cameras were set up. "This is supposed to be Tahiti."

We were so awed we could hardly speak. Later, however, I did ask him as he signed an autograph for me: "Do people like us follow you around?"

Looking at me straight in the eyes, he replied: "Tonight at the hotel, check up on me at dinner. You can see for yourself."

We were in the dining room early, and so was he...to avoid the crowd. He looked great, all showered and polished after sweating on the set. Wearing a freshly pressed white linen suit, he fairly sparkled. He sat dining alone at a corner table ... well, not quite alone, for a small crowd had gathered to watch him eat! His corner had been roped off to keep oglers from mobbing him, and probably snatching the knife and fork out of his hands to take home as a souvenir.

Clark seemed to take it all in stride, and when he saw me, he nodded in the direction of the onlookers and winked.

I winked back knowingly.

Later, in the hotel lobby, we were introduced to Al Jolson and his bride, Ruby Keeler, along with Jack Kirkland author of the hit play about Georgia white trash TOBACCO ROAD.

"We're not all like that in Georgia, Mr. Kirkland," I told him.

After that "spotting stars" became a sport with us Caravaners. Like keeping score of animals seen on an African safari after each day's game run. We would plop onto our cots at bedtime, each camper out-bragging the other.

"Guess who waved at me today on Hollywood and Vine: JEAN HARLOW! Gorgeous! Driving a red Dusenberg convertible. Her hair was real platinum, too, and she wore a low-cut satin dress with white dots. She was just great!" one would tell you.

"That's nothing. At Twentieth century Fox I met a really cute new star named Betty Grable ... and she kissed me on the lips ... full. Boy, did she have hot lips!" I replied.

One day at Paramount Studios, after watching Margaret Sullavan and Randolph Scott filming SO RED THE ROSE, I strayed away from my companions to get a thick milk shake and hot dog in the studio's commissary. Carrying a tray with my lunch from the counter, looking for a place to sit, I spied a booth occupied by only one person, a man in a khaki uniform. I thought he might be a Boy Scout master, so I approached him with "May I share your table? I'm a Scout, member of the Galloping Ghost Patrol, Rome, Georgia."

It turned out that he was a Navy officer, not a Scout master, inviting me to join him saying "Rome, Georgia! I have a friend from Rome, Georgia. Andy Cooper, do you know him?"

Of course I knew Mister Cooper who lived on East 9th Street and had three daughters Nancy, Alice and Anita, all pals of mine. I felt right at home with this nice man, for he had a Southern accent, too. Said he was from Virginia, knew Cooper at Pensacola Navy Air Base. In the course of our conversation I asked what he was doing at Paramount (still thinking he was a Scout master).

"We're making a film about our experiences exploring Antarctica."

"Wow, what's it called?"

"Temporary title is WITH BYRD AT THE SOUTH POLE."

Realizing I had to hurry and join my friends back at the set, I bid my new friend goodbye.

"Tell Andy that Dick Byrd sends greetings!" he called. Then I looked at him closely. Gosh. This man wasn't a scout master. He was ADMIRAL RICHARD BYRD.

By the time I returned to Rome, Admiral Byrd, Clark Gable and most top Hollywood were my new best friends (to hear me tell it.)

And tell it I did, thanks to the editor of the local newspaper ROME NEWS TRIBUNE. Since he was a friend of my family, I had asked him about the possibilities of my writing a story about my trip to Hollywood. He seemed highly amused at my name-dropping, especially that I had met Clark Gable, the king himself.

It so happened that the editor's daughter would be on

vacation from her chores as film critic, so I could take a whack at writing her column SCREENINGS. He felt that readers would be mightily impressed with a columnist who had just returned from meeting Clark Gable in Hollywood.

Soon I found how much fun it was to be a published writer.

Thanks to Clark Cable, my adventures in the "pen trade" had begun.

THEN CAME THE SIAMESE TWINS

I discovered early in the game that one of the great joys in journalism is people-meeting. I couldn't have Nunnally Johnson along to provide introductions and open doors, but I did have my newspaper credentials. So when a "celebrity" would come to Rome, whether in a vaudeville act or to see a cousin, all it took was a phone call from the Rome News-Tribune and... "open Sesame!"

That is how I got to meet Roy Rogers and the Siamese twins.

My movie column, SCREENINGS, not only provided me with free passes to the Rivoli, Desoto and Gordon picture shows, it also allowed me to go back-stage and interview the stars of the acts out front. In SCREENINGS, I made a point of "localizing" every movie I possibly could to make it more personal for my readers. I would try to emphasize "the Rome connection." Sample: "Rome's-own Edith Sayre had a special interest in THREE COMRADES, currently playing at the Desoto. The MGM film starring Robert Taylor, Margaret Sullavan and Franchot Tone, was written for the screen by F. Scott Fitzgerald, husband of her sister-in-law the former Zelda Sayre, of Montgomery."

After giving it the home-town touch, I would then go into my critique.

My mother's bridge-playing pals were constantly amazed

and amused at my deep knowledge of film folk. Little did they know that from the age of five I probably hadn't missed a flick in town, thanks to my nurse and pal, Ninny. While Mama (who Ninny called Miss Liza) was off to a bridge luncheon, Ninny and I would hitch up my pony Mickey, hop into our little British wicker pony cart, and off we'd dash to the Rivoli. We'd be home before Mama had collected her winnings at the bridge table, and she'd never dream what we'd been doing. Besides, it only cost a dime to see the show, and since Ninny could carry me in, children in arms didn't have to pay. That is why it was easy for me later to write knowledgeably about Douglas Fairbank's interpretation of ROBIN HOOD compared to Errol Flynn playing the same role many years later. Of course, when I mentioned "Errol Flynn," I usually made some reference to the fact that I had seen him filming on the set at Warner Brothers Studios when I was "last, in Hollywood." Of course "last" was my first-and-only ... but what the heck?

As a tot, not only would I see the movie, I would usually come home and act out the part that impressed me most ... and, believe me, I was most impressionable.

After TARZAN OF THE APES, I would dash for the woods nearby, throw off my clothes, and in my little knit underpants, climb a tree, hoping to find a vine to swing from, and maybe grab an ape along the way. Sometimes, I'd convince my neighbor Ella Jane, to strip to her underpants, too, and play "Jane."

Ninny and I had great fun driving Mickey around town. My Daddy adored horses and bought me, his first child, a pony as soon as I could walk to the stable. Along with Mickey-the-pony came an open wicker two-seater cart featuring a huge Japanese lacquered parasol to cover us from the scalding Georgia summer sun. Consequently, we were quite a sight as we jogged along over the seven hills of Rome.

That's how Rome got its name ... because it, too, had seven hills like that other Rome, in Italy. Mussolini even made us a "sister city" and presented our Rome with an exact bronze replica of Romulus and Remus suckling a wolf. When a hillbilly woman saw it unveiled, she spit out a wad of tobacco exclaiming loudly "Them little boys ain't got no pants on." Her husband poked her whispering "Hush, woman. That's how you know them are boys."

My pony Mickey not only provided me transportation around town, he also played "Tony" to my "Tom Mix." After seeing cowboy star Tom Mix and his faithful horse Tony in their latest Western, I would dash home, don my little cowboy suit, hop onto Mickey's back and gallop over "the range" (a mound of red dirt left over from an excavation down our street.)

During these cowboy forays, my neighborhood cronies had to assume the roles of Indian savages on foot, since they didn't have a horse. Sometimes I would let Ella Jane Maroney play Billie Dove's part, for I thought Billie Dove was the most beautiful star on the screen. Besides, Ella Jane was easy for the "Indians" to capture so I would have someone to "free" from a fate worse than death.

Thanks to Mickey and my pony cart, I had a set on-the-ready for my starring role. When I became Buddy Rogers in WINGS, I used the cart as cockpit for my World War I fighter plane, erecting a machine gun, made from a discarded carpet tube, on the rear.

Fifty years later I was to meet both Billie and Buddy in Palm Springs and they still looked wonderful. But I never came even close to Tom Mix.

However, I did catch a glimpse of Colonel Tim McKoy when he came to town with Barnum and Bailey Circus. Daddy loved to watch the circus unload, so he would wake me up at dawn, and I would tag along shivering with cold and slightly sick-at-stomach with excitement. We would go down to the railroad station and stand by quietly as elephants and horses descended one by one from their garishly-colored freight cars. Down the tracks I heard bystanders clapping and cheering. Word passed down the line that Colonel Tim McKoy had arrived. The Colonel had fought in the U.S. Cavalry with my friend Nick Featherstone's step-father, and Nick's parents were entertaining him at a cocktail party after his performance that afternoon. Somehow, I talked Nick into spying on the action with me, perched on the roof of his garage.

With such an illustrious background in movie Westerns, I could really "talk shop" with Roy Rogers when he came to the Gordon Theater plugging his first starring musical Western, UNDER WESTERN STARS. Trigger, his horse, had evidently been left "back at the ranch," but Roy did bring along his "gee-tar" to sing about tumbleweeds and bein' in the saddle under starry skies above.

Roy, having been born in Duck Run, Ohio, probably hadn't seen a saddle pre-Hollywood, but he sure did look good in those tight cowboy pants. After my interview, to be featured in a forthcoming SCREENINGS, I ran into Ella Jane waiting at the stage door to get Roy's autograph.

"Ella Jane. What are you doing here? I asked, then a senior in high school." I didn't know you were a cowboy fan."

"Well, to tell the truth," she blushed. "I heard Roy sing on the radio and kind of wondered what he looked like. So I caught his act at The Gordon, and I think he is a dreamboat. I just love the really sincere way he crinkles his eyes, and I don't know if you noticed or not, but he has the cutest fanny I ever saw on a man." It made me wonder what my fanny looked like...but then, I didn't even own a pair of tight cowboy jeans.

The Gordon had another act, later, so sensational that my reportage of it catapulted me from inside-column to front-page feature story headlined "World-famed Siamese Twins Visit Rome." The twins, Daisy and Violet Hilton, were joined at the hip, but they didn't let that impediment hold them down. They were early believers in "if you've got it, flaunt it." Born in Brighton, England, they were "groomed for the stage" at an early age. They learned to play the saxophone and sing duets, accompanying themselves on the accordion. They would glide onto the stage sideways, swinging and swaying smartly in sort of a subtle soft-shoe routine, tooting their horns with a flourish. No one cared if they had talent. Just to see them was enough. They wore low-bodiced satin evening gowns one plain, one flounced, to de-emphasize they were all-in-one. They must have had a wow of a dress designer.

Audiences gave them encore after encore for they loved to watch them bow, which they made in perfect tandem, naturally.

My reporter friends made up all kinds of stories about Daisy and Violet's love life.

One said that Daisy had a lover, and every time he made love to her, it was Violet who kept sighing "Ahhh." I just couldn't imagine what they would do on their honeymoon. Golly, it would be hard enough just going to the john.

However, I'm most indebted to those joined British twins for providing me with the story that led to my promotion as Feature Editor. I not only got free tickets to the movies with my column, now I pocketed $18 a week as both columnist and feature editor of the biggest circulated newspaper in northwest Georgia.

Being in the "pen trade" was getting to be more profitable, and fun, especially when I went to war....

THE P.A.A.F. GAZETTE

VOL. I - NO. I   NOVEMBER 12, 1943

THE
SPECIAL SERVICE OFFICE
OF
PAMPA ARMY AIR FIELD
PRESENTS

'TAKE IT OFF'

a Burlesque of Burlesque

BURLY-CUE & WORLD WAR II

There was a slight interim between columning SCREEN-INGS and my rather bizarre role in World War II.

The years in between were spent "finding myself" at prep school, then college.

At Darlington School for Boys, an absolutely wonderful boarding school overlooking a lake outside Rome, I was a day student. Every day there I would walk past entrance gates inscribed with a quotation from HAMLET: "To thine own self be true, and it must follow, as the night the day, thou canst not then be false to any man."

Not only did that bit of advice become tattooed on my brain, it made me curious to read more and more Shakespeare, especially, HAMLET.

At Darlington, I developed my love of literature. Our English prof, William Dix, who later headed the library at Princeton, read us poetry. Mr. Yankee, my geometry teacher and wrestling coach, would reward us for good work with his hilarious interpretations of Ring Lardner's baseball stories.

I became inspired to write a few short stories myself, with titles like FIGHT TEAM FIGHT. I even contributed an inspiring editorial to the school newspaper, which no doubt helped win me a scholarship to Washington and Lee

University in Lexington, Virginia.   In fourth grade, Washington was the focus of my project combining history-composition-art "about a historical subject." I chose "The Father Of The Father Of Our Country," frankly, because my Great-aunt Gertrude had brought me some colored postcards of the Washington family homestead in England.   Aunt Gertrude, widowed and quite well-off, traveled extensively and was always bringing back exotic gifts ... wallhangings from China and Egypt, art reproductions from Florence, carpets from Turkey.   So with those postcards in hand, I headed for the Carnegie Library to find out who were the Washingtons who produced Our Hero.

Because my contribution was "so original," it won first prize.   Miss Florence Smith, my most perceptive teacher chose appropriately enough as my prize, a book, GEORGE WASHINGTON. When word spread among the family that they had a budding genius in their midst, ME, my cousin Sara Ellington telephoned to tell me that "we Bests are related to the Balls of Virginia, and Martha BALL was George Washington's mother." So, off I went to Washington and Lee to learn more about my illustrious connections right on Washington's own turf.

It was at Washington and Lee, also, that HAMLET came back into my life, and I became fascinated by all aspects of the theater.   Until college, my only theatrical experience had been to see Beatrice Lillie and Bert Lahr in a musical review THE SHOW IS ON, when my family descended on New York en masse on the occasion of Cousin Harry Elkins graduation from West Point.   We all just loved Bea Lillie, and I became intrigued with the way words-music-dance worked together in telling a story.

So, in my sophomore year, when we could get credits by attending the 7-hour uncut version of Shakespeare's HAMLET in Washington, D.C., I jumped at the chance, not only to relish more HAMLET but to experience the theater again. The production starred Maurice Evans and played from 1:00 to 5:00 in the matinee and 7:00 to 10:00 evenings. It was a long haul, but I amused myself in between soliloquies by training my opera glasses on the very-exposed bosums of Mady Christians, who played Hamlet's mother, Gertrude.

For English Composition upon my return, I re-wrote HAMLET as a ballet, receiving an A-plus. My English professor Dean Frank Gilliam, kept me trying to outdo myself, boosting my ego by reading my "works" to the class from time to time. Also, at Washington and Lee, I wrote the lyrics for QUEEN OF THE FANCY DRESS BALL. This came about, probably, after a few beers in the bar at my Phi Delta Theta fraternity house. Here, after study hours, a fellow pledge, Paul Thomas, from Bluefield, West Virginia would "tickle the ivories" on the upright piano. Paul was the complete musician; he had his own orchestra all through college and could play every instrument in it, expertly, and did, as part of the act.

Deciding that perhaps journalism might make an interesting career, I changed colleges and entered the Henry W. Grady School of Journalism at the University of Georgia, noted for its illustrious Dean John Drewry and Peabody Awards. Dean Drewry truly opened up the world of writing to us, bringing in the great editors, advertising copywriters, novelists, poets, columnists to speak and hold seminars. Among our honored guests were historian Hendrik Willem Van Loon, novelist Thomas Mann, cartoonist John Held, Jr., foreign correspondent Vincent Sheean and Georgia's-own Margaret Mitchell.

These were the days of "casting GONE WITH THE WIND," when seemingly everyone alive had in mind who they wanted to play "Scarlett O'Hara" in the film version of Margaret Mitchell's colossal-selling novel. Some of us at The

17

University wanted Georgian Miriam Hopkins as "Scarlett" and Macon-born Melvin Douglas as "Ashley." When they chose non-Georgians, what's more, non-Americans, for the leading roles, I dashed off this verse to THE NEW YORKER Magazine:

Shades of Scarlett

Mah name is Miz Scar-lett O'Hara
Come from Jaw-jah and deah old Tara,
I'm just as mad as I can be
They gave my part to Vivie Leigh
And for Ashley, they picked Leslie Howard
Who do they think wrote this thing ... Noel Coward?

As luck would have it, I did see Viv Leigh and my friend Clark at the film's premiere in Atlanta. The parade of celebrities ended at a reviewing stand directly under Aunt Gertrude's corner apartment at the Georgian Terrace Hotel. What a scoop for SCREENINGS. Before I could start my career in journalism, however, I rushed to defend my country's honor after the Japanese attack at Pearl Harbor. I was so infuriated when that report came over my car radio (as I was enroute to the Coosa Country Club for a Nine O'Clock Cotillion dance-planning meeting) that I swerved off the road in search of the Army Recruiting Office. The Tarleton Twins in GONE WITH THE WIND had nothing on me when it came to patriotism. I was off to tackle those nervy-Japs single handed. It wasn't as easy as that.

Not only was the Recruiting Office closed on that December 7, 1941 Sunday afternoon, it took me months before I was accepted by the U.S. Army, and more months of training.

Waiting to be called up, I tried writing a novel DARK CHANNELS, about an illegitimate mulatto's passage through life in the South. It was based on something my father had witnessed while growing up on his family's plantation "Grassdale," near Cartersville, Georgia. Since hot-passion was very much on my mind at the time, this story teemed with sex....certainly not based on the author's experiences.

Even though I was only on Chapter Six when I got my call to report to duty, I listed "novel-in-progress" on my business description application for Officer's Candidate School. I had also included ROTC, Cavalry; served on newspaper, magazine staffs Darlington School for Boys; Washington & Lee University; University of Georgia (graduated AB Journalism '41); Feature Editor/Columnist Rome News Tribune; published short stories ... then... added "novel in progress."

So it is not surprising when the Commandant of Pampa Army Air Field, in the Panhandle of Texas, needed someone with writing experience, he honed in on my record, probably thinking that Rome News-Tribune was the internationally-acclaimed chief newspaper of Rome, Italy ... and with that "novel in progress," this Best fellow must be another Ernest Hemingway.

Whatever, as it happened then, and on many occasions later furthering my career, I was in the right place at the right time.

The time was winter, and arctic winter it was. The field was located north of Amarillo at the top of the Texas Panhandle plains with nothing to stop wind-ice-sleet-snow rushing in from Canada but a howling prairie dog or two. Most of the shipload of fresh personnel (there to service Advanced Pilot Training) were Aviation Cadets who had just flunked flying school. I was one of them, having landed my plane several times about ten feet off the ground. Something had gone awry with my depth perception.

All of us "wash-outs" had morale as low as the temperature. We were despondent, cold and frantic about what would happen to us now that we no longer would be Thors in our Thunderbirds.

One night, the Colonel came up to me in the Post Exchange, seeing all my gloomy compadres crying in their beers, and said: "Best, what are we going to do to snap these men back into shape, there's no esprit de corps. What can we do to make them work together on a big team project?"

Having just come from a Judy Garland-Mickey Rooney MGM musical at the Post movie house, I suavely suggested "Why not produce a soldier show? We could air our gripes in skits on the stage, get together an orchestra, artists to paint sets and give the field personnel something positive to do after duty hours, rather than just sit around moping."

"Great," clapped the Colonel. "Do it."

"What do you mean, do it, sir?"

"Just what I said. You are hereby assigned to do whatever it takes to put on the blockbusterest soldier show these parts have ever seen."

And he meant it.

First, I had to make the idea of being in a big show exciting. So I started a post newspaper, building up plans for the forthcoming show, along with local news, and asking for volunteers. So I became Editor and Publisher, with my own office and secretary, a marvelously busted Swedish blonde from Minnesota. Next, of course, I had to write the show. What would interest every man on the base? SEX! Girls, girls, girls. I would create a Ziegfeld extravaganza, a burlesque of burlesque using the toughest guys on the air base as burlesque "queens." We would have blackout skits poking fun at our superiors and our plight in this Siberia of a place.   Thus, TAKE IT OFF took off.

Believing that everyone wanted to do "something for the boys in uniform," I contacted Manhattan's top burlesque queens, asking for any blackout skits or discarded costumes that we could copy for our big "burlesque of burlesque." They were delighted to supply.   Everytime we would get an acceptance I would post such headlines as: GYPSY ROSE LEE SENDS G-STRING FOR UPCOMING TAKE IT OFF SHOW.   Or, LILY-THE-DOVE-GIRL ROUTINE TO APPEAR IN POST MUSICAL.   After several blasts like that in the paper everybody wanted to get into the act.

I adapted scripts and burlesque numbers that could be performed by my raw talent.   Since our band leader had played in the pit of many a Broadway show, he could orchestrate songs I would make up.   Creating all the tunes and lyrics was great fun.

Also, to publicize the show in advance, I staged a weekly radio broadcast from the USO in town.   This brought other talents to the fore.   By then I was also putting my new experiences as newspaper editor, publicist, producer, director, writer of radio and stage shows into play.

We had a "beef-trust" chorus line of the porkiest guys on the field wearing wigs made from shredded cellophane gas-mask bags.   Our chorus cuties' "bosoms" were made of mess kit tops.   G-strings were jock straps covered with satin roses sewn by ladies volunteering at the Red Cross.   They also made jazzy costumes copied from those supplied by Gypsy Rose and Georgia Southern.

Producing TAKE IT OFF I learned early on that the written word is the most important thing.   Without the script, what have you got? Yet the writer is usually the last to get paid and the first to be let go if there is a money problem. Also, I experienced the power of advance advertising. Without it, who knows or cares about the product? In this case, the product was TAKE IT OFF, so while the show was being put together, I gave it a strong build up, or "teaser" campaign, in "my" paper, Pampa Flyer, and "my" weekly radio show from Pampa USO, CONTACT.

Headlines told: "Gypsy Rose Lee Assists TAKE IT OFF." Bold ads all type with lots of white space, read "Coming Soon, TAKE IT OFF, A BURLESQUE OF BURLESQUE featuring Miss Pampa Army Air Field (wait til you see her landing strip!)" The same layout would follow each week only the name of the featured burlesque queen would change. Instead of "Miss Pampa Army Air Base," for instance, we might spotlight "Belle Bomber (wait til you see her take off!)"

I had George Wilson, a commercial artist from Boston, design the program cover and a huge backdrop to look like the front page of the old Police Gazette...only re-entitled "The P.A.A.F. Gazette." For my chorus line I named the beauties for the little towns near the base: Mobeetie, Panhandle, Borger, White Deer and listed them on the program as "The Vamps Around Pampa." And my prize of them all was a 6-1/2 foot-tall beanpole, Private Eddleman. At first, when he dropped by to say he would like to be in the show, I couldn't envision him in my beef-trust chorus. He was twice as tall as the rest of my "girls," and certainly pounds too thin. Then, he told me that his specialty was tight-rope walking. Plus that, he could get his equipment very quickly, for his home was a tiny Texas town not too far away.

"Can you dance on a tight wire?" I asked, hopefully.

"I can try," he assured me. "What would you want me to do?"

"A strip polka!"

Eddleman would be my surprise "star"!!!

There, as he stood, I could see him strutting on the wire, peeling off feather after feather.

It would be the first tight-rope striptease in the state of Texas (or anywhere else, for that matter.)

Excitement about the forthcoming production became so intense that all the townfolk wanted to come...and people from surrounding communities let it be known that it would be "good public relations" if they were invited, too.

Opening night, the Post Theater was jammed. A "barker" stalked the aisles handing out our Police Gazette-replica programs shouting "Program! Get your program! Can't tell who're the cuties without a program!"

Technical Sergeant Albert Fish and the Pampa Army Air Field Orchestra "struck up the band" in the pit with a wham-bam overture. The curtain parted to reveal "gorgeous" Ziegfeld girls (my beef-trust chorus line) posed on steps leading out from a giant Police Gazette cover, then, to the tune of "A Pretty Girl Is Like A Melody" they descended one by one as the tenor held up a placard introducing "Miss Mobeetie" etc....each getting whistles, shouts, applause from the hysterical audience. Then, "les girls" lined up across the stage a la Rockettes, tore off their trains, tossed them to the boys and became Burlesque Queens singing:

> To you who labor on the line
> To you who fly or work behind
> The desk
> We bring to you burlesque
> We bring to you burlesque
>
> We bring to you a putty nose
> Girls who throw away their clothes
> Jokes that everybody knows
> We bring to you burlesque
> We bring to you burlesque

Burly, burly burly burly burly cue burlesque
The dances that we'll try to do
Aren't samples of Nijinsky
Instead we try to bring to you
Routines straight from Minsky
We bring to you The Burly Cue
We bring to you BURLESQUE!!!!!!!

HAPPY DAYS AT HOLIDAY

After the tremendous success of TAKE IT OFF, the Air Force Training Command had me writing-directing-producing a series of shows for raising soldier-morale and War Bond purchases throughout Texas, then the Caribbean.

I ended up on the island of Trinidad with the title "Entertainment Director of U.S. Army ATC," scouting for talent on such neighboring islands as Barbados and Tobago. Naturally we picked the most beautiful native girls who were dying to get into the act. If they looked like Hedy Lamarr as Tondelayo they were hired.

Thus we had incomparable companions dancing with us through downtown Port of Spain celebrating Japan's surrender on VJ Day. We formed a Conga line and snaked through the streets; villagers rushed to bring us cups of their best rum. Carnivale was a bachannal: Calypsos beating out ALL DAY ALL NIGHT WITH MARY ANN non-stop for two days.

After the war, when my sons would ask: "What did you do in the Great War, Pop?", I would reply in a "top-secret tone": "The President sent me on Special Service in the German-submarine-infested-waters of the Lesser Antilles."

My "special services" with Army Special Services led me to believe that I had a very special talent, a Rodgers-Hammerstein in one. So after The War, I headed for

Broadway where it soon became apparent that I needed very special training.

With G.I. Bill backing, I enrolled in courses at Columbia University. My professors included playwright Lynn Riggs, whose GREEN GROW THE LILACS became the huge hit OKLAHOMA; NBC's radio-script genius Max Wiley; and professor-of-stage-performing Mady Christians, recent star of Lillian Hellman's WATCH ON THE RHINE, whose bosoms I had watched all through HAMLET in her role as Queen Gertrude.

One night, walking by The Roxy Theater, I heard my name being called. "BEST!"

I looked around and didn't see anyone looking in my direction.

"BEST! Over here. I'm at attention!"

My God, it was Private Edelmann in a flamboyant door-man's uniform, more got-up than a drum major.

"Come over and talk. I have to look straight ahead. Management rules."

"What are you doing HERE?" I gasped.

"Well, after my big hit in TAKE IT OFF, grease paint really got into my blood. I'm here trying out for a Broadway show, and because of my height and all, I got this job as doorman at The Roxy. If you've got a part for me in one of your shows, ever, contact me here. I don't have a permanent address yet."

Dear Lord. I probably ruined that poor boy's life taking him away from tight-rope walking in Texas. He may spend the rest of his days as a doorman, but at least he's had a starring role at The Roxy.

I soon realized that show biz really wasn't for me. Everything took too much time. I had been spoiled by having everything at my command, so I began to inquire about the advertising agency business, or possibly, radio writing.

Max Wiley had assigned our radio script-writing class to create TV spots (probably the first in history) for John Wanamaker department store on Astor Place. Television as an industry had yet to be born. Wanamakers had installed a production unit in the store and presented tiny entertainments on it from time to time as a store attraction "more contemporary than organ playing."

In my rounds hunting for employment in the ad business, I dropped by to see a friend of my mother's, Frances Heard, grande dame of HOUSE BEAUTIFUL and the home furnishings trade. Those were the days that all the lady editors at Hearst wore elegant hats at all times at their desks, lunch or ladies room. Frances and I were talking about my job prospects at, say, J. Walter Thompson when in walked her publisher, Richard Hoeffer. When Frances asked Dick who-did-he-know at J. Walter that I could tap for a writing job, Hoeffer questioned my experience. After hearing about my illustrious career (to hear me tell it), he inquired, looking me over: "How would you like to work for me?"

"Writing my speeches, sales letters, promotion pieces," he continued, after I asked "Doing what?"

And that's how I entered the magazine world, as "Assistant To The Publisher of HOUSE BEAUTIFUL."

Those days in New York were glorious. Dick's ad agency account executive, Ned Doyle, who later started the famed "creative" agency, Doyle Dane and Bernbach, instructed me in speech making, whenever I had to fill in for the Publisher, say, at a Home Furnishings Convention in Atlantic City or High Point. In my building were other Hearst Publications ...HARPER'S BAZAAR, TOWN AND COUNTRY and MOTOR. I quickly developed a network of friends in all aspects of publishing, broadcasting, public relations and advertising. So I was one of the first to hear about a new concept in magazines, an elegant slick-paper, expense-be-

damned, sophisticated publication called HOLIDAY, devot-
ed to the joys of leisure. HOLIDAY was to join THE SATUR-
DAY EVENING POST, THE LADIES HOME JOURNAL and
COUNTRY GENTLEMAN as another star in Curtis
Publishing Company firmament. All Curtis magazines were
acknowledged to be the biggest money-makers in the field.
So, HOLIDAY would have the total financial backing of this
prestigious and very-rich organization.

HOLIDAY's New York space salesman, Ralph Hench, told
me about it one night with my good pal Woody Armstrong,
who controlled several accounts that Ralph wanted at Foote,
Cone & Belding Advertising Agency. We were at The
Biltmore Bar, and by the second martini, Ralph had set up a
date for me to talk to HOLIDAY's Advertising Promotion
Director John Veckly.

Since I had a lead on others in applying, and with my
Hearst/New York credentials, I soon found myself moving
to Curtis headquarters in Philadelphia.

Soon I was creating happenings that would spark attention of advertising   agencies, staging shows at conventions,
writing direct mail copy and publicity.

HOLIDAY was edited by Ted Patrick, a man of exquisite
literary taste and far-reaching ideas. It was his notion that
authors best identified with a subject should be assigned to
cover it for HOLIDAY. William Faulkner wrote about The
South; James Michener, The South Pacific; Ernest
Hemingway, Cuba. In no time at all, HOLIDAY had quite a
stable of literary thoroughbreds Ludwig Bemelmans, S. J.
Perelman, John O'Hara, E. B. White, V. S. Pritchett, Irwin
Shaw, James Thurber, Ogden Nash, John Steinbeck, Arthur
Miller...to mention just a few.

Our Food Editor, Elizabeth Woody, called me one day
and asked me "How would you like to go to New York and
take me to an awards luncheon?"

"Who's getting the award?" I queried.

Little did I know that she had written the Pocket Cook Book, which had sold over a million paperbacks for Pocket Books. Every year the publishers gave a "Golden Gertie," their Oscar for all authors whose titles had sold over a million copies. The "Gertie" was a small replica of a kangaroo with a book in its pouch.

We arrived at the Awards Luncheon and sat at the honoree's table. I quickly eyed the placecards to see who my table companions would be, spying the names of James Michener, Dale Carnegie, James M. Cain (our Elizabeth Woody) and someone I had never heard of, Dr. Spock.

James Michener arrived, and recognizing us from HOLIDAY asked if he could sit with us. I immediately whispered to him: "Who is Dr. Spock?"

"I take it you're not married?" smiled kind Mr. Michener. "If you were, and had a child, you'd know Dr. Spock. His paperback on Child Care is as indispensable to new parents as toilet paper. His book outsells us all."

Not too long after that encounter with Dr. Spock, I got to know his book first hand, for I became a proud papa.

All of us who were in at the beginning of HOLIDAY agree it was the halcyon days of our careers.

Everybody loved everybody connected with it, and we loved what editor Ted Patrick and art director Frank Zachary were doing with it. Ted saw it as not just a travel magazine, but also one devoted to "creative leisure" and all the good things of life.

Before HOLIDAY, Ted had been one of the great advertising copywriters at Young and Rubicam. A genius in his field, with super literary taste, he had served on the War Advertising Council during World War II, hence knew personally top talents on YANK and STARS & STRIPES.

Many of his close friends were writers for THE NEW

YORKER. A day at his house in Quogue, Long Island gave me a close view of his lifestyle. Early morning he walked the beach with his beloved Airedales, then breakfasted on the terrace with his wife. Errol Garner on piano was his record of the moment.

Ted loved jazz and had many Garner recordings. Ted was a big tennis fan, too, and played at The Meadow Club. During that day, George Nelson, the architect/furniture designer came over and we discussed his designing and actually building an ideal HOLIDAY vacation house right there in Quogue to dramatize the epitome of HOLIDAY living. Irwin Shaw and his wife dropped by for lunch of lobster, corn on the cob and a cold bottle of Pouilly-Fuisse.

One of Patrick's basic ideas was to devote a major portion of HOLIDAY to one subject, usually a fascinating city or country, produced by writers known for their understanding of a place. So Irwin Shaw would tell about his Paris; E. B. White his New York; Hemingway: Cuba, setting of his OLD MAN AND THE SEA. Ted collected fine writers like some collect fine wine and art. He had to pay top prices to get them, of course, but it became a prestige thing to do a definitive piece for HOLIDAY. Many HOLIDAYs became collectors items, cherished like rare books. Decades after Ted's April 1957 "entire issue on France" appeared, I pulled it from my saved-HOLIDAYs to enjoy once more. I have never seen any magazine equal its high-quality. To give the essence of France, its history, art, fashion eclat, the cover featured a collage by artist Georg Giusti, portraying "Marianne," the personification of France's hard-won Republic.

Andre Maurois, France Minister of Culture and renowned biographer, gave an insider's view of the Academie Francais, pantheon of France's greatest writers, statesmen and soldiers. Who better to tell its story than Maurois, a member himself of that exalted group. And what writer more entertaining than James Thurber to share the first time he saw Paris.

What gave this and every issue special eclat was its look, thanks to the genius of art-director Frank Zachary. He gave HOLIDAY its glamour, and went on to do the same for TOWN & COUNTRY and TRAVEL & LEISURE.

His major coups, as far as I'm concerned was having photographers Arnold Newman and Slim Aarons stage their photographs in settings that told their whole story. They knew everybody from prime ministers to party girls. Newman's portraits were Rembrandts of photography picturing George Duhamel resplendent in his hand-embroidered uniform, holding hat and sword, in the private study of the French Academy; Dior in his Paris salon; Bernard Buffet in his studio; prima ballerina Zizi Jeanmaire posed en pointe front curtain on stage; chef/owner Alexandre Dumaine in his kitchen at the famous Hotel de la Cote d'Or at Saulieu.

With Slim Aarons' photographs you always felt you were THERE as a private guest at the manor, hunting lodge, with the Duchess, Marquis or Baron.

But what really "knocked my socks off" in that issue on France were incredible on-the-spot photographs of French people doing-their-thing by that country's legendary Henri Cartier-Bresson. Page after page of Cartier-Bresson, 22 pictures by the best cameraman in the world!

How did Patrick and Zachary keep up this quality issue after issue? Ted Patrick would have his staff bring an "interesting person" to his monthly luncheon at New York's Hotel St. Regis. A sample group might have Ted with John Steinbeck, Harry Sions, S.J. Perelman, photographer Tom Hollyman, Angier Biddle Duke, Frank Zachary, Al Herschfeld; Lou Mercier bringing Andre Francois or Ronald Searle. Everyone brought new ideas and anecdotes to the table.

Equally, in fact VITALLY, important was the exciting advertising in HOLIDAY master-minded by publisher Ed Von Tress. "We had to recruit a new type of advertising salesmen," Ed related. "And set up promotion, research and merchandising departments to generate enthusiasm for the HOLIDAY idea and demonstrate the opportunities such a dynamic magazine could bring. There had never been anything like HOLIDAY before, and with the drab World War II years just over, the world was ready for ways to enjoy life to its fullest."

When HOLIDAY began hiring its people in 1945, a young generation was just returning from the wars. There were great numbers of brilliant young men around age-thirty looking for new careers, but who may have had no experience in marketing, merchandising, selling OR advertising. So from this wide field, Von Tress could select people on their personality, character, ability and natural enthusiasm. "The end result" said Ed, "was the most remarkable group of young people with whom I had ever been associated. It was rather like a club, we all became very close friends. Putting HOLIDAY over-the-top was a sort of game for us."

To get advertising for clothing, HOLIDAY hired Orrin Spellman, a man well-acquainted with top stores in all major cities Orrin created in-store promotion packages consisting of blowups of HOLIDAY covers, and counter displays tying-in with a giveaway booklet "What To Wear Where." As HOLIDAY Merchandising Director, Spellman first went to his friend Stanley Marcus in Dallas, whose Neiman-Marcus store was then considered the most stylish in America. What Neiman-Marcus did others were sure to follow. So when Stanley Marcus had departments and display windows featuring EVERYDAY HOLIDAY LIVING as the theme of an all-store promotion advertisers and their agencies quickly got the idea that being in with HOLIDAY was the IN-thing to do. After all, when people are in a holiday mood entertaining or traveling, that's when they are in the mood to buy "the best, smartest, most fun." We delivered a slogan: THE HOLIDAY MOOD IS A SPENDING MOOD.

Several months in advance of special issues, HOLIDAY Editorial Promotion Director Jim Powell would send stores offerings of HOLIDAY cover blow-ups and photographs to create their own tie-ins. To point out the quality of HOLIDAY's writing, he sent out a series of pocket-size pieces SPEAKING OF HOLIDAY, interviews with HOLIDAY authors and artists by witty reporter Caskie Stinnett (who later became editor of both HOLIDAY and TRAVEL & LEISURE). Powell also produced perhaps the prototype of today's Audio Books: a record of authors reading from their works in HOLIDAY, with each segment introduced by editor Ted Patrick.

My role as creator of advertising promotions had me writing and staging shows at Travel Agent Conventions, making "happenings" that would spark attention in ADVERTISING AGE, whether it be a show with performers from smart supper clubs like The Blue Angel, or promoting THE HOLIDAY MOOD IS A SPENDING MOOD at exclusive parties to attract "top brass."

Dramatizing everyday HOLIDAY LIVING, we had George Nelson create the perfect vacation house, building it in stylish Westhampton, Long Island. We featured it editorially, picturing its new ideas in home furnishings, gardens, appliances, foods, beverages and "time-savers." Then, we invited key prospects to "A Holiday On Long Island" giving them a day away from the office at this model house; flying them out in a special jet, transporting them in a fleet of convertibles and sports cars being advertised in HOLIDAY.

While Jim Powell and I were developing contests, art

shows, direct mail pieces and convention displays, Zelia Zigler was heading Holiday Information Service, giving out information to readers wanting to know where-to-go, where-to-stay or how-to-travel. "Z" had been head of the travel information bureau for Shell Oil Company, and she was as enthusiastic about HOLIDAY's prospects as the rest of us. When it became evident to the advertising staff that some classifications required special attention, Zelia was put in charge of creating and selling such special advertising sections as Places To Stay; Schools and Camps; Tours and Cruises, plus a mail order ad page, The Holiday Shopper.

We all worked as a team, became sort of a "HOLIDAY family."

At the time, I was single, going back and forth to my apartment and girl friends in Manhattan. I had shared a town house on East 49th street with my best friend, Woody Armstrong, an account executive at Foote, Cone and Belding. He later married Leonard Bernstein's sister-in-law. Our digs had special cache because they overlooked Katherine Hepburn's town house just across the street. We never once saw her, though.

In Philadelphia, I shared an apartment near Rittenhouse Square with a HOLIDAY advertising-space salesman, Al Johnson, whose dad was a founder of LIFE magazine and at that time served as president of Temple University. Al and I were very footloose and fancy free until love walked right in and took our bachelorhood way, way, away.

Ed Von Tress had invited me for a dinner party at his country place to meet a new girl in town, Barbara Thornburgh. Ed had been a friend of her father way back in the Indiana University days. The Thornburgh's had recently moved to Philadelphia and Ed was introducing them to a few special friends. Since Ed was my boss, of course I could come—which meant giving up my weekend plans in New

York. Only when I arrived at Ed's, Barbara was a no-show. She had a date in New York!

When I did finally meet her, it was just like Oscar Hammerstein put it in song "Some enchanted evening...you may see a stranger...and somehow you know...you know even then...you'll see her again and again." Once I had found her, I never let her go.

We were married within five months after that meeting. I had found my true love!

MADISON AVENUE'S ELEPHANT MAN

Part of my job in promoting HOLIDAY, was to create direct mail pieces that would attract advertising agencies into recommending our new-concept magazine as an ideal medium for their clients' advertising campaigns. Media directors are very cautious about buying space in new publications, preferring to wait-and-see-if-it's-a-success. At last, after four years of great selling by our ad reps, HOLIDAY was out of the red and into the black. Our ad lineage had spiraled, and we couldn't wait to shout the news out to Madison Avenue's bevy of ad agencies.

I was en route to our Mad Ave agency, Batten Barton Durstine and Osborne, when a promotion idea flashed... hell, exploded...in my brain. Our next issue was devoted to Africa, noted for Big Game. I had just read a story by Hemingway about big-game hunters and their trophies. Wouldn't it be sensational if we ran a full page in the New York Times promoting our upcoming Africa issue along with our advertising success and grab attention by having a mounted elephant head with a headline WE'VE REALLY SHOT A-HEAD! Then, we could send out those big elephant-gun shells with our message to ad executives, and they would keep this unusual conversation piece as a paper weight .

First, of course, I'd have to find elephant-gun cartridges. Where? Of course, Abercrombie and Fitch, the Madison

Avenue purveyors of deluxe sporting goods. Also, it was most conveniently located just across Mad Ave from BBD&O.

I went directly to the store.

"Big Game Department?" I asked the elevator operator, who ushered me grandly to an upper floor.

I walked towards an area bristling with mounted heads of bear and deer.

"Big Game?" I ventured, as a British Colonel-type sales-clerk approached.

"Indeed," he clipped. "What is it that you want?"

"Elephant-gun cartridges. You do sell them?"

"We do. How many would you like?"

Quickly I totaled our promotion list, thinking the cartridges would make a first rate enclosure for our mailing.

I then let him have it: "NINE THOUSAND."

Whether it was the thought of nine thousand elephants hitting the dust, or whether he thought I was some kind of kook, he suddenly paled and then almost whispered "May I ask why you want such a large number? You see, they have to be ordered from England, packaged separately..."
I didn't have time for all that, so, with nothing to lose, I looked him squarely in the eyes and replied "Because, well, I just can't stand elephants. Sorry you don't have 9000 cartridges in stock, for I need them now!"

I bowed, squared my shoulders, and walked briskly towards the exit.

When that story echoed around Mad Avenue, some nick-named me "Elephant Boy." I would walk into an advertising party and people would point me out and snicker. So in my anonymous role as writer-without-byline, my name became known in advertising circles.

I reached almost immortality as: "That guy who left the oyster carton on the bus."

That happened when I was en route to deliver my stool

specimen to the Pennsylvania Hospital Clinic. It was to be the grand finale of my annual thorough physical exam, required for all our company executives. It is a rather indelicate maneuver, but I managed to package my specimen in the oyster carton supplied by the Clinic. On the lid, in bold script, the nurse had penned BEST. So it sort of appeared like a first prize.

I put the carton in a brown-paper shopping bag, caught the bus and became so engrossed reading my New York Times that I almost missed my stop. Realizing it, I dashed off the bus leaving my "package" on the seat.

Before I could stop it, the bus roared off and away. Damn! I would have to "produce" all over again. So I waited until my bus circled its route of ten blocks, then waved it down, only to discover that someone had taken my package.
Ha! I envisioned what that thief must have felt when he opened what he thought was BEST OF SHOW.

When it was learned that Elephant Boy and the Oyster Carton Kid were the same person, I needed no introduction when I changed jobs to make more money, and joined the copywriting staff of N. W. Ayer, the nation's oldest advertising agency.

At N. W. Ayer, I could put all of my skills to work, including the television commercial-scripting I had experienced as a project of my journalism class at Columbia.

There were few writers anywhere with "TV experience" then, and from all the requests I was receiving from ad agencies about town, I was probably the ONLY one in Philadelphia.

Shortly after Barbara and I were married, I welcomed any "moonlighting" job to supplement my modest income. I had been delighted when Ken Keen called and asked me to create a weekly western 15-minute TV show for his ad agency's client, Ranger Joe cereal. It was to air at noon on Sunday, for

15 minutes. Will Rogers' fifth cousin "from Oklahoma" was to play "Ranger Joe," and since Jesse Rogers sang, I was to provide space and action for him to get in a little song or two. Plus all that, there could be no chase in this Western for we only had one set, a "prairie" with a cactus and a big fake boulder. We could use no film footage "to bring on the horses"; we had to create suspense so viewers would "tune in next week." Furthermore, our director suffered from shell shock and would go into a writhing fit at the sound of a gun shot, so we could have no shooting. Indians (local rug salesman in wigs) would be provided, however. Since I am very fond of our Native Americans, I did not want to make them villains, rather victims, so I had Jesse protecting them from mean cowboys somewhere off camera, with the sound of hoofs approaching. It was simply terrible, but since no one watched it (few had television sets), it established me, in the eyes of a resume scanner, as a TV writer of Westerns, sit-coms and commercials.

Soon I was called on to write a LIVE Western, telecast over CBS five afternoons a week. Nights and weekends I labored over situations that would save the hero from lynchings, stompings, knifings, burnings, drownings...even, landslides.

Due to my HOLIDAY connection, I also created a weekly travel show, the sort of thing we saw later as "Sophia's Rome"; "Elizabeth Taylor's — London"; and "Gene Kelly's Paris."

All this background contributed to many assignments developing TV commercials for such clients as Bachman pretzels and Fels soap (my ballad "Gentle Fels" sung by, Rosemary Clooney was so gentle-icky-sweet it wouldn't lullaby a baby to sleep, it would make it throw up.)

At N. W. Ayer we had wonderful talent and clients. Weekly, it seemed, we would chug out to Detroit and show our latest masterpieces to our big $22-million account,

Plymouth Automobiles. When introducing a new model, our creative team had to work in complete secrecy, behind closed doors, using code words in our telephone conversations, for industrial spying from rival companies ran rampant. At night, before leaving the office, we could leave no clues about what we were working on, for even the cleaning woman might be a Mata Hari.

I created campaigns that ran exclusively in THE NEW YORKER for Yardley of London and Hanes Custom Quality men's underwear, banks, towels, telephones and newspapers. However, it was Whitman's Chocolates that took me back to Hollywood, following The Yellow Brick Road.....

MY PHILADELPHIA STORY

THE PHILADELPHIA STORY, Katherine Hepburn's smash hit movie and play depicted the way of life enjoyed by an upper-crust family on Philadelphia's Main Line. To a world just emerging from the devastating depression, it seemed about as real as Cinderella. But it was true! Philip Barry, who created the play, described a lifestyle as he saw it when his Harvard class-mate Edgar Scott was courting Helen Hope Montgomery at her family's 750-acre estate, "Ardrossan," near Wayne. Hope Montgomery became the prototype for Tracy Lord, the Katherine Hepburn role. In real life, Hope and Edgar married and lived happily-ever-after on those same 750 acres surrounded by loving family and friends. And like Hepburn, Hope was scintillating, gung ho, very much her own self...a legend in her own time.

But the Main Line that PHILADELPHIA STORY depicts has gone with the wind. It still represents suburbia at its most superb...beautiful people in beautiful homes surrounded by beautiful land. But those days of 30 servants minding 750-acre estates live on only in memory, or on the VCR. So when a magazine asked me to write "a piece about the Main Line," I decided to tell the way I saw it when I first came there in 1947.

The only thing I knew about the Main Line then was what

I had seen in the play. Those names tossed about...Biddle, Drexel, Cassatt and all that...meant nothing to this product of the Old South and New York publishing. Philadelphia, to the rest of the world, at that stage in time, had a reputation about as inviting as China's Forbidden City, where natives spoke another language totally undecipherable to outsiders.

But fortunately for me, I had good friends who were Main Line natives, very high up in Philadelphia peerage, so they acted as my High Interpreters.

"What is the Main Line?" I asked them when invited "out to the Main Line" for my first weekend as the new bachelor in town.

"It gets its name from a freight track," they explained. "It's to Philadelphia what Long Island is to New York, a whole chain of rather fashionable stops along the Railroad's main line. So when you come out for the house party, take the train called Paoli Local and we will meet you at the Radnor station. Just remember the phrase Old Maids Never Wed And Have Babies Then Three."

It was a way to remember the station stops...Overbrook, Merion, Narbeth, Wynnewood, Ardmore, Haverford, Bryn Mawr—then three to Radnor.

I was met at the station in an open Pierce Arrow phaeton, circa 1929. Gleaming, enameled, old, elegant, it set the tone of what was to follow. We drove past rolling fields and estates that might have been transported, intact, from the English countryside I had seen in Kent. Later I was to learn that those palaces behind the gatehouses we passed belonged to families named Chew, Dorrance, Berwind, Walton and Hare. We were headed for the Drexel Paul's. My hosts lived, along with several others of the young social set, in a former servant's cottage, left vacant like so many others after World War II. It seemed that EVERYone there was either named Biddle or related. My host, a Biddle, had married his cousin, a Biddle, who introduced me to his brother, a Biddle, who was marrying her sister, who was, of course, a Biddle. Then Mrs. Drexel Paul dropped by, just in from Palm Beach, and it turned out that she was born a Biddle, too. It seemed just like my South...everyone was a kissin' cousin...connected. And they all couldn't have been more charming, urbane, secure "doing interesting things." Unlike the ambitious, rat-racing, trying-to-make-it bunch I had left behind in Manhattan, these Old Main Liners were at ease, relaxed, unstriving, whose main mission in life was to enjoy it and see that others did, too. Also, I noticed they spoke a language of their own. For something that was "absolutely very very exquisite or marvelous-right-down-to-the-toes," established Main Liners had a special word: "gluss."

So, "How was Doty's party before the Assembly?" might have been answered "It was just GLUSS!" And the dress Mrs. Duskin found to match her Maw's emeralds was just...just...GLUSS!

The men talked about "beagling," which was about as unknown to me as Biddle-ing. Little did I know that beagling was chasing a pack of beagle hounds who were chasing a hare. Also, they had their code-word for places where they vacationed, as if to keep anyone from trespassing on their territory. Hence, "going to the camp" meant "going to our Maine summer place near Northeast Harbor." And, "How would you like to go to the river with us?" referred to their Island cottage in the St. Lawrence River.

Now, where I grew up, we called the ledger in which we registered our bulls and stallions *The Stud Book.* That's their name for the Social Register.

Indeed, here they spoke another language.

Soon thereafter I returned to the Main Line scene to attend the coming out party of a Kate Hepburn-type at Gulph Mills, a very unpretentious golf club for a very privileged few. En route to get the girl I was escorting, we stopped at my friend's home to meet his family and pick up a "few orchids for the girls" at their conservatory, past their gatekeeper's up the long drive next to the gardener's cottage, past the nice little pad they had built on the premises for their off-springs' Fraulein—their children's governess. Mom and Pop's house seemed sort of like Sandringham, summer palace of Queen Elizabeth and the Prince. On the third floor was a gilt-mirrored ballroom encircled by quaint gold-gilt chairs, where Meyer Davis and his orchestra played for private balls, and Cliff Hall "down from Newport," batted out Cole Porter on the Bechstein. It we had the time, we could have bowled a few frames on the parents' basement bowling alley, or had a massage, for dad's valet also served the family as a masseur. We passed all that up, but did return at dawn for nightcaps and skinny dips in their Romanesque swimming pool. We didn't have to worry about the 4 a.m. chill, for their poolhouse not only had its own kitchen but was heated when needed.

Later we headed out to the Merion Golf Club, which was not in Merion, but in Ardmore. When I asked why, then, it was called the MERION Golf Club, my host explained "because it is a spin-off from the Merion Cricket Club," which is not in Merion either, but in Haverford, To make it even more confusing, the Cricket Club is a tennis club. "You see, it started as a cricket club in Merion, then moved. On the Main Line we hate to change names. We have Gulph Roads running into Gulph Roads, and at least six Bryn Mawr Avenues."

At the Golf Club, instead of Merion's East Course, where Bobby Jones completed his famous Grand Slam in 1930, we opted for the much-less demanding West Course, where everyone stood aside to "let Mr. J. Howard Pew play through." Mr. Pew, major domo of Sun Oil and the sacrosanct Republican Party had quietly kept the Club afloat during War time, and it was taken as a matter of course that The West was Mr. Pew's course.

There, too, on vacation from her Tallahassee, Florida plantation, was Miss Frances Griscom who, in 1900 became America's first Woman Amateur Golf Champion. Miss Griscom, reportedly, was the first woman to drive a car in Philadelphia. When her shipping-tycoon father, Clement Griscom, had the car delivered to their Haverford estate "Dolobran," the mechanic came with it. They kept him, too. Later her nieces and nephews told me that Aunt Frances carried her own martinis in a vial secreted in her walking cane. When she entered the club bar, all she had to do was wave the cane and the bartender would "bring on the rocks."

I was given to understand that Merion was THE club for serious golfers; Philadelphia Country Club for those who wanted everything—"Swimming, tennis, trap, bowling, golf— the works"; and the Cricket Club strictly for racquet sports and "young" social activities, especially its porch dances and dining.

I learned, too, that to "play the Philadelphia game" or "to make it on the Main Line" one should follow a certain pattern. A lady we know did just that, and set aside one day as "Boxing Day," reserving her box for the Philadelphia Orchestra, Charity Ball, Merion Tennis Week, Radnor Races and Devon Horse Show all at once, before her social secretary "might forget."

On my first Main Line year, I was introduced to the Art Scene. Occasion: a retrospective of Matisse, with his son Pierre in the receiving line. It was a "pull-out-the-family-jewels" affair, and some of the grand dames descending the steps of the Philadelphia Museum of Art appeared to have taken their evening gowns out of long-neglected closets, too, wearing probably "Cousin Katherine Cadwallader's Poirret peau-de-soie from Paris." In the locker room at Philadelphia Racquet Club, jammed with gentlemen in underdrawers changing into "black tie," topic of conversation centered around "wonder if that old sonovabitch Dr. Barnes will be there." Dr. Barnes, it turned out, had commissioned Matisse himself to come out to his Merion mansion and "do the murals for his art gallery." Snubbed by Main Line society for his "new rich" boorishness, Barnes' collection of art did not gain him entrance into Philadelphia's inner art circle. That was "Whistler's Mother"-time, pre-Picasso. So despite the fact that Barnes was a friend and early collector of Matisse, and, in his private gallery on Latches Lane, personally possessed 180 Renoirs, 60 Cezannes, numerous van Goghs, Gauguins, Rousseaus, Monets, along with Matisse's largest mural, he was not invited to "join the Club." Consequently, he was "out to get 'em," so his appearance at the Museum's Matisse gala was as feared as a Margaret Thatcher teaparty invaded by Irish Terrorists.

Dr. Barnes didn't show, but "nearly everybody" who was anybody in town did, including, of course, courtly Henry Clifford, who had put the Matisse retrospective together. The Clifford's maintained quite a nice modern-art collection, themselves, at their Mediterranean-style villa, "Rock Rose," in Radnor. He also lived the life of a grand duke at his petit palaces in Florence, Vevey and Mexico. Much later, after a burglar climbed to their second story and stole Mrs. Clifford's pearls while they were at dinner, keeping such valuables at home was no longer safe. He sold his huge Henri Rousseau painting of "a tiger in the rain" to Britain's National Gallery, who bought it with the financial assistance of another Main Line collector of Impressionist art, Walter Annenberg, then our Ambassador to the Court of St. James's. The Cliffords later sold "Rock Rose" to the Norman Cohns, who immediately established themselves as the Main Line's premier hosts, a mantle once held by the late Tootie (Widener) and Cortright Wetherill. In the days of Philadelphia's very exclusive Piccadilly Dance crowd, an invitation to the Wetherill's annual ball in a tent set up on their "Happy Hill Farm" was considered top ticket. However, to a first-time invitee, it was confusing finding the way there since some said the farm was in White Horse, others Sugartown and, some, Newtown Square. Such address-confusion is typically Main Line. Adolph Rosengarten, whose "Chanticleer" estate and gardens are superb examples of Old-Main-Line lifestyle, said that many of his neighbors, at "Ravenscliff" and the Montgomerys across the road at "Ardrossan," received mail at several post offices. In order to avoid mail mix-ups with his parents who lived in 'the big house', Mr. Rosengarten kept a mail-box in St. Davids rather than Wayne. Such estates in his area are so vast that they are considered part Radnor, St. Davids, Ithan or Villanova, all "mailbox villages."

Before I knew what was happening, I had said goodbye to bachelorhood, and was to become a Main Liner myself. Our wedding by candelight at 8 p.m. in Old St. David's Church in Wayne (not in St. Davids), was a shocker. "We marry in daylight, here" we were told by our proper social director. "Well, we are not YOU, yet," was our thought, so we had all the men getting out their white tie and putting on their tails.

Getting married on the Main Line was especially glamorous because of the personal attention, then, of the trade. Starting with J.E. Caldwell. In this one store, beginning with Mr. Lutz and the engagement ring, you would pick out your wedding invitations, silver, china, and bridesmaid-groomsmen gifts. It was especially exciting to see Caldwell's unique elegant maroon delivery van heading up the drive with gifts personally delivered by a chauffeur in livery. It made recipients feel true "carriage trade."

Then, when we had children, they had their own "clothes friends" who always waited on them at Best's in Ardmore. The milkman delivered right to the refridge and became everybody's welcome good friend. Our doctors, Pancoast Reath, old Doc Truxal and pediatrician Stewart Polk, made house calls. You could always get a check cashed in an emergency at Park Hardware, Wack's Pharmacy or Delaware Market because "they knew you." And Mrs. Franklin in Haverford knew just who she was buying those dresses for. After a big ball it wasn't a bit surprising to meet fellow ball-goers shopping at 7 a.m. at the Farmer's Market, still in evening clothes, and very nonchalant about the whole thing. Too, most of our best Old-Main-Line friends had set an example we had not found in other places: they had a feeling of obligation to their community...a deep social concern. Working committees for the church, the school, hospital, United Way...wherever you could "do your thing," gave a great sense of satisfaction. It's this giving of oneself that brings all the best people together and makes the Main Line not just a bedroom community but a "family." You could live as far away from the railroad as Unionville or Chadds Ford and still feel "Main Line." Once a local debutante, curtseying to Queen Elizabeth, replied when asked where she was from, "I live on The Main Line, m'am." That seemed to say it all.

Looking today at those places I saw on my first Main Line encounter, I discover that the Drexel Paul estate is now a residential development, "Fox Chase." Stately "Woodcrest Farms," once home of John Dorrance, the Campbell Soup founder, has been re-vamped into Cabrini College. Nearby, the Walton Estate, with its swan lake and duck pond, has become campus of Eastern College.

Biggest change: the Main Line is no longer tied solely to the city. We've become self-sufficient. Starting with the

50

world's first suburban shopping center, in Ardmore, the area now boasts the largest, stretching from Valley Forge to King of Prussia. Ladies-who-lunch no longer have to train into town; elegant places to dine have bloomed in the 'burbs. Acres of farm fields now sprout corporation headquarters, office malls, or residential villages such as Hershey's Mill and Chesterbrook. So you see, the Main Line is no longer that exclusive world of those types we saw in THE PHILADELPHIA STORY. Today we all can participate in living The Philadelphia Story Part II, and share most of the goodies Philadelphia's Main Line has to offer. Thanks to the Benefit, we, too, can go to the Ball, the steeplechase at Radnor Hunt Club, the garden party at an exclusive estate, the art gala and mix with The Swells. Glamour events are open to anyone for a price of a ticket to benefit either The Hospital, The School, The Orchestra, The Horticulture Society, The Museum or The Church. No matter what color or religion, our boys and girls can attend the best private schools (both Episcopal and Shipley have gone coed). The presidents of the old-line institutions rather than fifth-generation Philadelphia Bluebloods, are more than likely dynamic Newbloods. The Gladwyne-to-Paoli circuit is no longer strictly the province of the Upper Upper. Now Middle Middles hob nob with Biddle Biddles...to a point. The Old Guard is still on guard, but the New Guard doesn't seem to give a hoot. Mutual interests have created new social circles within circles and more circles. Close friendships are formed volunteering to serve at the Devon Horse Show, University Museum Antique Show, Philadelphia Museum of Art and Philadelphia Flower Show. Then there are tennis, golf, squash and horse groups; the choral societies; amateur theatricals; antique car clubs. From Colonial Dames to Wine and Food societies such as Chevalier du Tastevin, there's something for everybody's interest on today's Main Line.

Despite all the changes, there's no more beautiful place on earth to lead the good life.

I still have my Southern accent, but I notice that my vocabulary has gone "Main Line." When questioned what it's like living here, I now find myself answering: "I think it's GLUSS!"

Behind the scenes Bossy resists stepping out on the 19th floor balcony during the shooting session.

Cow and friends, Jim Fowke (left), president of BF&J Productions, Baltimore, unidentified cowhand, and Hugh R. Best, vp-creative director, Arndt, Preston, Chapin, Lamb & Keen, pause during tv filming.

Cows Star in TV Commercial; Cast Upsets Staid Baltimore Citizens

19th Floor Balcony Scene Stops Woman, Decorator in Tracks

PHILADELPHIA, Aug. 29—Hugh Best, vp-creative director, Arndt, Preston, Chapin, Lamb & Keen, keeps a meticulous on-the-job journal, and some recent entries about an on-location tv commercial filming in Baltimore are a bit out of the ordinary.

They're all about cows standing on a 19th story apartment balcony, riding a self service elevator, being walked like poodles on crowded city streets, grazing on the front lawns of nice residential sections, posing in a typical kitchen and being milked in a mid-city drugstore.

"Pamplona may have its bulls, but they certainly couldn't cause more excitement than the 'bossies of Baltimore' did when we filmed our tv commercial for Interstate Milk Producers Cooperative," Mr. Best said. The commercials will be aired in the Pennsylvania-Delaware-Maryland-New Jersey market beginning in September.

■ The objective of the commercial was to show what a mess people would all be in without

Cows Star in TV Commercial; Cast Upsets Staid Baltimore Citizens

■ "Are you Mr. Levine, the manager?" she asked one of the camera crew.

"No Ma'am. He may be inside."

"Well, I have brought my decorator along to measure my new apartment . . . what's that?" She suddenly noticed a bale of hay being hoisted by pulley to the 19th floor.

"A bale of hay."

"But what is it doing *there?*"

"Oh, it's for the cow up there on the balcony on the 19th floor."

"A cow on the 19th floor, huh," scoffed the decorator. "What color is it?"

They spied the cow and froze in their tracks.

Later, when the cow was descending, the self service elevator stopped on the third floor. The door opened for an elderly woman, who stared incredulously at the cow passenger, gulped, and said, "I'll take the next elevator, thank you."

■ In the drug store scene, a man

One of the stars of the Milk Producers tv commercial takes time out for primping before going in front of the cameras.

Looking as nonchalant as any of the bus or airline travelers at the terminal in Baltimore, two cows relax before their next stint in filming Interstate Milk Producers' new tv commercial.

COW INVASION OF BALTIMORE

Creating "The Wizard of Oz" commercials in Hollywood may have been my most glamorous TV-writing experience, but unleashing cows onto an unsuspecting Baltimore was certainly my most bizarre.

In the first place, I knew nothing about cows. No one told me that they have to be milked at dawn and again at dusk. Otherwise their udders might swell up and burst. It's what my mother-in-law Julia Thornburgh would refer to as "udder neglect."

Besides being very placid, which is nice, they are also not toidy trained, hence leave cowplops whenever or wherever nature calls, which is messy.

Also, their brainpower doesn't measure up to their milk-producing ability, hence you don't see cows performing in circuses, do you? Have you ever heard of a cow walking a tightrope or riding a tricycle like those Russian bears? Nor do they pirouette and dance La Conga like Barnum and Bailey elephants do.

All I knew about cows was that they gave milk (and fertilizer). Which is wonderful enough, for where would we be without milk? More than that, where would we be in this citified world without our dairymen? Suppose you had to tend your cow living in a condo on Madison Avenue. Can you imagine La Cote Basque with residence cows waiting in the alley out back?

That was the point of my TV spot for Interstate Milk Producers Cooperative, supported by dairymen of Pennsylvania, Maryland, Delaware and New Jersey to promote their industry.

"We're having a problem," their Advertising Director told us at my advertising agency. "Our young men go off to college and come back to the farm feeling like a boob, rather than a hero. They keep saying they want to go into something to help humanity, like the Peace Corps. Cowboys get more respect, at least in the mind of the public. We have to build the image and importance of our dairymen. People just take for granted that milk will be delivered at their door or supermarket, sure as sun-up. There's no thought of what goes on to get that milk to them."

Frankly, I hadn't thought about it either.

When I did, I suggested: "Why don't we make a television commercial showing a mass audience what would happen if we didn't have a dairy doing our dirty work? We'll make The Man Behind The Cow a Robert Redford-type hero. We'll show him proudly shooing in his herd, happy, healthy and virile, in a lush Lancaster County landscape, with oh-what-a-beautiful-morn background music. Then we'll cut to a city-street scene, a whole block of row houses, with a cow hitched out front of each one of them. Can't you just picture it ... cows parked on both sides of a city street? And we'll show men dressed for the office milking frantically so as not to miss the commuter train. We'll have cows looking over top-floor balconies on apartment houses .... it will make your message unforgettable!"

The more I talked, wilder and wilder scenes emerged, for I could see that the client was going along with it all.

"We can certainly provide the cows," said the Milk Cooperative's representative. "It all depends on how central your location would be to our dairy farms. It is important to truck them in and back by four in the afternoon. Also, what city would give us permission to bring herds of cows right into the middle of town?"

"You leave that up to us," we assured, and immediately wondered "What in hell have I done?"

Fortunately, two weeks prior to my meeting with our dairy clients, Jim Fowke, president of BF&J Productions in Baltimore, had shown me a reel of their latest television spots. They had produced the most "with-it" work I'd seen in years. So I called Jim, told him about the idea, and asked if they could do it.

Timing and luck has a lot to do with success in the ad game, and as it turned out, Jim's company could do no wrong in the eyes of Baltimore's progressive mayor. He knew that if Jim was in charge, everyone would benefit... especially Baltimore's image way out there in Televisionland. Also, Baltimore was only an hour's truck-drive away from cooperative farms sure to cooperate. This was most important, for each cow to have a tender in attendance, along with a "pooper scooper" to keep those Baltimore streets spotless. Assuring Baltimore's powers-that-be that they had nothing to worry about safety and sanitation (after all, these were peaceful cows, not raging bulls) they gave us permission to use their fair city as our prime location.

On the day of the shoot, truckloads of Holsteins arrived from the farms of Interstate, descending on the city like lumbering army tanks. A caravan of actors, handlers and television crew zoomed across Baltimore with cows mooing behind.

I was in my glory playing a C. B. de Mille in a Brooks Brothers suit, standing right by the cameraman as I spelled out the shot I wanted,

At a new high rise apartment house, we were shooting a

scene of a cow standing contentedly on the 19th floor balcony. As we hoisted a bale of hay up to the waiting cow looking down on the whole operation, a prospective tenant pulled up in her car.

"Are you Mr. Levine, the manager?" she asked.

"No, ma'am. He may be inside" we replied, whispering aside to the director "Zoom in on the hay as it heads towards the cow."

"Well, I have brought my interior decorator along to measure my new apartment ... and...WHAT IS THAT?". She suddenly noticed the haybale dangling high in the air as it headed heavenward.

"That's a bale of hay."

"What's it doing there?"

"Oh, its for the cow up there on the balcony on the 19th floor."

Then the decorator threw his limp wrists into the air and scoffed "How divine. What color is it?" then he spied the cow and froze in his tracks. "My God, it is a cow!"

Later, when the cow was descending, the self-service elevator stopped on the third floor. To get the cow into that elevator, we had to back it in and hold its head to the side, so the little old lady waiting for the elevator stood face to face with the cow when the doors parted. She stared incredulously at the cow passenger, gulped, and said "I'll take the next elevator, thank you."

In a drug store scene, a man asks for some cream in his coffee, and a waitress pulls a cow up to the table. The next thing you see is milk squirting into the cup.

Of course, what was going on behind the cameras was just short of pandemonium. At midday on Charles Street, the financial center of Baltimore, we had men in business suits walking cows like poodles, with local TV-news teams photographing us photographing the cow action. Naturally crowds had to be held back, people were hanging out of windows watching and cheering, and all the confusion set the cows off a-mooing.

Not only did the commercial turn out even better than we could have hoped, our client got a million dollars worth of publicity via the TV news of our filming, and big splashes in local newspapers. ADVERTISING AGE carried a page devoted to it, headlined "Cows Star In TV Commercial: Cast Upsets Staid Baltimore" with a sub-head reading: "19th Floor Balcony Scene Stops Woman, Decorator in Tracks."

YELLOW BRICK ROAD TO HOLLYWOOD

We were off to see The Wizard... the wonderful "Wizard of Oz." At the request of Bob Butler , N W. Ayer account exec, I received the assignment to go to Hollywood and 'be on the set' when my Whitman's Chocolates commercials were being taped at CBS studios there for our TV Christmas Special. It was to be the first time a major motion picture would be telecast to millions on a TV network. We were determined that our creations would match the quality and artistry of this 1939 film classic, starring Judy Garland.

After our producer Annette Bachner and I had screened sequences over and over to determine where best to cut into for our TV spots, we decided to let "the yellow brick road" lead right into them.

To open the show, I suggested having Judy Garland reading the original book to her little 11-year old daughter with the big-big eyes, Liza Minnelli. Judy nixed that idea, saying she didn't want to "commercialize her children." Everyone had liked the idea of a star opening, so we managed to sign clown Red Skelton with his delightful red-haired daughter, Georgia.

Everything about the project was first rate, including our accommodations at the legendary Beverly Hills Hotel. At a breakfast conference in the hotel lanai we spied Audrey

Hepburn talking-movie in a nearby booth. On the terrace sat Anthony Quinn. By the pool, Hoagy Carmichael seemed to be at work on a song in his cabana. Someone had me paged in the Polo Lounge. Gee it was good to be back again. Too bad I wasn't still writing SCREENINGS.

Answering my page, I was told that the background music tapes for my five commercials had arrived. Mitch Leigh (later famed for his MAN OF LA MANCHA) had orchestrated a score rippling with Christmas joy. Richard Maltby had given my lyrics "Wonderful Whitman's Sampler" a wonderful sound. So we had two of the best on Broadway composer-conductors providing the melodies for my words.

Producer Annette had also produced an exceptional cast, seemingly, overnight. "Hollywood is a supermarket of talent," smiled Annie. "Snap your finger and there it is. You should see the puppets they created yesterday for your Giftees jingle. Charming."

At the CBS-Television studios, they were taping DRAGNET on the next set. Across the way I heard a violin playing. It seemed so strange, so disconnected with the rest of the action around us, like one of those musicians who suddenly pop up playing "Flight Of the Bumble Bee" while sitting next to you on the subway. Out of curiosity I followed the scent of the sound. Sitting alone in a corner, soulfully sawing fiddle strings with his bow was Jack Benny.

Sometimes I had to pinch myself to realize I was hobnobbing and working side-by-side with the top talent of the day. Copywriters at N. W. Ayer set the mold. They had penned "A Diamond Is Forever" for De Beers; "In Philadelphia, Nearly Everybody Reads THE BULLETIN" and "They laughed when I sat down at the piano..."

My friend Comer Jennings, now one of Atlanta's best-known painters, had advised me when I arrived to write advertising copy: Keep on the good side of the artists. They can make You or break you. Heading Ayer's staff of layout artists, illustrators and calligraphers was Charles Coiner, who had designed the NRA-eagle symbol of President Franklin D. Roosevelt's National Recovery Act. Coiner was a believer that the manufacturer who dedicated his advertising to building the most consistent personality for his product or his company would get the largest share of market. No better example of this philosophy in action is "Great Ideas of Western Man," the corporate campaign for Ayer's client, Container Corporation of America. Coiner astonished the ad world by using exciting modern art to illustrate, not ad copy, but great quotes from great minds. No sell, just ads that stretched your mind, reminding you that any company that could command Man Ray, Ben Shahn, Rene Magritte and Feliks Topolski and their ilk to provide the graphics for such a high-level series, must be the best in the business. At HOUSE BEAUTIFUL, HOLIDAY and now, Ayer, I had the privilege of learning from "the best in the business."

No organization anywhere, that I knew of, had such a reputation for taste as Ayer's art department in the mid-1950s, and I was privileged to work closely with such artists as Donald Kubly, Tana Hoban, Edward Gallob, Wing Fong and Mary Faulconer. Each of them had illustrated the immortal words of William Penn, Woodrow Wilson and others in the Great Ideas series. Don Kubly, for instance, introduced me to the great photographer Irving Penn. We were working together on the Plymouth Automobile account, and Don somehow talked everyone into paying "extra for giving our car glamour-plus" by using the photographer who women recognized as the ultimate fashion photographer in Vogue. To give Plymouth that extra eclat, the model chosen to represent the smart Plymouth owner was Penn's wife, Lisa Fonsagrives. Later when we created a series of "ideas with paint" advertisements for our client DuPont Paint, Don

would take me along for the "shootings." While photographing Mary Faulconer's uniquely painted house in
Bucks County, her neighbor, the humorist S. J. Perelman,
dropped by for a chat. Most memorable of all in our Du Pont
Paint creations was by architect-designer Alexander Girard.
This association with Girard led to our great adventure into
collecting folk art.

Girard and his wife Susan had collected objects on their
world travels which they considered, in their own way, to be
masterpieces of form, color, whimsy or design. It may be a
barbershop sign from deepest Africa, an Indian doll from an
Acoma pueblo in new Mexico or a fanciful kite from
Bangkok.

Whether it was a native painting or wire funeral-wreath
frame discarded in a Paris cemetery, the Girards treated their
finds like jewels, and incorporated these objects in the most
charming environments my wife and I had ever seen.
Girard's ability to work in several disciplines...architecture,
fabric design, graphics...gave him complete control of his
project at hand. Hence his end product emerged as a three-
dimensional work of one artist, not a mish-mash weakened
by committee.

There was no better example showing the totality of
Girard's genius than the restaurant, La Fonda del Sol in New
York's TIME/LIFE building. When it opened in 1961, the
Kublys and the Bests were invited to make a grand tour. Its
influence on us is still exploding.

The Restaurant Associates had given Girard free-rein...the
menus, tableware, matchcovers, tiles, waiters' jackets, and
even the buttons on them. Here we saw in-toto the importance of color and texture, right down to the food on our
plates. Dining at La Fonda had all the fun of a fiesta, where
all ages, nationalities, walks-of-life joined together in a spon-
taneous celebration, sampling exotica of Latin America and

the joyousness of folk art. So entrancing was Girard's decor that diners wandered through the restaurant merry as mariachis, sharing together surprise after surprise in ingeniously lighted vignettes, whimsical south-of-the-border settings, colorfully inset in adobe walls. It gave us a life-expanding exuberance...instilling in us that zestful, imaginative informality is something to pursue in our own lives, rather than big-rich pretense. He whetted our appetites for more romantic, diversified interiors at home. Ones not depending on size or cost...affordable with a disciplined mix of color, pattern and art.

Soon we would be on a "yellow brick road" of our own, traveling the world to collect folk art right at the source. Thanks to the Girards and our new artist friends, we were to begin our odyssey hightailing it to Haiti for naive paintings direct from easels of Third World Rousseaus.

GEORGIA O'KEEFE MYSTERY

As Vice President Creative Director of Arndt, Preston, Chapin, Lamb and Keen, a Philadelphia-New York based advertising agency, I headed a staff of about thirty men and women. My role was somewhat akin to Leopold Stokowski's leading the Philadelphia Orchestra. Only, instead of violinists and oboe players, I led a symphony of copywriters, layout designers and commercials producers. One of my duties was to keep my creative band in tune with new trends in art, fashion, lifestyle, music, theater and media...anything that might inspire great ideas for our advertising. So, when our family took a grand tour of the American West, I had my antennae out for things to report in my talk to the agency when we returned.

In California, our children met Sidney Poitier lunching in the commissary at Universal Studios. Barbara and I were wowed when Diahann Carroll made a gorgeous entrance one night at Le Bistro. Equally exciting was my visit to see how a film studio made that cheering section of applauding hamburgers.

As we continued our Western odyssey, we rode horses over the Grand Tetons; floated on a raft down the Snake River with "Cookie,"(Queen of Sikkim Hope Cooke's father) as our guide; climbed Mesa Verde Indian ruins; and called on artist Georgia O'Keefe.

It was a surprise visit, mind you.

Impromptu.

When I told a friend in Santa Fe that I was gathering material for a report on what was happening in the art world of the West, he suggested "If you are going near Abiquiu, why not stop by and talk to Georgia O'Keefe? She has a fascinating studio-compound right on the tip of a mesa."

"Are you kidding?" I replied. "Everybody knows her passion for privacy makes her as unapproachable as Garbo."

"Well, do what you wish, but since you know two of her close friends, I'm sure she would be glad to see you. It gets lonely in those quiet hills."

Thus encouraged, I hustled my wife and three children into our luggage-jammed rental car. We headed up Highway 84, turning off at the exit marked "Abiquiu," then bumped down a road lined with dusty juniper and pinon trees leading past a soaring wall, imposing as the prow of a mighty ship.

O'Keefe's compound turned out to be a virtual fortress. Undaunted, I parked our car at the entrance portal and approached the tall, bolted, cedar-paneled Spanish gate, pulling the bell cord with my fingers crossed.

Soon an Indian woman appeared, peering at me through a slit in the door.

"Yes?" she inquired suspiciously.

I handed her my business card, saying I only wanted to ask Miss O'Keefe two questions, and bring her news of her friends Henry and Sandro. If she was busy, of course, I would understand, but being from the East Coast, it would be most disappointing not to see her for at least a minute or two ....

Before I could finish, the Indian greeter disappeared.

"Daaaaad, come on, let's go" my children pleaded, appalled by my brashness, sliding down in the seat hoping

66

they couldn't be seen.

Then, my wife looked past my shoulder and whispered: "My God, it's her!"

There she was, silver hair pulled tightly back; fierce, inquiring eyes; ramrod-straight, unsmiling, attired in a long flannel robe, wearing beaded Indian boots.

Reading from my calling card, she muttered: "I see you know my sister's friends, Henry and Sandro."

"Your *sister*?" I inquired, taken aback.

"I'm sorry. My sister is at her Ghost Ranch several miles away, but I'm sure she will be happy to speak to you on the telephone. Come in and follow me."

Once inside the enclosure, what seemed an identical twin of Georgia O'Keefe had me wait on the stoop of a slatted-blind doorway. "I'll get my sister on the telephone," she called over her shoulder.

After an interval she shouted from behind the door: "My sister will speak to you now. Here is the phone." With that, the receiver was handed to me through one of the slats.

"Miss O'Keefe?" I asked, speaking a bit too loudly into the mouthpiece.

"Yes," came a voice almost exactly like the one I had just heard.

After explaining the reason for my visit, and how I knew her two friends, we had a jolly good chat.

"When I first saw a painting of yours," I confessed, "your hills reminded me of big bosoms rising out of the desert."

She chuckled: "My, I didn't have that in mind."

She seemed very witty and fun-loving, telling me that she had recently returned from her first visit to Japan; that on the return flight, clouds below her made such a vivid impression she could not get the scene out of her mind, and they were emerging now on her canvas, inspired by the floating world of Japanese prints.

"I always paint from inside my head," she confided, then thanked me for calling, wished me a happy journey home, and hung up.

I pushed the telephone back through the door slat, saying "Here is your phone. I had a delightful talk with your sister. Thank her for being so gracious. "

"Goodbye" said the voice from the other side of the door. But only the Indian servant appeared to usher me out past the steer skulls and piled-up stones, to the gate.

Later, in Taos, I asked an acquaintance if Georgia O'Keefe had a sister living with her.

"She has a sister, but she lives in Palm Beach" I was told in reply. "And she looks nothing like Georgia. Very soigné; she is married to a railroad president."

I then related my "experience."

"Oh, that's an old Chinese trick," he laughed. "When a stranger suddenly appeared unannounced in a remote outpost, the owner would pretend to be someone else, either in fear of being robbed or whatever. She didn't want to be rude in case you were acquainted with her old friends, yet she wasn't sure of you, either." Then he added-with a shake of his head: "Yep, that was Georgia, all right."

THE WYETH WHO WENT WEST

On another trip to New Mexico, we visited another artist legend-in-her-own-time, Henriette Wyeth Hurd.

We had admired Henriette's portraits of her famous brother Andrew Wyeth and late husband Peter Hurd at Washington's National Portrait Gallery. Never did we dream that one day we would be her house guests. And, at the very same ranch she had painted that very same portrait of Peter.

It all came about under a hair dryer.

At "Tilli of Strafford," having her weekly coiffeur, wife Barbara mentioned to her friend-in-the-next-booth, Joyce Lewis, that we were planning a trip to Santa Fe. Joyce then suggested: "Since you're going to New Mexico, why don't you drive down to San Patricio and have Hugh interview Henriette Wyeth? She and her son Michael Hurd have recently opened a new gallery and I'm sure they would welcome a bit of publicity."

"Why that would be wonderful" countered Barbara "but how would we arrange to meet her?

"Well, I know her," said Joyce. "Her brother Nat Wyeth and our family have been friends since his college days. I'll call Nat and see what he says about it."

So, she did, and we were invited to be Henriette's guests.

All this led up to further interviews with Andrew Wyeth

at his Chadds Ford retreat, The Ark; also with Pulitzer Prize winner Paul Horgan, and "first lady of the American stage" Helen Hayes. Each of them gave me revealing background material on "the grand dame of America's royal family of art."

Henriette, first born of N. C. Wyeth's extraordinarily gifted children, grew up as darling of a social world with such friends and neighbors as the du Ponts of Delaware. Admired for her beauty, humor and talent at the easel, she had many beaus, including screen-idols John Gilbert and Richard Barthlemess. Never a day went by that the Wyeth domain wasn't exposed to stimulating talk. Her father, Newell Convers Wyeth, was perhaps America's most celebrated and best-financially-rewarded artist of his time. Her mother, Carolyn Bockius Wyeth, presided over a household noted for its exuberant lifestyle and gracious, informal hospitality. One day a guest at table might be author-grandee Joseph Hergesheimer or Baltimore iconoclast H. L. Menken or the editor of The Saturday Evening Post. Then, Peter Hurd came out of the West, lassoed Henriette and they rode off into the sunset of his beloved New Mexico.

"Peter was a charmer," Henriette's younger sister Ann McCoy told us. "Gary Cooper-type cowboy. Tall, lean, blonde. He had dropped out of West Point, on his own accord, attended Haverford College and Pennsylvania Academy of the Fine Arts to begin his career as a painter. Henriette was enrolled there, too, but they hadn't met until one day he was coming out for an interview to study painting with her father. They got off the same train at Wawa. Since they were the only passengers at the station, he tipped his Stetson and asked if she knew how he could get to N. C. Wyeth's studio explaining he had an appointment with him. Conveniently, N. C.'s driver was waiting to take her there, too.

"Well," Ann continued. "That was it. The rest is history. Peter became N. C.'s devoted pupil and Henriette's steady Mr. Right."

As we drove out to the Hurd ranch to visit Henriette, we wondered what she thought six decades ago when she first saw her new home-to-be. En route from Albuquerque, we had driven mile after mile without seeing a soul.

Spectacular vast landscapes, yes, but an infinity of stillness and silence. Here all the action was in an endless sky, stretching like an ocean overhead, with occasional lightning fireworks streaking across waltzing clouds. Then we came to a crossroads with a sign pointing to San Patricio, and looking down from a high ridge into Hondo Valley, we spied Sentinel Ranch. Covering over two thousand acres, it seemed like a Brigadoon in bronco country. Truly a verdant oasis in the Plains.

As we drove off the road towards the town of San Patricio, population 167 (but no one in sight), the only movement apparent was a huge flag flapping atop a sign reading "Hurd-Rinconada Gallery by the Polo Field." We had reached our destination!

The Gallery featured works by N. C. Wyeth, Henriette, Peter Hurd and son Michael.

"This is not your usual ranch" the Gallery hostess told us, after walking us past Henriette's full-length portrait of brother Andrew Wyeth posing as a young soldier in a Civil War uniform when he was a teenager. "Here we raise apples and artists."

"It looks like you have a nice crop of polo players, too," we remarked, noticing a game in progress on the polo grounds outside.

"Oh, yes," she smiled. "Polo was Peter Hurd's passion, as well as painting. It's the same with his son Michael, who has taken over the reins here since his father died."

Someone had told me Michael had designed this charming gallery-guest house, where we were to stay. It combined Swedish-modern efficiency with Santa Fe style, including an adobe corner fireplace in its living room, its cathedral ceiling had sort of a skywalk stretching across its center on the second floor. This led from our upstairs bedroom right onto a roof porch. Henriette had stocked the kitchen with food, beverages and breakfast staples for us, in a completely equipped kitchen. Henriette, now in her eighties, had left word to join her for breakfast in the main ranch house, where she lived nearby in a 19th-century adobe compound, completely sheltered from prying eyes of curious visitors.

Her hacienda seemed right out of Old Mexico, with its red-tile roofs and long portals encircling a patio garden. Peacocks paraded and preened across the yard, occasionally splitting tranquillity with their piercing shrieks. Henriette's German Shepherd "Greta" slept in the shade, while the gardener's obese dachshund "Maria" romped with Mike's mixed-breeds "Viva" and "Polo."

Like Henriette, herself, the hacienda had grown old with grace and charm. Her flair and imagination gave every room a special glow. Family antiques from Pennsylvania and New England stood side-by-side merry Mexican folk art. In the grand sala, N. C. Wyeth's "The Giant" hung over the mantel, and Jamie Wyeth's sketches of Rudolph Nuriyev had a place of honor next to Henriette's painting of Brazilian lilies.

The house meandered over several wings. Peter Hurd, an avid botanist, had erected a thriving Orangery near his studio and Henriette's indoor swimming pool. The studio was kept just as he left it, with-a small alcove outside the door containing his polo tack.

Henriette greeted us enthusiastically, attired in a quilted house coat, still very much a belle-of-the-ball. Over breakfast around an Amish table in her Spanish beamed kitchen, she had us chuckling with her anecdotes about people and places of her past. A great mimic, she gave a marvelous imitation of Truman Capote.

Capote, a special pet of hers, had visited there and asked her to paint one of Sentinel Ranch's green apples for him. When she sent him her rendition of "Truman's Apple" he was so pleased with the painting that he took it along with him to show the television audience when he appeared as guest on Johnny Carson's show.

Like Truman Capote, many of the Hurd's ranch guests were "legends" themselves.

Helen Hayes and husband, playwright Charles Mac Arthur were comforted there right after their only daughter, Mary, had died of polio. During that stay, Helen had her portrait painted by Henriette.

Another great chum, who visited months at a time with the Hurds, was Eric Knight, author of "Lassie Come Home," "The Flying Yorkshireman" and "This Above All." While there, he brought polo to San Patricio.

British born, polo-playing Eric had accepted the Hurds' invitation to come rest-up from the drudgery of writing screenplays in Hollywood. Seeing that the ranch had a wide, level field, several scrappy quarter horses and neighboring rancheros who could ride like the wind, Knight suggested they start a polo club, and enlist players and equipment from Peter's alma mater Roswell's New Mexico Military Institute. Ever since, Sentinel Ranch has been headquarters for San Patricio Polo Club. While we were staying at the guest house overlooking the polo field, we watched vans of visiting polo ponies arrive, filling 78 paddock stalls prior to a match with a team from Argentina.

Michael Hurd captained the San Patricio team, and lived in his studio residence, The Polo House, adjacent to the field.

Michael found "cowpasture polo" brought in paying visitors from neighboring states as well as close-by towns.

For years, crowds had come on weekends to watch Peter Hurd and his players pound the turf in heated matches. In turn, people would ask to purchase paintings direct from Peter's and Henriette's studios. So Michael decided to take advantage of their visits by creating Hurd-Rinconata Gallery, a place to browse before, between and after chukkas.

"For years people came to know this valley through my father and my mother," Michael told us. "The legacy of Peter Hurd still casts a long shadow over all southern New Mexico, and Henriette has brought the Wyeth mystique right here to Hondo Valley. So why discontinue the tradition they created?"

Thus, Henriette's transplanted Wyeth roots keep sprouting anew, way out West.

Adventure in Maya Land

ADVENTURE IN MAYA LAND

Rising out of Mexico's massive Yucatan jungles one can spy silhouettes of a vanished civilization... the ancient Maya's Cities of the Gods...mysteriously abandoned about 800 A.D....covered under centuries of vines... recently-sighted matching hillocks deep into a rainforest are thought to be twin towers of the legendary 'lost' Temple B..."

We were watching a fascinating film, MYSTERY OF THE MAYA, being shown by its producers, Suzanne and Hugh Johnston of Princeton. As we sat transfixed in that darkened University Museum auditorium, we didn't dream that a few months later we would be part of an expedition to rediscover Temple B.

Arranged by The Mexican Society of Philadelphia, expedition members included the Johnstons, who pulled all the strings with Mayaites; Dr. Victor Segovia, chief Maya archaeologist-in-the-field for Mexico City's Museum of Anthropology; a PBS producer; a honey-mooning couple; suburban Philadelphia adventurers and Rittenhouse Square sophisticates. Among them was white-gloved "Mrs. Perfect Hair-do" with her Gucci parasol to ward off that tropical sun. Of course we had no idea of what to expect.

No mention had been made that we might encounter scorpions and tarantulas dropping down our collars; that we could be covered like chain mail by swarms of stinging ants or killer bees. Did we even think about those swift-striking snakes, or steel-jawed jaguars, lurking in the bush?

Or that this jungle might be harboring tomb robbers, drug dealers or escaped convicts? Oh, no. In our minds that rain-forest would be an Eden flowered in exotic blooms, with Birds-of-Paradise, toucans and parrots tweeting in the tree-tops.

True, we were told to wear "protective" clothing: socks covering trouser cuffs; cotton gloves over long shirtsleeves secured by rubber bands; bandanas around neck; wide-brim hat to block out fierce sun rays; sturdy shoes for our hike over rough terrain. We would also pocket a potion of SCAT, plus a tube of sun-protector...but it never occurred to holster a gun, sheath a hunting knife, or carry along matches in case we lost our way.

Talk about innocents abroad!

Our game plan was to assemble in Merida, capital city of Yucatan, then fly to the just-completed Cancun Airport. Here we would be met by a fleet of taxis taking us to a sea-side fishing camp, complete with thatch roof roundhouses, or palapas; a Caribbean beach, and its own "tortuga farm" a pool-pen of giant turtles. (Here, turtle steak is as plentiful as chicken is in our cuisine.) "Primitive potluck" might well describe our accommodations. Beds and bathrooms depended on luck-of-the-draw. Some found they had creepy-crawlies as bedmates. The hairy spider in our cot seemed big as a crab, but at least we weren't stung by a scorpion, which accounted for the screams next door.

At dawn on our first day, after a sleepless night expecting more tarantulas, we wandered through a Mayan village towards the beach. Along the way, beautiful Mayan girls were washing their clothes and themselves in a shaded stream, their long, lustrous black hair gleaming in the rising sunlight. Gauguin hadn't fared better in Papeete!

On the beach, just as the sun rose out of the turquoise ocean like a giant yellow egg yolk, thousands of butterflies fluttered up as one, briefly blacking out the sky. From then on, we fully expected the unexpected.

Certainly not violence.

Yucatan seemed the last place in the world you'd expect violence. The Yucatecans are such gentle, beautiful people. Clean, quiet, God-fearing. They dress in spotless white, and live in houses surrounded by palms, built just the way Mayans designed them thousands of years ago. Archaeology confirms that a culture has existed on the Yucatan peninsula for almost twenty-thousand years. Centuries before Christ, astonishing cities covered its isthmus. When Europe was dragging through the Dark Ages, Yucatan's Mayas had mastered mathematics and astronomy. What's more, the Mayas stayed put. Why, remains one of the many mysteries that makes Yucatan ever intriguing.

You can bet they didn't stay because of ample water. You won't find a river in the whole of Yucatan. The natural water supply comes from deep underground streams. Rainfall seeps through porous limestone, bedrock of the entire peninsula. Occasionally, the earth caves in, sliding into the subterranean waters a hundred feet below, forming a well, or cenote (chen-oh-tee). Where there's a big cenote, you'll usually find remains of a big Mayan city close by.

We were to learn that ancient Mayas found their wilderness very generous, providing an abundance of fruit, game and corn. It took only half a year's work to fill their basic food and shelter needs. That made a short work week, with lots of leisure time to learn, think, build — even to invent rubber balls for games. They excelled in building and carving in stone. Soon, science and religion took over. Priests became powerful potentates presiding over spectacular

79

white temple cities towering over the lush landscape. A network of remarkable road systems (sakbe) linked these cities together.

All this in the big toe of Mexico, completely isolated from the rest of the country. With the Caribbean and Gulf lapping at its shores, a golden civilization flourished in Yucatan until 800 A. D., then something calamitous happened. Everything stopped. Seemingly overnight, millions of Mayas totally abandoned their colossal city-states. Nothing in world history compares with the mysterious Maya exodus.

Why? Many believe a class struggle was the main cause. Mayan aristocracy may have been swept up in keeping-up. The elite got greedy. One city tried to outdo the other in the lavish splendor of their architecture, monuments, jade and feather work. This led to inter-city warfare, draining manpower and food reserves until famine swept their cities clean. There's also a theory that this aristocracy kept peasants uneducated, so when the starving masses rose up and killed all the leaders, no one was educated enough, or strong enough, to keep alive the whole superstructure of trade, political administration and religion.

Thus, peasants scattered, deserting those ceremonial centers, leaving no one to take over.

No doubt we saw some of their descendants when we stopped in Merida, their capital city. Our distinguished archaeologist Victor Segovia, for instance, had a profile exactly like those of ancient Mayans depicted in petroglyphs and on wall friezes.

Merida seemed a most civilized town. Very Seville-like, fringed with wedding-cake Spanish Colonial buildings in blues, yellows, pinks and whites. Horse-drawn carriages clop-clopped through tree-lined streets. Markets lured with goods from all Yucatan: hammocks, huaraches, Huipiles, Guyaberas, embroidered cotton dresses, pottery, tortoiseshell combs, Panama hats.

Leaving Merida for Chichen-itza, as we bussed down a smooth Maya road, "lecture en route" became the order of the day. Oswaldo, our guide, loved to shock us with all the gory details about ancient sacrifices.

"Sacrifices!" he smacked. "Sacrifices! Those Chac Mool statues were used as sacrificial altars. The supreme sacrifice was human life. Children were preferred — because of their virginity. Sometimes they bought them from neighboring cities, paying usually five or ten red beans per child.

Then they would strip the victim, paint his body blue, lead him to the top of the pyramid and, with great ceremony, he would be stretched over a stone alter. Four priests (or chacs) would hold his arms and legs in a hammer-lock grip. Then the priest known as a nacom would step forward with a dagger of flint or obsidian, slash the victim's chest and tear out the heart. It would still be beating when he handed it to a high priest whose job it was to dip his fingers in the blood and anoint the faces of idols with it..."

"That's enough! Stop it!" ordered Mrs. Perfect Hair-do, having turned slightly pale.

"But that's not all!" guide Oswaldo shushed for attention, continuing: "they would toss the corpse down the temple steps to a waiting priest, who would skin it and dance in the skin. The onlookers ate the rest of the body — or almost all of it. They'd save the hands and feet for the officiating priests..."

"I said ENOUGH!" shouted Mrs. Perfect Hair-do, covering both ears.

Undeterred, Oswaldo kept on orating dramatically. "There were loads of other rituals. Dancers shooting arrows into sacrificial victims tied to a stake — and, as you will see in Chichen-Itza, there's The Temple of the Nuns, where virgins were kept before they were sacrificed and thrown into

The Sacred Well."

Not only were these 'sacred spots' reconstructed, so was most of Chichen-itza, laying before us to explore as an open-air museum. Lording over it all was a 100-ft. high pyramid, El Castillo, looming sunward above a base 180 feet square. On each side, flights of steps totaling 365 (days of the year) led to a platform at its peak. The surface of this mighty edifice was faced with 52 stone slabs, representing the number of weeks in a year. Steps were so narrow we had to climb to the top sideways. One could easily see why so many had tumbled down, descending from the peak, and broken their necks.

Naturally, we had to see what was inside, for there is a perfectly preserved temple right at its center. To get to it, we slid through a slit in the side, crept down a long dark gallery, climbed a narrow, steep, stone stairway to enter an inner chamber guarded by a red-stone jaguar. This ancient cat had the fanciest spots ever: 73 inlaid jade chips.

Upon leaving, we patted the Chac Mool at the entrance, hoping it would bring us luck in the impending jungle journey. The Chac Mool is a reclining figure representing Chac, god of rain, and Mool, Mayan's sacred jaguar. On its back, carved as a stone dish, is a depository for freshly torn-out hearts.

Chichen-Itza was especially interesting because it represented three periods of the Mayan Civilization. Founded by Itza-Maya emigrants from central Mayadom in the fifth century, it existed peacefully until the blood-thirsty Toltecs charged in from Mexico and took over between the 10th and 13th centuries. That's when all the pyramids, jaguars and sacrificial altars entered into the picture — and their soccer-like ball game.

Chichen-itza's Ball Court of the Gods is big league. Here the ball game was seen as a religious rite, played on a field

272-ft. long and 199-ft. wide.   A heavy stone ring protrudes at right angles from the midpoint of the arena's side walls, each decorated with reliefs of snake designs and rising 23 feet from the ground.   The object of the game was to get a hard rubber ball through the ring using only the knee, elbow or hip.   If you lost the game, you lost your head.

By the time we reached the most impressive of all Mayan city-states, Uxmal (ushmawl), we thought we had done more than enough pyramiding.   But we were in for a delightful surprise.

Before descending into our rainforest searching for Temple B, archaeologist Segovia invited us to see his dig, Kohunlich. He had named it for the kohun palm grove surrounding the site of a once mighty city near the Guatemalan border.   No one knows just when this city started, but it had been recently discovered when looters tried to sell a giant mask off one of its pyramids to the Metropolitan Museum of New York.   It came to the attention of Mexico City's Museum of Anthropology, which immediately contacted their Mayan expert in Merida, Victor Segovia.   He went to investigate and, voila!, found his life work, unearthing what might have been a metropolis as long as Los Angeles.

Right from the start there was excitement since we would be the first Americans to see it.   What we saw had us frozen in our tracks, as if we had unexpectedly turned off a road and run smack into Shangri La.   We walked down a ridge covered by palm trees and wild orchids towards the giant Pyramid of The Masks at the end of a long ball court. Suddenly, rockets started flaring into the sky; sounds of our Philadelphia Orchestra boomed Beethoven's Third from the tree tops as stunning Mayan maidens in brilliantly embroidered cottons walked towards our ladies, presenting each with huge bouquets of multi-hued zinnias.   Then one in our group pointed to a Mayan, all in white, descending down the steps from atop the towering pyramid. He held high a big placard-on-a-pole inscribed: WELCOME, PHILADELPHIA GRINGOS.

We were almost intoxicated with delight at our spectacular and unexpected greeting. Segovia had hitched his stereo speakers to his Jeep battery, and had all 150 of his workers make ready for us. We had a luau under the palms, complete with fresh pineapples soaked in rum; imported pate, cheeses, meats, beer, native fruits and soft drinks.

It was quite different the next day at Temple B, the target of our expedition. Everyone was up at sunrise, dressed so all exposed parts, other than faces, were covered to keep out ticks and other undesirables. A ragtag caravan, seven vehicles in all, had been assembled to the edge of our jungle. An open truck came equipped with a thrift-shop assortment of broken rockers, car seats, and straight chairs lined up in the back as sort of an in-transit conversation pit. Most of us packed into rusty VWs, which natives here call "bellybuttons" (since everybody has one).

We rattled-jostled-and-bumped over washboardish roads to the beginning of an abandoned logging trail, then hiked right into the rainforest. Sort of like going through a Disneyland spook show with ant hills, tree trunks needled with thorns, weird sounds, and animal tracks. We marched single file, our chiclero guide cutting a path ahead with his razor-sharp machete. He was also carrying a Nan Duskin shopping bag for our Rittenhouse Square gardener, just in case she found a rare orchid or two to put in it.

After a few hours, several stumbles and cries of "Slow up!" we heard Segovia call out: "There it is — Temple B! A jewel in the jungle!" (only he pronounced it "yool in the yungle").

And a jewel it was. Twin towers still intact. Pulling off its covering of old vines, we discovered a wall of latticework in stone.

84

We climbed over ramparts and into small chambers to make rubbings of its ancient graffiti: a Maya god, a nude woman, a cat, two square-headed peasants carrying a Mayan ruler on a litter.

All of us gathered in front of Temple B for an official photograph. Quite a feeling to know that we were the first to visit there in 1,000 years. We put "lost" Temple B back on the Mayan map.

AN X-RATED CELEBRITY

There I was, bigger than life, spread across the FRONT PAGE of The Philadelphia Inquirer, my picture, double column, captioned "Hugh Best in his Main Line living room."

And under that in big, bold headline type: "SEX IN 1776," subheaded "HE'S AN X-RATED CELEBRITY."

Me, nice little Sonny Best of Rome, Georgia. "G. I. Billy Rose," "Elephant Boy" and now, X-RATED.

It's all George Washington's fault.

In fourth grade my paper on George Washington, written on his birthday, won me my first writing prize: a child's biography of George Washington. Even though it was due more to my illustrating it with postcards of Washington's ancestors' English home Sulgrave Manor, sent to me by my surrogate grandmother, Great Aunt Gertrude, than brilliant text, I viewed my award second only to a Nobel.

All through life I walked in the path of Washington. At Washington and Lee, I hiked to Natural Bridge where he had carved his name as a boy. In World War II, I happened to be stationed at his old stomping grounds, Belvoir, and spent many a Sunday leave exploring Mt. Vernon.

So it's not surprising when my country's Bicentennial approached that I felt it time to write The Great American Book on George Washington.

But how did he - and I - get X-Rated in the process?

You see, in my research, I found his life story in that era of erotica, to be, well, sexless. And I wanted my book to be read.

"A Dirty Book Never Goes Unread" is a proverb that popped into my memory. However, I continued my pursuit of producing something straight and noble about my hero. In searching for anecdotes at Washington's headquarters in Valley Forge National Park, I discovered that his troops sang this barracks ditty to the tune of "Yankee Doodle":

> Sir William, he
> Snug as a flea,
> Slept in his bed a-snoring.
> He does no harm
> As he lays warm
> In bed with Mrs. Loring.

Exploring further, I found Sir William to be Commander-in-Chief of the British forces in America, and Mrs. Loring, his camp-following mistress. More than that, he had been a member of a notorious sex-fraternity, "The Hell-Fire Club" back home in jolly-old-England. In fact, many of the British elite, including Lord Sandwich and Sir Francis Dashwood, fellow members with Howe of Brooks's Club, had reveled in orgies as "Monks of Medenham," at Dashwood's country seat, West Wycomb Park, in Buckinghamshire. Why, most of those Redcoats were randy rakes, three thousand miles from home!

That's how my "Red Hot & Blue: An X-Rated History of the American Revolution" was born. And here's what that story in The Philadelphia Inquirer said about it—unexpurgated.

Sex in 1776.
He's an X-Rated celebrity
By Susan Q. Stanahan
Inquirer Staff Writer

"Reeves Wetherill, the publicity director of Wanamakers, is describing the long-time Philadelphia tradition of a celebrity autograph party in the Grand Court:

"I do this sort of thing all the time, with every celebrity who comes to Philadelphia, whether it is Zsa Zsa, Yul Brynner, James Michener or Hugh Best."

"Hugh Best?

"You know, Hugh Best.

"Last year, he wrote a book commemorating the 100th anniversary of his Main Line Presbyterian church. It did not make a big splash. This year he just published a history of the Revolutionary War: "Red Hot and Blue, an X-rated History of the American Revolution." It is making a big splash.

"Hugh Best, possessing the expected Main Line credentials of Racquet Club membership, impressive art and antique collection and all the right connections among Philadelphia's movers and shakers, has written, and now is out hustling, a 205-page dirty history book.

"So far, the book has won a deafening silence from the city's book reviewers.

"But Best has gotten celebrity treatment from two staid old Philadelphia institutions — Wanamakers and his own Racquet Club.

"For what? Well, for coming up with a new angle to work the Bicentennial for bucks. That angle: Sex; raw sex.

"'It's straight barnyard sex throughout the whole thing," says Best, a silver-haired, impeccably dressed former Georgian, sitting for the moment in his elegant Wayne home, adjacent to the campus of the Valley Forge Military Academy.

"'Frankly, it wouldn't sell if it wasn't written this way.'"

"Best, who 25 years ago was writing scripts for a Western filmed in the WCAU-TV parking lot, has described a colonial world in which there were no flat-chested women, where George Washington had to change into his uniform before entering Philadelphia because he had been hit by a flying chamber pot and where a New York City house of ill repute was operated by a woman named Madame Triks.

"He has given real-life historical figures, such as Capt. John Andre, later executed for his role in aiding Benedict Arnold, such memorable lines as: 'Man cannot live by bed alone,' and has described Howe as 'Lady Killer Numero Uno.'

"British are bad guys

"To keep from offending any of his friends—some of whom can trace their heritage back to the signers of the Declaration of Independence—Best portrays the British as the transgressors, with Benjamin Franklin—who will be remembered for better things—as the only wayward American patriot.

"The tone of the book is set on the very first page:

"'Mr. Benjamin Franklin: a lady greets as she sweeps open the door.

"'Lady Caroline.'

"They stand in the door eyeing each other. She smiles and bids him enter.

"'You were so kind to invite me for a little game,' Franklin whispers.

"'You were so kind to come. I get lonely here on Thursday when the servants are off. The house is so empty.'

"They look knowingly at each other, chuckle, embrace, kiss, tussle and grapple in the entrance hall. Franklin pulls down her dress and fondles her ample bosom.

"'Mr. Franklin,' she said archly, 'I asked you here to play

a little chess...not chest.'

"You get the drift. And that's just the part we can print.

"What Best has done in RED HOT AND BLUE etc. was take a few shreds of historical evidence that indicate the British in the American colonies may have originated the slogan 'Make Love, Not War' and written an account of their escapades.

"'The purpose of the book is to make the Bicentennial fun, to get people excited, to make it a spicy hors d'oeuvre to the feast of the Bicentennial,' explains Best.

"Actually, another purpose of Best's book was suggested by a legitimate historian on a recent Washington, D.C. talk show, when Best was featured in a segment of the show on 'kitsch souvenirs.'

"'I came on as comic relief,' recalls Best, who was roundly criticized by Thomas Fleming, author of 1776: YEAR OF ILLUSIONS.

"'He claimed I am not a historian, which I am not, and that all I am is a salesman trying to cash in on the Bicentennial, which I am, telling the history in the idiom of today which is, unfortunately, pornographic'...

"Other than some expressions of 'shock' among neighbors in the wealthy enclave where Best lives, he says the only negative reaction to RED HOT AND BLUE has been an oft-asked question: 'What's a nice man like you doing writing a book like that?'"

Well, after that, all Hell broke loose.

My brother Jim in Birmingham, Alabama kept my book locked in his car trunk, hidden from his darling daughter, Ann.

My cousin Gertrude Smith in Rome, Georgia, always a sister to me, tried to block it from local bookstores, warning friends DO NOT READ THIS BOOK. IT'S UGLY!

My dear minister at Bryn Mawr Presbyterian Church, David Watermulder, referred to "that book" in a sermon, and he didn't mean The Bible.

"Red Hot" became the chic book to read during Bicentennial days.

Colonial Dames of America would see me coming and duck into the nearest doorway, so they must have read my book.

College newspapers gave it rave notices. Princeton's Whig Clio (history) Society tossed a Madiera party in my honor.

I appeared on WHAT'S MY LINE with Arlene Francis; PANORAMA in Washington with Margaret Truman; CBS with Harry Belafonte, Pete Seegar and Paul Robeson's son; and radio talk shows over the USA, even though in Bible belt areas, only adult bookstores would stock it.

After its first 100,000 copies sold out, my publishers printed more, and more and more.

It's still selling.

And I'm still X-rated.

HOUSEPARTY AT BUFFALO BILL'S

After my RED HOT book made its big splash, I kept getting intriguing complementary invitations. ALITALIA gave me a first class trip to Milan-Florence-Venice. The President of Peru, Governor of Veracruz, tourist bureaus, hotel and resort publicity offices made similar offers. I accepted them all.

Buffalo Bill Historical Center IMPLORED me to come see and write about them, due to the insistence of gorgeous Leigh Gamble Peralta-Ramos an old pal of my son Don who seemed to always have loyal and lovely girl friends.

"Why should I write about a Buffalo Bill museum in Cody, Wyoming?" I asked, imagining it to be a display of his spurs and saddle in a remote filling-station. However, when The Center pelted me with handsome books, beautiful publications, plus asking Barbara and me to a gala houseparty, and we saw who was on the guest list , I changed my tune.

Here was a great article-and-photo op!

First I asked my friend from HOLIDAY days, Frank Zachary what he thought about it. Frank, then Editor of TOWN & COUNTRY, reacted with instant enthusiasm when I showed him Cody's past characters which included Gertrude Vanderbilt Whitney; "Sonny" and Mary Lou Whitney; Vogue-editor Diana Vreeland; Brooks Brothers-heir Win Brooks and so many other socialites that little old Cody,

Wyoming seemed like Park Avenue West.

"Go! Do it!" he directed, slamming hand on desk. "Bring us back a great story."

So I did.

Cody was a complete surprise. Not the looks of the town itself, but its inner life and sensational surroundings. All around it, grassland rolled up into forested foothills and snowy peaks, close to where the Big Horn Basin bumps into Wyoming's Rocky Mountains. Yellowstone Park was less than two hours away.

We discovered that Cody-area ranches belonged to scions of Rockefellers and Wideners; CEOs of Coca-Cola, Morton Salt and such.

When we first walked into Cody's night-and-day gathering spot, The Irma Hotel, fellers in fancy boots and bola ties turned out to be General Jimmy Doolittle; James Michener; film-actor Slim Pickens; sportscaster Curt Dowdy; Willard Marriott; Senator Alan Simpson; Ray Hunt, of the Dallas H. L. Hunt oil clan; sculptor Harry Jackson and Peter Kriendler, major domo of Manhattan's "21."

The Irma's gigantic cherry-wood back bar had a celebrated background, too. It was a gift to Buffalo Bill from Queen Victoria!

Buffalo Bill lived like a king, himself, with the world's great and near-great as his courtiers. He hunted with the Prince of Monaco and Grand Duke Alexis of Russia.

During his Wild West Show decades, he accumulated millions of dollars, plus several hundred thousand acres of ranch land, and had such friends in high places as Teddy Roosevelt. They say that Roosevelt borrowed the name "Rough Riders" from Bill Cody and also some of his Wild West Show horses for that charge up San Juan Hill in Cuba.

Hunting with Buffalo Bill was de rigeur with wealthy sportsmen. Among them was W. R. Coe, chairman of

Johnston & Higgins Insurance Company, and married to the daughter of Rockefeller's partner, Henry Huttleston Rogers. Their Standard Oil fortune was considerable, and the Coe's Long Island estate "Planting Fields," a showcase. When he experienced life in Cody country, he was hooked.

In 1913, Mr. Coe bought land from Buffalo Bill, built a lodge, and every summer the Coe entourage, with family doctor plus a full staff of servants, would arrive from New York in a private railroad car, with their automobiles strapped on flatcars.

His son, the Honorable Robert Coe, former Ambassador to the Court of Denmark, asked us to have lunch with him at his lordly Coe Lodge. Coe's spread, considered to be the most beautiful in all the West, covered a 500-acre mountaintop surrounded by the snow-topped Rockies in one direction, with the valley of Cody and Yellowstone Park beyond.

His driveway from off the main road to the Lodge's front door was eight miles long, with deer and antelope at play on either side.

Coe Lodge, itself, was no Lincoln log cabin.

Its vast hewn-log living room, with its great stone fireplace, bear rugs, paintings by Bierstadt, Catlin and Coe himself, was crammed with family memorabilia. Beside a photograph of his maternal grandfather, Henry Huddleston Rogers, was a sketch of Roger's steam yacht, circa 1900. We also noticed a signed formal portrait of the King and Queen of Denmark, and another of Bob's glamorous first cousin, Millicent Rogers.

Millicent and Bob had grown up together on Long Island and we surmised he had always been in love with her.

Millicent Rogers was one of the most exotic, commanding social figures of her time, with such legendary style that her jewelry and gowns set fashion.

"Millicent was the most extravagant person on earth,"

Bob Coe told us. "She stacked her Monets on a floor in the corner."

It looked to us that his lifestyle wasn't exactly pinch-penny.

Every year he brought his household staff over from his winter villa on the Riviera. So Coe Lodge's cuisine was more Cannes than Cody.

Bob Coe's Swiss valet/butler, Vincent Bassin, had been with him for over forty years. The first maid had served for years at Blair House in winter, Coe Lodge in summer.

Our luncheon, announced promptly at one, began with a perfect souffle served on limited edition china decorated with art by Frederic Remington.

It didn't take long to see that Coes certainly live well in Cody.

Bob's sister-in-law, Margaret Coe, lived in a town mansion more Whitney-Long Island than John Wayne-Western.

Its spacious rooms, paneled walls, Coromandel screens, English antiques, Romney painting made a great setting for entertaining visiting big-wigs. Peg Coe, as chairman of Buffalo Bill Historical Center's Board, held Cody's social reigns with the dexterity of Buffalo Bill driving his Deadwood stagecoach. A welcome-reception at her place set off a series of events for our celebrity houseparty—square dancing, fly-fishing, barbecues and rodeo.

Buffalo Bill's grandson, Fred Garlow (Irma's eldest boy), gave Barbara and me a private tour of "his" Yellowstone. Fred's younger brother had his name changed from Bill Garlow to Bill Cody, giving his Bill Cody's Dude Ranch a touch of authenticity. He had grown billy-goat whiskers and shoulder-length hair to even look like his famous grandpa.

Most glorious of all our festivities was the official opening of the Center's $3.75-million complex: The Plains Indian Museum. Leaders from 14 Plains tribes helped in the planning of it right from the ground up.   Representatives of the Blackfoot, Cheyenne, Crow, Gros Ventre, Shoshone, Arapaho and Sioux nations served on the Indian Museum's advisory board, with a distinguished Gros Ventre anthropologist, George Horse Capture, as curator.

Peter Hassrick, the Center's dynamic Director, had been curator of Fort Worth's Amon Carter Museum of Western Art before Cody corralled him, so he knew where the best Indian collections could be found, and what Indians were most qualified to plan the displays.   An absolutely stunning museum resulted.   So when it opened, Cody had the greatest pow-wow imaginable.

Members of fourteen tribes came on horseback in full Indian regalia, setting up tepees on the Museum grounds. Their leaders held open house in each wigwam.   Sitting on heirloom blankets, they looked magnificent in their feathers, furs, turquoise and silver finery.

We all joined hands and snake-danced together around ceremonial bonfires to the beat of tom-toms and chants.

We had a ball , and began our delightful association as a writer for TOWN & COUNTRY.

PEER-ING INTO TEXAS

TOWN & COUNTRY ran my Cody story in an unprecedented two-parts as THE CODY CONNECTIONS and THE CODY COLLECTIONS... all in the same issue. Many pictures, many pages.

On the day our copy arrived, I received a phone call from my good-ole-boy Texas buddy Lon Hill.

"You old son-of-a-bitch" he drawled. "I just read that piece of cow-plop you wrote about Coe-dee, Wyomin'. Cody!! Why we got lots more exciting stuff to tell about, down here in Corpus Christi country — King Ranch, Padre Island, Farrah Fawcett, more oil money than you can shake a stick at. Now you just get your tail down here and start tellin' tale. We'll tell you who's-who and what-to-do. Philip Johnson designed our new museum and it's a knock-out. Now you start packing."

I had remembered that THE BRAVE BULLS author Tom Lea had written THE WONDERFUL COUNTRY, a biography of the King Ranch. Edna Ferber had based her novel GIANT on it, too. I looked up some articles about Senator Lloyd Benson, and, remembering what Lon said about that "beautiful museum by Philip Johnson," we called Johnson himself.

"I need help," I implored. "TOWN & COUNTRY wants me to do a story about Corpus Christi and your new museum. Who were the mover-and-shakers back of it there?"

Right off the bat the great architect replied "Ed and Patsy Singer. Let my partner John Burgee tell you about it."

Burgee agreed. The Singers were the money force and driving force. "They came direct to our offices and asked us to build them an art museum, for they liked what we had done in Houston and Museum of Modern Art. Well, we didn't know whether Corpus was big enough to afford it, so told them we would have to have a million dollars in advance. They didn't bat an eyelash. 'That's no problem,''' said Patsy. 'Ed get out your checkbook.' And you can bet, money was no problem—-you'll find Corpus great story material."

We discovered that sort of Big Money-thing prevailed around Corpus Christi. No sooner than Jean and Lon Hill announced we were on our way from TOWN & COUNTRY , Texas hospitality rose to new heights.

First, Patsy and Ed Singer invited 150 of "the folks you want to meet" to a swank dinner dance in our honor. French cuisine, black-tie, champagne, caviar, Cole Porter music—-the works.

Next day, King Ranch-scion B. K. Johnson and his wife Patsy had us for lunch at La Puerta de Agua Dulce, their historic turn-of-the-century-style ranch mansion, key in the King family saga that led them to build a ranch empire spreading over thirteen-million acres worldwide.

That night James Storm and his Argentinian bride, Chela, entertained us on their 112-ft. yacht, CELIKA S. anchored at a Corpus Christi marina. Twenty-six were seated at dinner served by members of their five-man crew. Afterwards we had a moonlight cruise into the Gulf of Mexico.

As we drifted past Ed Singer's line of oil-refineries, each outlined in lights so they reflected in the water like a parade of July 4-fireworks, we got to chat with our fellow-guests intimately. We learned that our host personally owned more off-shore drilling rigs than any individual anywhere, renting them to nations and potentates from Arabia to the North Sea. He represented Corpus' "international importance."

At this yacht-party we met Lawrence Wood and his wife Leonora Yturria, whose great-grandfather Don Francisco Yturria had come up from Mexico and made a fortune in banking during the Civil War. Richard and Leonora were elegant examples of "the Texas-Mexico connection," and added Old World dash to the social scheme of things. Lawrence and his brother added even more: a restored period country village, Sunshine Place.

Lawrence took us out to see this town they owned lock, stock and liquor barrel. Here, they had built the state's first legal distillery, TEXAS SPIRIT, capable of producing Scotch, bourbon, tequila and vodka, as well as gasohol!

Another local big-wig, Charlie Butt, sent a boatman to ferry us to a Padre Island landmark, the pre-Civil War Arkansas Pass Light Station which Butt converted into his private retreat, a great place to entertain friends at beach parties.

Our resulting article, LONE STAR PEARL, was given a 10-page Texas-size spread in TOWN & COUNTRY, illustrated with 22 four-color pictures. It appeared when DALLAS was red-hot TV fare, worldwide, including Great Britain and its colonies. In London, it caught the eye of Debrett, British publishers planning a book with Tex-appeal.

DEBRETT'S PEERAGE AND BARONETAGE for centuries had been the bloodstock register of Britain's titled lords and ladies. Now they were ready to do the same on the "aristocracy" of the United States. What better way to give it world interest than by making its first book showcase Texas "nobles." And, who better to do it than that writer who wrote about Texas patricians so prominently in TOWN & COUNTRY: Hugh Best?

"Why me?" I asked Debrett's director of the project, Martin Stansfield. "I am not a Texan, or a genealogist."

"We could tell by your coverage in TOWN & COUNTRY that you would be accepted by the Texas elite. We checked and heard you had the right connections. Besides, you have a Southern accent, and we like your style."

"My style?"

"We want our books to attract the leisured, well-off and fashionable reader—to be about stars of American social leadership," he explained. "We don't want a directory. We want to entertain with a jolly-good read."

Since Texas is about the same size as the whole country of Spain, writing such a book was a tall order, but I accepted it as a challenge. Opportunity for more "adventures."

Fortunately I had good friends who "knew-the-territory."

Peter Kriendler of "21," watering hole for rich Texans in New York, brought me up-to-date on who-was-who-where.

Frank Zachary reminded me that TOWN & COUNTRY tried to list Texas richest families, and found it so long that his magazine had to limit it to families with fortunes over $30 million. At the top was the Hunt clan of Dallas. Their combined wealth exceeded $8 billion!

One of them, Stuart Hunt, was my fraternity brother and crew mate at Washington and Lee. We pledged Phi Delta Theta together as freshmen. He helped with introductions to his uncles, cousins and aunts.

Lon Hill-the-Third's granddaddy had headed Central Texas Power and Light, and was credited as opening up South Texas to commerce. So the son of "Mr. South Texas" led me through that area's social strata.

B. K. Johnson steered me straight about his King Ranch family members, and who in Texas was considered "true peerage."

Neiman-Marcus provided a great source of anecdotes about Texas big-spenders past and present.

Manhattan art dealer Clyde Newhouse, over lunch at Le Cirque, brought me up-to-date on Texas important collectors, and gave fond recollections of legendary Miss Ima Hogg.

Those sources handed me the keys that opened doors of the high-and-mighty of Houston, Dallas and beyond.

I started in Dallas, for the "Dallas" TV series had inspired our book, and the Hunt family was hot-copy. Especially, Caroline Hunt. She's the Hunt behind THE hotel: Dallas' ultra-chic The Mansion On Turtle Creek, an intimate world-class hostelry with an award-winning restaurant.

When Caroline inherited $2 BILLION from her daddy, H. L. Hunt, she called her sons and daughter together and held a family conference to decide what enterprise would be interesting, productive and pleasurable for them to share as a family.

Her eldest son, Stephen Sands (by her first husband) said he felt Dallas needed an elegant small hotel " like The Connaught in London." To Steve, a real-estate man, hotel returns looked better than the standard real-estate transaction. Sons Bunker, David and Patrick liked ranching, farming, timber, oil and gas. Her only daughter, Laurie, loved remodeling old houses for resale, and mama-Caroline's special interests were interior-decorating and cooking. In the world of cuisine, she was one of three American women elected to the Commanderie des Cordons Bleus de France.

Caroline and family decided to embark in the hotel business under the name Rosewood Hotels, Inc., Rose being Caroline's middle name.

For their first venture they found a Mediterranean-style mansion with a glamorous history and fashionable address: Turtle Creek. Purchasing the house with its four-and -a-half acres for $1.6 million, they invested $19.4 million in restoring it and building a 143-room hotel addition.

To create "timeless classic interiors with understated elegance," they turned to Robert Zimmer. By the time we checked in there to interview Caroline it had become the most talked about luxurious hotel in America.

Caroline, pretty, unassuming, unpretentious drove us around Dallas in her station wagon. We told her to show us what Hunt owned, and she did so —pointing out skyscrapers, stadiums, properties in much the way my Aunt Maude would point out varieties of petunias in her garden.

In the course of our Hunt tour of Dallas, Caroline talked about what she hoped to do now that The Mansion On Turtle Creek was off and running. "See that block" she said, "I would like to level all those tacky buildings and build a stylish Rodeo Drive type shopping area with boutiques and a luxury hotel."

"Oh you plan to have other hotels?" we asked.

"Oh yes. Maybe one in Houston, perhaps a Hawaiian resort. Also, do you know The Bel-Air in Los Angeles? I wish we could buy it, and it would be wonderful for us to have a grand hotel in London."

Years later all those wishes came true. Everything Caroline touched seemed to bloom.

We stayed at The Bel-Air after she put millions into redecorating it, and we loved The Lanesborough in London. All had her touch.

Stu Hunt suggested we drive over to Kerrville and talk to Charles Schreiner at his YO Ranch. Charlie, known as Charlie Three, raised nearly-extinct animals.

When we were let past YO's electric gates, we gasped in seeing giraffe striding across the landscape, co-mingling with zebra, ibex, emu, blackbuck antelope, ostrich—exotica from nether reaches of the globe.

"Once a Zulu chief visited here, " Charlie III recounted. "He couldn't believe what he saw. Said if he had landed by parachute, he would have sworn he was back in Africa."

There were some 10,000 animals on The YO, including javelina, jack rabbits and more than 400 head of Texas long-horns, a nearly extinct breed of cattle he rejuvenated after breeding his first longhorn bull in 1960.

Exotic animals added a dash of panache to other Texas ranches, too. One of his neighbors had a one-horn rhino that escaped and charged into YO property. No problem. YO had its own game warden from Kenya, and he knew just what to do. That rhino was escorted home without further ado.

While Charlie collected kudu in Kerrville, attorney Gib Denman was rounding-up Roman and Grecian marbles, Egyptian burial art and Etruscan ceramics and bringing them back to his private museum overlooking San Antonio's pic-turesque Riverway. He took us to see his classical antiqui-ties, dramatically lighted and displayed in his town pied-a-terre a few miles away from his white-columned antebellum mansion on a lake.

Knowing that his law firm administered the estates of Texas most prominent families, we asked about the late Miss Ima Hogg, whose American antiques collection was leg-endary. And so was Miss Ima, often called "The First Lady of Texas," but more often known to the outside world for her unfortunate name. Mr. Denman told us it was not true that her father, a governor of Texas, had named her brothers Heza Hogg, Sheza Hogg and Ura Hogg. However, it was true she spared no expense to get the quality she wanted.

"We went hunting for antiques together in Munich after the Bayreuth Festival one year," Gib Denman recalled, "And I was stunned at the cost of a complete set of Nymphenburg porcelain on her shopping list. When I told her the price was

105

eighty-thousand dollars, she just smiled and replied 'I thought it would be something like that. Buy it.'"

Getting the best didn't stop another Houston grand dame, Sarah Campbell Blaffer, heiress to a Humble oil-Texaco fortune. In her five generations of collecting art, when truly fine art was available to buy, she gathered a phenomenal collection of Old Masters, Impressionists, American Abstract Expressionists which she loaned free to Texas schools, colleges and museums that didn't have collections of art. "Most of her buying took place before World War II," said Denman, who was her lawyer, too. "And she would buy de Kooning and Pollock when almost no one else in Texas shared her understanding. Now her "museum without walls" with its Goyas, Tintorettos, Rothkos, Munchs travel all over the state bringing the fine art experience to far-flung Texas areas where there are no art treasures."

We found that Sarah's daughters, Jane Blaffer Owen and Her Serene Highness Princess Titi Von Furstenburg, were chips off the old block. Jane restored the utopian community of New Harmony, Indiana. She felt the entire village had been just waiting for her to adopt it. She took it all under her wing, renovating old buildings but adding such inspirational contemporary architectural innovations as Philip Johnson's "roofless church"; Richard Meier's dazzling-white library; and Jacques Lipchitz's Ceremonial Gates.

When Jane Owen and a friend pulled up in a new Mercedes 450 SL convertible to show us "her Houston." First thing we noticed was her hat swooping almost the width of the windshield.

"That's what I call A HAT," I remarked, admiring it.

"Mr. John makes them for me," she laughed "I've named this one for my old neighbor Howard Hughes' megaplane SPRUCE GOOSE. When the wind hits it —- crash!"

While Jane and her sister Titi collected art, another

uniquely Texan heiress, Electra Waggoner Biggs, created it. Electra lived on the 500,000-acre Waggoner spread in northwest Texas. Everything in site, she owned. The town of Electra, Texas, was named for her. So was Buick ELECTRA. She studied sculpturing while living at Hotel Carlisle in New York, and went on to create portrait heads of Eisenhower, Truman, Knute Rockne, her chum Mary Martin and a life-size statue of Will Rogers on his horse.

After becoming friends with Electra, we'd see her in New York. One day over lunch at Le Grenouille, she told us that the horse in that statue was a police horse she had borrowed from Mayor La Guardia when she was modeling the Will Rogers statue at her Manhattan studio.

"Every day a mounted policeman would trot across town to deliver his horse to pose for me," Electra remembered. "Then he had to wait until the horse had finished. To pass the time, the cop would visit a nearby tavern and tipple. Each night, he'd ride back to the police stables swaying in the saddle."

Another glamorous Texas achiever featured in our TEXAS PEERAGE book was Martha Hyder. To establish Fort Worth as home to the Van Cliburn International Quadrennial Piano Competition in 1962 she corralled 48 grand pianos for the contestants converging there from all over the world. She helped us in suggesting appropriate Texans for our book.

While interviewing Martha Hyder at her Park Avenue apartment she said, "With a title like TEXAS PEERAGE you definitely should include Viscountess Rothermere."

She explained that Mary Murchison, of Dallas, had married Viscount Rothermere, owner of London's DAILY MAIL newspapers.

"Here, I'll call her for you" offered Martha, dialing the telephone. "She's now in Palm Beach."

Soon Viscountess Rothermere and I were chatting on the

phone and I asked her if I could interview her when she next came to New York. "I'll be there Monday" she answered. "my son and I are flying up in our plane for lunch."

"Oh, I can't on Monday, for I'll be in Yugoslavia on a job for ABC-Sports prior to The Olympic Winter Games in Sarajevo," I answered, very disappointed.

"Yugoslavia! I was just there visiting my great friend Sir Fitzroy Maclean. Tito gave him the most divine estate for his help in the War, and you just must see it. I'll phone him right now and tell him you may call him."

Thus began, another adventure. This time in Yugoslavia.... Thanks to those Texas ladies, a whole new story fell into my lap.

I HAD TO ESCAPE IN YUGOSLAVIA

Needless to say, if you've read this far, my career in the pen-trade (writing) involved my creating newspaper features, sports, movie reviews, magazine publicity, sales presentations, TV and radio commercials, scripts, stage shows, song lyrics, ad promotion, business letters, public relations campaigns, juvenile fiction, novels, biographies, social histories — just about anything that required putting pen-to-page.

One of my jobs was producing corporate promotion for Chilton, publishers of such trade magazines as HARDWARE AGE, AUTOMOTIVE AGE, FOOD ENGINEERING and JEWELER'S CIRCULAR-KEYSTONE. When American Broadcasting Company acquired Chilton publications, sales representatives saw it as a great opportunity to cash-in on their connection with ABC-Sports. Suddenly I found myself writing and producing a series of mini-magazines THIS IS CHILTON, tying in with such major sports events as the World Series, and the Olympic Games "as seen by ABC-Sports." Gathering material for ABC-SPORTS COVERS THE WINTER OLYMPICS, took me to Lake Placid in the Adirondacks and across the ocean to scout Sarajevo where the Winter Games were being held in Yugoslavia.

In order to get there, I had to join a press trip sponsored by Yugoslavia Travel Bureau, going along with a busload of journalists and TV camera crews. Once there I found myself a captive of the Bureau, confined to their bus or lecture schedule. I had no free-time to do what I wanted to do, only what Big Brother dictated.

When I couldn't stand it any longer, I escaped when The Group left the bus to take film footage of a ski slope atop a mountain miles from Dubrovnik. I only had one more day left to find and interview Sir Fitzroy Maclean, who Mary, Viscountess Rothermere had told I would be calling.

Leaving a note that "urgent business required my being in Dubrovnik, will see you tonight at our hotel there," I jumped ship, and began hitch-hiking across the Yugoslav mountains towards Dubrovnik.   I could not speak Serbo-Croatian, Slovenian or Macedonian, that country's recognized languages, nor did I know directions or even where I WAS at the time. I just hoped for the best. I now knew what it must be like to be a kidnapped-victim or prisoner-of-war. I couldn't take being cooped-up one second more, especially since I thought Sir Fitzroy Maclean was expecting me for cocktails

When a car approached I waved frantically, obviously looking like a well-dressed American in distress.   The car braked immediately as I ran towards it shouting "DO YOU SPEAK ENGLISH?"

Fortunately, the driver spoke perfect English. He was an Italian honeymooning with his bride and would be happy to take me to my hotel, where they were also staying.   Talk about luck!

Once there I implored the manager to find me an English-speaking driver who knew where Sir Fitzroy Maclean lived. After a phone call, he told me: "We have just the person who can take you there, Mike, who meets the Macleans at the airport. Mike was also the driver for Elizabeth Taylor and Richard Burton all the time Burton was here starring in the film TITO."

While waiting for Mike I ambled into the ancient walled city of Dubrovnik, swept into an undertow of shoppers, strollers and sightseers scurrying along a cobblestoned "miracle mile" of medieval shops. Every building, far as the eye could see, had a shop opening right onto the curb. No cars, only pedestrians. No trees, no plants, just stones, stones, stones. Stones-built 4-story buildings; stone-paved narrow alleys that separated block after block of matching stone structures. In Dubrovnik, I felt completely separated from today's world, even closed-off from the Adriatic Sea, which was just outside a stones-throw from the city wall.

When Mike appeared in his local limo, I sat with him on the front seat. He chuckled when I did so, saying that Richard and Elizabeth always rode in the back with Jack Daniels.

"Who was Jack Daniels? The Burtons' dog?"

"No," he answered, "The Burtons' bourbon."

Mike had once been a New York cab driver, and unknown to his passengers on the backseat understood every profanity they uttered. He regaled me with tales of riding with the superstars as we soared towards Sir Alistair's seaside palace. Time flew by, then we turned into what reminded me of a canalside cottage neighborhood in Ocean Park, New Jersey. Its mailbox bore a bold-lettered name MACLEAN.

I was more than disappointed. I was shocked, having expected something sumptuous, not salt-box. Too, no one was at home. Then after snooping around, I discovered Mike had taken me to the Yugoslav retreat of another British celebrity: ALISTAIR MacLean, the novelist. Not FITZROY, the WW II hero.

Since I had hired him for the day, and not wanting to waste a minute of my Yugo-visit, I then directed him to drive me to Mostar, a town about 80 miles north of Dubrovnik, and then to the Adriatic island of Sveti Stefan, the same distance south. Granted my stay in each would be short, but I just wanted to see what they were like.

Mostar on first glance, seemed like a set for THE TAMING OF THE SHREW, architecture circa 1468. Lying in a limestone gorge, it was kind of a dream city with slender minarets, graceful mosques and an enchanting arched bridge spanning the rushing Neretva River which emptied into the Adriatic Sea. The Old Bridge, as it was called, had stairsteps that met in a steep Gothic arch, unsupported by pillars. Villagers used it to walk from one side of town to the other. The more I saw of Mostar, the more I thought that Ali Baba could have lived in this Turkish town with its bazaars, samovars and scimitars.

Once a crossroads of the spice trade, conquered by the Turks in the 15th century, Mostar retained a Turkish air. It's local head-shop still sold hookah pipes. Evidently, opium passed through here as well as spices.

I ended up buying an antique opium-purse made of a solid shell with a metal fastener. Hanging from a silver chain, it was probably worn on the belt of a sheik next to his scimitar.

I had never known any place like Mostar. Even its cemetery was different, with tombstones shaped like turbans, pomegranates and bell jars. They buried men vertically, women horizontally!

When I had tea in a restored Turkish merchant's house, my surroundings seemed even more Ali Baba-ish. Sitting on a banquette covered with Kilm carpets, sipping tea served from a brass samovar, I noticed a whitewashed courtyard with a splashing fountain and exotic plants in pots. Green and white latticed balconies, with narrow stone steps leading to them, had been used by the merchant's many wives and concubines who had lived there screened from outside view, a harem custom.

When we left Mostar, driving through Yugoslavia's bare jagged stone canyons and moonscapish terrain, I could understand how in this nature's fortress Tito could entrap the enemy.

Once out of stoney landscapes, we drove past lush vineyards, tobacco fields, Gypsy encampments with tents made from Oriental carpets, then arrived at Sveti Stevan, a whole fishing village made from rock, just off the Adriatic coast. Here every house had been gutted, made habitable to sophisticated tourists, turned into a modern-but-medieval island resort.

When I rejoined my press-bus buddies back in Sarajevo, I learned we were to fly to Belgrade with Yugoslavia's Olympics basketball players, all tower-tall, clones of Clint Eastwood. Watching them play made up for my missing having that interview with Sir Fitzroy Maclean.

AS I REMEMBER MICHENER

I t seemed that I would run into James Michener every other decade.

When we first met, his TALES OF THE SOUTH PACIFIC had won a Pulitzer Prize, been adapted into the blockbuster musical SOUTH PACIFIC, and inspired HOLIDAY to send him back to the area described in his TALES. Michener's HOLIDAY articles later became a book, RETURN TO PARADISE, and a movie starring Gary Cooper.

He always credited HOLIDAY for opening new opportunities writing for both magazines and films.

We had probably given him his first magazine assignment: an article about the epitomy of HOLIDAY LIVING, Philadelphia's aristocratic middle class suburbia, The Main Line.

Michener didn't miss a trick, covering everything: lawn tennis, riding to hounds; coming-out parties; WASP lifestyle that made The Main Line so unique. "The storied Philadelphia suburb," he wrote, "long domain of the wealthy, has taken off its diamond tiara, rolled up its sleeves, and fashioned for itself an admirable way of life. Here there is no wrong side of the tracks, people decent, homes friendly, beauty of land something rare."

This was the forerunner of Michener things to come: novels fashioned from intense research. His Main Line story was

so complete we devoted nearly all our April 1950 issue to
it...60 illustrations plus a charming cover showing a whimsical angel-winged commuter choo-choo floating on a cloud
over a Never-neverland of rolling greensward, country clubs
and families at play.

Often, I saw Michener at HOLIDAY functions. He seemed
to be part of the HOLIDAY team; always gracious as honor
guest at our editorial-promotion parties; swapping jokes
with the boys in the downstairs bar at "21."

Also, I would run into him when he dropped by to discuss an assignment at our editorial offices overlooking
Independence Hall.

Once he told me: "When TALES OF THE SOUTH PACIF-
IC came out in 1947, it was one of the UGLIEST books ever
printed. Wartime restrictions curtailed using decent paper.
I was devastated to have my first book look like it had been
printed on toilet paper. Chapters had almost no margin...
some had been started where another ended, just to save a
smidgen of paper. Reviews, too, were skimpy. In those
days, nobody seemed to be buying hard-cover books, anyway."

As luck would have it, SATURDAY EVENING POST had
bought two of his TALES, and POST-editor Harold Latham
saw that they received first-class treatment. Oscar
Hammerstein read them, and tried to find the author to discuss stage rights, not realizing that Michener lived just down
the road from him in Doylestown.

"Hammerstein couldn't have been more gracious or GEN-
EROUS," Michener revealed. "He insisted in lending me
money to invest in SOUTH PACIFIC. Income for that invest-
ment allowed me to devote full-time to my writing."

From then on, Jim Michener whirled into being a one-man
writing industry...with more than 40 titles to his name.

He lived in every part of the globe he wrote about:

Hawaii; Japan; Korea; Hungary; Afghanistan; Spain; South Africa; Colorado; Poland; Israel; Chesapeake Bay; Alaska; the Caribbean and Texas.

Almost 25 years had zoomed by until we encountered Michener again, in Cody, Wyoming. He had come there with his Japanese-American wife, Mari, to deliver the inaugural address opening Buffalo Bill Historical Center's spectacular Plains Indian Museum.

It was most appropriate that he did so for he had researched his western novel, CENTENNIAL, there. Plus, he was noted for his ideals of tolerance and universal brotherhood, qualities greatly respected by the Plain's tribes.

Over and over again in his fiction and nonfiction; in his philanthropy and everyday interactions with people, Jim had been a spokesman against prejudice and injustice. He told me that his favorite song from SOUTH PACIFIC was "You've Got To Be Taught."

Watching him dedicating the Plains Indian Museum, we realized that since our last meeting he had published 17 more books, including HAWAII, CARAVANS, THE SOURCE, IBERIA, THE DRIFTERS and CENTENNIAL. In creating each of them, he immersed himself in the cultures of his settings. His curiosity about people and nations, his passion to explore, truly made James Michener a "citizen of the world."

He personally covered the tragic events surrounding the Hungarian Revolution in 1956. Between 1972 and 1981, Jim visited Poland more than 10 times.

Early in his writing career, he published a widely read essay on Islam which later helped him gain acceptance during his travels in the Arab world gathering material for THE SOURCE.

Even as a boy, James Michener had a passionate urge to wander. At age 12, he began to hitchhike across the country "to see what was beyond Doylestown." By the time he

117

entered Swarthmore College, Michener had thumbed his way to 45 of the 48 states.

Wherever he went, Jim made a pilgrimage to the great art museums, carefully analyzing the paintings, then buying postcards with reproductions of those that excited his interest. They became his portable art gallery.

"Ever since my childhood," he said, "almost no day goes by without my looking at some piece of art. The riches and colors of paintings have accompanied me on all my journeys. They have echoed in my mind when I needed consolation, and been at hand when I required dedication to some old task or needed inspiration for a new one."

The Micheners devoted much of their spare time acquiring rare Japanese woodblock prints. He authored several acclaimed texts on the subject, including THE FLOATING WORLD.

After his book HAWAII became a best-seller and film, Jim and Mari donated 6,000 of their Japanese prints to the Honolulu Academy of Art.

"My husband made his money in the arts, so we return it to the arts," Mari told reporters when they gave more than 300 paintings from their 20th Century Collection to the University of Texas at Austin. They made Austin their main home after working there on his longest book, TEXAS, in 1985. TEXAS, 1,096 pages, sold over 1-million copies. The University received over $37-million in gifts from the Micheners, including a $15-million donation in 1992.

Since they lived very simply, Jim and Mari used income from his writing to fund projects and programs relating directly to the ways his money was made. Each of his books brought money to support a university writing program in the location of the book. The Micheners provided more than $75-million supporting young writers throughout the world.

Nor did they forget his hometown, Doylestown. Their

$1-million endowment gift enabled Doylestown to create its museum for preserving and presenting works by Bucks County artists, writers, craftmasters and composers. In 1996, Michener contributed $3.5-million to the art museum.

All this is housed in the charmingly renovated former Doylestown Jail, a Gothic structure built in 1884, modeled after Philadelphia's Eastern State Prison. Michener remarked when it opened as The James A. Michener Museum: "When I was a troublesome boy growing up in Doylestown, many had predicted that sooner or later , I would end up in that old jail on Ashland Street. Now, 80 years later, here I am doing exactly that."

Jim lived to be age 90 and never quit working. The year he died, 1997, he said: "As long as the old brain keeps functioning, I know the desire will always be there. I can hardly wait to get up in the morning to get back to work."

MR. DU PONT OF WINTERTHUR

D o you mean that Mr. du Pont LIVED here? My God, the house has 196 rooms." A friend from Houston was calling. She was on a winter tour of Winterthur, America's superstar house and garden display near Wilmington, Delaware.

"He certainly did," we replied. "And it's pronounced 'winterTOUR' not 'winterTHUR.'"

"I know that," she grumbled. "But I lisp."

Our friend is one of thousands who pour in annually from all over the world to wonder at and wander through our "Taj Mahal-Buckingham Palace-Versailles, all in one."

For seventy years, it was the private home of a timid genius: very-very rich, Henry Francis du Pont (Harry or H. F. to his friends). Now it's a museum, but when he lived there with his wife and two daughters, it was considered the most exclusive fiefdom on the Eastern seaboard, with its own private railway station, post office, fire department, golf course, farm, dairy and security force. Ninety-nine cottages housed 250 of du Pont's personal staff, all totally dedicated to maintaining the nine-story house, the 2,400 landscaped acres of gardens, and this planet's utmost collection of Americana.

Not only did Mr. du Pont collect the best quality American decorative art that dated from 1640 to 1840, but he bought entire rooms where Washington and Jefferson no doubt danced and toasted the New Republic. He had the rooms moved cross-country, installing them in his house...paneling, ceiling, staircases, and in some cases, the whole facade. For example, he adorned each wall of his indoor badminton court with actual fronts of four historic dwellings, assembled brick by brick, from as far away as New England and North Carolina.

Harry du Pont's neighbors around Chadds Ford spread tales about his buying habits. One recounted a story about a Southern lady whose run-down plantation was slated to be sold or wrecked. She answered a knock at the door to be greeted by du Pont's chauffeur. He tipped his cap, informing her that a "Mr. Francis" had come to see her about purchasing her front parlor, since he understood her house was to be razed.

"My parlor!" she is said to have exclaimed. "Why, there's nothing in it but some old chairs."

"Oh, he only wants the paneling and mantel, and perhaps the ceiling," said the chauffeur.

John Sweeney, Mr. du Pont's assistant and close confidant, doubts that this happened. Sweeney does point out, however, that whenever an architect or an antique dealer reported on a doomed building worthy of Harry's attention, he usually followed up pronto with a personal visit.

"He would arrive in a 16-cylinder Cadillac driven by his chauffeur, and think he was incognito by using his middle name," says Sweeney. "He wasn't fooling anyone in those Depression days. However, when he did purchase a room, you can bet he would pay enough to refurbish the whole plantation."

Money, certainly, was never a deterrent for Henry Francis du Pont. World War I had made his father, Colonel Henry Algernon du Pont, one of the world's wealthiest men. The colonel was earning over $1-million annually just from the shares in the Du Pont Company, which provided gunpowder and chemicals for the entire war.

Winterthur had initially covered 3,200 acres acquired by Eleuthere Irenee du Pont between 1810 and 1818. The house was built by his daughter Evelina and her husband, James Antoine Biderman, who named it WINTERTHUR after his family's ancestral hometown in Switzerland. It had passed down through du Pont uncles and aunts to the Colonel, a West Point graduate, Civil War hero, railroad president, political boss—and tyrant to his two children, Henry and Louise. The Colonel ruled that, even as toddlers, they speak to him in French at all meals. Living under his tyrannical thumb turned shy Harry into a totally insecure child with a speech impediment. So extreme was his tight-lipped, rapid, low mumble that, all his life, only those closest to him could make out what he was saying. John Sweeney relates that one time H.F. handed a rare just-purchased bowl to his driver, saying, "Bought this in self defense." The chauffeur understood him to say, "Toss it over the fence." So, he did. Fortunately, the bowl didn't break.

Early in Henry's childhood, his father was determined to "make a man" of his timid son and heir, so he sent him off at a very young age to Groton, the New England boarding school noted for headmaster Endicott Peabody's emphasis on athletics. Introverted Henry hated sports and loathed the regimen the school demanded. Being forced into playing competitive rough-house games made him even more intimidated. His handwriting, as well as his speech, got worse as he grew older.

Homesick for his beloved gardens at Winterthur, young Harry chose to spend his spare time not "with the boys," but helping the local nurseryman to plant bushes and flowers. In the 1890s, this was considered very odd, indeed, for a rich boy to do while attending one of America's most exclusive boarding schools. Even so, from that experience he went on to become perhaps the greatest horticulturist this country has ever produced. For the next twenty years, gardening continued to become his all-consuming passion. That is, until he discovered the joys of collecting great "Americana."

Until then, his life path led in no direction, other than "country gentleman." Since he had no interest in business nor public office, he holed-in at Winterthur after graduating from Harvard in 1903. His mother died while he was still in college, so when his father was elected Senator in 1906, Harry had Winterthur all to himself. For something to do, his father made him manager of the estate's farm and dairy. He became a pioneer in crop rotation, and developed the most prized Holstein herd on the continent. Yet he was a very lonely young man until he met Ruth Hale, niece of Elihu Root, secretary of state while Colonel du Pont served as Senator in Washington. No doubt, the Secretary of State's unmarried niece and the powerful Senator's unattached son were seated together at Capitol dinner parties. A romance blossomed, and they were married in 1916, when the bridegroom was 36 years of age. They complemented each other perfectly: he, an aesthete; she, down-to-earth, humorous, and lots of fun.

Harry and Ruth returned to live with his father at Winterthur, spending summers at Southampton, where she had spent many a Long Island summer with her parents. In 1918, a daughter, Pauline, was born. Four years later, they were blessed with another girl, Ruth Ellen. Still into his forties, he had no life-mission whatsoever. Then, suddenly in 1923, the solution for what to do with his talents loomed up like a genie from a bottle in the shape of an early-American cupboard, displaying plates, platters and pitchers of pink Staffordshire. This first encounter with "Americana" came about while the du Ponts were visiting the Watson Webbs at their 110-room, four-thousand acre country place in Shelburne, Vermont. Electra Havemeyer Webb was among the first of Harry's friends to become fascinated with early-American craftsmanship. Besides hooked rugs, patchwork quilts and carved eagles, Mrs. Webb would later acquire barns, schoolhouses, a covered bridge, and the 892-ton S.S. Ticonderoga among her other 125,000-or-so American antiques.

When H.F. du Pont began his own collection, rare American antiques were in abundance. The Henry Fords, Abby Aldrich Rockefellers and Ima Hoggs of the world weren't yet big in the market. The first piece Harry bought was a Pennsylvania walnut chest-of-drawers, inlaid "1737," the date it was made. Soon, he had no other place to store his antiques except his Southampton, Long Island, summer place. He installed his first period rooms there.

Harry's collection kept growing at such a pace, it needed a home of its own, and quite a big one. That problem was solved when his father died in 1926, leaving him the Winterthur estate, along with $50-million.

Now he was free to make his dreams come true at his beloved ancestral home. Right away, he rounded up interiors from ten doomed early-American homes, and from those, installed 23 period settings in which his family could live and guests could enjoy.

What was it like living in a house with all that going on?

The du Pont's eldest daughter, Pauline du Pont Harrison, remembered that as children she and her sister Ruth found it all perfectly natural. "After all, we had grown up that way. One year, however, because of all the building of additions, our whole family had to move into a smaller house at the foot of the hill near our creek. It was very cozy. We loved sharing a tiny cottage, bright with chintz and firelight."

She adds: "You couldn't help but be inspired by our

father's energy and enthusiasm. He really was a great artist, but instead of painting or sculpting a landscape or room, he created the real thing. His eye for proportion, his ability to remember and match colors, textures and shapes was truly remarkable. He alone formed the Winterthur collection and spent hours each day working on it, making each room a work of art."

Mr. du Pont would arise at dawn and delve non-stop with his helpers into his projects. Nothing escaped his notice: the most subtle match between fabric and bowl; the correct piece for the period; the most perfect placement for the right tree.

At the age of 48, he came to be recognized for what he was accomplishing. He, who had never been sure of himself, was now a "star."

His "eye" for beauty and quality, combined with his horticultural and farming expertise, turned Harry into a whirlwind. By 1946, he had installed 80 period rooms. His ever-increasing collection had become so mammoth that he hired a full-time cataloger, Joseph Downs, curator of the American Wing at New York's Metropolitan Museum of Art. Downs, and his assistant, Charles Montgomery, told du Pont that Winterthur had surpassed the Metropolitan in preserving for all time this country's early lifestyle, giving future generations a broader definition of American history. They urged him to consider making Winterthur a "center for the study of American arts."

Fired by the enthusiasm of these expert antiquarians, H.F. turned Winterthur into a learning place, not only for decorative arts, but for American horticulture as well.

"Before too many years, Americans will forget what a country place and its countryside once looked like," he predicted at that time. "At Winterthur, therefore, we will not only preserve the livability of our country's best colonial interiors, but its landscape as well." Even the flowers from a

1640-garden would grace the table of his 1640-room setting, suitably arranged to reflect the style of that particular period—not fake flowers in "embalmed bouquets," but living flowers, freshly changed week after week.

Within six months after deciding to change Winterthur from his private home into a public museum and study center, he had ninety-nine gardeners working full-speed transforming the grounds. He built a mile-long walk through his woods where visitors could hike in peace in the shade of American forest trees, among native ferns, mosses, laurel, wild flowers and bushes.

Ponds, lakes and streams were enlarged and diverted to provide water power aplenty, with a sophisticated sprinkler system servicing thousands of acres. One reservoir on the property could provide as much as eight-million gallons of water, more than enough to put out fires in case of emergency. Every day, H.F. would make the rounds of his grounds, most of the time with his British-born head gardener, Gordon Tyrrell. (For the contributions du Pont made to horticulture, the Garden Club of America, the New York Botanical Society, and the National Association of Gardeners bestowed on him their highest honors. Also, the Royal Horticulture Society of Great Britain elected him vice-president.)

Mrs. Vincent Astor, in a forward to a handsome book on Winterthur hospitality, *American Elegance*, tells about observing H.F. at work. "The du Ponts were marvelous hosts," says Brooke Astor, "and would have as many as forty guests for weekends...friends and family arriving from New York, Philadelphia, Washington, New England, old England and France...presidents of corporations, princes, counts and countesses." Mrs. Astor observed H.F. and his staff plan the meals and the table settings for the ensuing houseparty. H.F. kept a list of menus and table arrangements so that guests would not be presented the same things twice.

Every day, at both lunch and dinner, the dining room table arrangements were carefully changed. Mr. and Mrs. du Pont would discuss menus at length, then plot the meals with the cook and Emil, the major-domo. As Mrs. Astor watched, a footman climbed a ladder in the enormous china closet and handed down the centerpieces as directed by Mr. du Pont. All the shelves were filled with banquet-sized services of Crown Derby, Lowestoft, Spode, Worcester and Wedgewood, so choosing the right china for a series of meals and cocktail parties was hardly a problem.

H.F. would have his butlers place his selected table settings on a large table in the pantry so they could study the effect. Once satisfied that the silver, crystal, china and centerpiece were placed properly with the linens, he would summon the head gardener and the greenhouse man to bring in flower samples that would complement the china service.

Since opening his home to the public in 1951 and until his death in 1969, Mr. du Pont was in total command. Everything at Winterthur was done according to his wishes.

Mr. du Pont wanted Winterthur to keep the ambiance of a private family house, hence there are no ropes, fences or do-not-touch signs. Tour takers, just a few at a time, feel like privileged guests being escorted by their gracious hostess.

Acres of gardens, too, are being renovated making them even more inviting for people who just want to stroll. Under the direction of horticulturist Thomas Butcher, groundskeepers have cleared out areas that might have obstructed vistas from visitors.

"Mr. du Pont was careful to protect those vistas," Butcher told me. "Long ago he made plans to keep the countryside around Winterthur free from encroaching commercialism. He sold adjoining land to Wilmington Country Club for a golf course and rented other acres and his private golf course to Vicmead Hunt Club. He sold more property to his cousin John du Pont, who build the Delaware Museum of Natural History on it. That totaled forty percent of the original acreage, leaving us the view without the upkeep. Now we are an island between two golf courses."

And so it goes. Winterthur is ever evolving and involving...for expert and amateur alike. What began as a hobby for a shy man who hadn't found his niche, is now a national treasure, open for all to enjoy again and again for it is always changing, always fascinating.

For Henry Francis du Pont, truly "life began at forty," when he discovered "Americana," setting him on a course that produced a wonder of the world.

DR. BARNES & HIS DOG

One of the most unforgettable characters I never met was Dr. Albert C. Barnes. He seemed to haunt person after person right from the grave.

I never met him, but I certainly heard enough about him. In fact our Wayne neighbor, Cynthia Stine wrote an article about her experiences as his executive assistant in the 1930s. Called MY PRIVATE WAR WITH DR. BARNES, it appeared in Harper's magazine and described him as a devil. Fiske Kimball and Henry Clifford, major players at the Philadelphia Museum of Art, told me he had given them nightmares in connection with their major retrospective of Matisse's works. He even plagued me decades after his death, even though I had never even seen the man, much less had dealings with him personally.

I did meet his caretaker, Gar Reed.

Gar had grown up as the boy-next-door to Barnes' country place in Chester County, and it was he who told me about Dr. Barnes and his last love, Fidele.

It all began in France.

France had always lured Dr. Barnes like a Lorelei. It was in Paris that his first grande passion ignited. The year was 1913. With new millions in the bank from his patent medicine business, he was there exploring the art scene.

An artist friend took him to Leo and Gertrude Stein's

Saturday night salon at 27 rue de Fleuris. Brother and sister expatriates from San Francisco, the Steins entertained rich art-prospects (and hot-painters-of-the-moment) in their cluttered two story apartment. Here, Barnes found what he unknowingly had been seeking all his life—paintings pulsing with a fierce new energy. Whole walls filled with them. Picassos, large and small. Melodious Matisses in birthday-ribbon colors. Rosy-plump nudes by Renoir. Sun-splashed Monet landscapes. Serene Cezanne still-lifes. With Barnes it was love at first sight. From that night on, Dr. Barnes and his "magic checkbook" brought back home perhaps the greatest private collection of modern art in the world.

Bought when affordable and plentiful, his collection included 180 Renoirs, 69 Cezannes, 60 Matisses, 44 Picassos, works by Monet, Manet, Degas, Gauguin, Roualt, Utrillo, Rousseau, van Gogh, Seurat, Modigliani, Soutine, The Ashcan School painters, as well as such Old Masters as El Greco—more than 1,000 paintings in all.

For years, Dr. Barnes with his wife Laura or assistant Violette de Mazio, would spend each summer on art-buying sprees in France. Their base of operations was Port Manech, a seacoast village in Brittany, where a new great love entered his life: Fidele.

It happened on his morning walk across the sea escarpment. A neighbor 's black-and-white dog leapt over a wall and began trotting beside him, looking up at Dr. Barnes adoringly, tail wagging joyously.

Every day this pattern continued. Barnes became so attached to this mixed-breed mutt that he begged to buy it. But the owners wouldn't sell. However, touched by their dog's affection for the visiting American, they did allow Barnes to take their pooch along on his art excursions.

Soon, everywhere that Albert went, fido was sure to go, no matter if to Matisse's studio, or dinner at The Ritz.

When Barnes and his entourage departed for the States, the dog pined so that it almost died, seemingly with a broken heart. Consequently, when Barnes returned to Brittany, the owners gave him their dog gladly. Barnes named his pet "Fidele," the French word meaning faithful.

Returning to the States with this animal presented a problem. Dr. Barnes feared it might be impounded for a period of waiting when they passed through customs. So to avoid red-tape, he formulated a plan of escape. The doctor would go ashore ahead in a pilot boat. Mrs. Barnes would walk down the gangplank holding Fidele on a leash, and once spying her husband waiting on the dock, would let the dog loose. Dr. Barnes knew his adoring pet would jump ship and rush through the crowd into his waiting arms.

Sure enough, his plan worked, and they took off in their chauffeur-driven black Packard for Philadelphia's exclusive Main Line suburbs—and a new life together.

Many happy times were spent at Barnes' weekend place, a historic 1795 Chester County farm.

Barnes named this 165-acre estate "Ker-Feal" (kerr-fee-all, meaning "Fidele's House" in Breton patois). Fidele's picture was printed on the house stationery. Fidele and Dr. Barnes bunked together in a boudoir adjoining that of Mrs. Barnes. Fidele had his own French-Provincial dogbed, with "Fidele" carved across its headboard. Above Fidele's bed, Dr. Barnes hung an ancient map of Brittany "so Fidele would feel at home." Over his own bed, Dr. Barnes had a sketch of Port Manech, Fidele's hometown.

The doctor on several occasions signed his diabolic correspondence: Fidele-de-Port-Manech, secretary.

Fidele curled in the doctor's lap when he sat, and rested at his feet while Barnes gave his art lectures. Noted as "the great possessor," Barnes was now possessed—by his dog.

Life ran placidly at Ker-Feal. On Saturday mornings,

Albert and Laura Barnes would arrive for a weekend of rest from running their classes at the Barnes Foundation in Merion—hers in Horticulture, his in Art. Ker-Feal, with its beamed ceilings, wide planked floors, walk-in fireplaces had become a perfect setting for their priceless collection of Americana: 18th century country furniture; ironwork; locks; clocks; wool-and-linen rugs. Especially noteworthy was red-ware made in Jamestown, Virginia as early as 1680; a Kentucky sideboard made of holly wood; Lancaster County dower chests; old pewter. One room had been converted into a solarium for Mrs. Barnes' orchids and other plants brought from her greenhouses.

Occasionally they would have weekend guests, but not more than two at a time. This because their round William and Mary table in front of the massive fireplace could only accommodate four people.

Showing up often as a weekend guest was their close friend, actor Charles Laughton. He became such a regular that his bedchamber was designated "Laughton's Room," with a tin cookie cutter in his shape tacked to the door.

Sometimes this Captain Bligh of the movies had the pleasure of sharing his room with a Renoir nude. Dr. and Mrs. Barnes were so attached to their paintings that they would bring along a masterpiece or two to hang for a privileged guest, or just to enjoy themselves away from their gallery.

Always, Fidele came, too. Always beside the doctor, even while they dined.

Fidele and his master were inseparable even until death. On the afternoon of July 24, 1951, they were killed together in an automobile accident while turning out of Ker-Feal's driveway onto a main road. Fidele lingered long enough to protect his master from state troopers and rescue squads called to the scene. Even though barely alive, Fidele was so vicious a protector that he had to be destroyed on the spot.

HOUSE WITH 13 CHRISTMAS TREES

Do you mean you have 13 Christmas Trees? In your house?" the lady exclaimed incredulously, when she inquired if a tour group could visit us for a "benefit."

"Well, yes," we answered, almost apologetically. "But some of them are small. You see, we collect whimsical folk toys and have to have a place for them all to, er, enjoy Christmas with us."

Little does she know that we have HUNDREDS of hand-crafted "little people" in our attic that have taken on real personalities and fairly scream to get out and show off with their peers all through the holidays.

What do we mean "taken on real personalities?"

Take the animals seated around our dining room table, for instance. That big llama with the knitted Andean cap on his head is Fernando, and Fernando Llama has llama beans on his plate. Across the table from Fernando are the pig ladies, Mary Roberts Swineheart and Tammy Faye Bacon, chatting across their pork crisps with Alice Aardvark. That teddy bear, Bear-y Manilow at the head of the table, sports a hand-made sweater with bear buttons, all made by a mother-daughter team in Mendocino, California. The big stuffed animals came from the wild imagination of a lady on Lookout Mountain, Tennessee. That big lamb with a red velvet bow is Meryl Sheep, a life-size handpuppet from a Lancaster craft show. So you see why it's rumored that we are somewhat wacko?

And the Christmas trees!

One year in Oaxaca, Mexico, we visited a village of tin-smiths and decided we should have a "tin tree." It's in our dining room, too, surrounded by wooden carousels, Ferris wheels, navy boats, animals and peepshows made by Oaxacan toymakers and wood carvers.

In our "ethnic" den, is our Tribal Tree, adorned with trinkets of silver, beads, feathers, along with stone fetishes we have gathered from various Indian tribes in New Mexico, Arizona and North Carolina. The tree is topped with a silver-star wand made for us by Jonny Woodenlegs of the Taos adobe. One of our prize small trees is atop the den's TV. From its branches dangle woolen birds, animals and Santas made by Peruvian Indians. Also, the "magical" walnuts of Mexico. Inside the walnuts are charming mini-scenes of weddings, bullfights, serenaders. We bought them from prisoners in Guanajuato.

Then, on deep windowsills in the living room are four other trees, each with a "theme." There's the African Tree, loaded with native carved animals picked up on our safari in Kenya. When we found a Masai Santa Claus made of grasses, you would have thought we had discovered King Solomon's diamond mine. It's a treasure.

We like our British Tree, too, loaded down with clothespin dolls made by fisherwomen from a fishing village near St. Andrews. Some came from Liberty of London.

Norwegian, Swedish and Danish craftspeople created the tiny trolls, soldiers and Vikings for the Scandia Tree. Pigs from everywhere make up our prized Pig Tree.

And so it goes, all through the house, all through the holidays: a Farm Tree of old-quilt ornaments in a bedroom; a

Haitian Tree in the upstairs hall; on the breezeway, a Centennial Tree of Uncle Sams, Miss Liberty and American flags; a Utensil Tree in the kitchen and, lording over them all, our ceiling-high tree jam-full of "character" dolls.

We are among the millions of doll collectors who seem to have emerged from all corners of the globe during the past decade. Ask any auctioneer or antiques dealer and they will tell you that, these days, doll collecting is *big*.

Our collection started two decades ago, while visiting a toy shop in Bern, Switzerland. There, sitting spread-legged atop the counter, a charming wooden Swiss-miss dolly, all pigtailed and ginghamed, had her arms opened wide as if to say "love me and take me with you, please, please, please." Well, who could resist? Much later, in Salamanca, Spain, another handmade doll caught our eyes. She seemed the spitting image of a gossipy village woman we had seen in Mijas the day before. She had to go back home with us, too. Thus, as mementos of our travels, began our huge collection of "character" dolls. Ours aren't the pretty, sweetie-pie type. Especially those made by the mountain folk of West Virginia and North Carolina. Barefoot and overalled, they would probably be a-bootleggin' and a-feudin' in them thar hills back home if they weren't with us. Now, they are sidling up to the likes of an Italian vamp from Venice; Betty Boop, out of Hollywood; Pierre-the-gendarme stocking doll purchased in Paris; a Nantucket old-salt in a sou'wester; Mayan maidens made in the Yucatan; a doll dressed in ancient textiles found in Cuzco. Peru; Swedish grandmas and grandpas; toughie Australian soccer players; a mustachioed wrestler from Bangkok...there's also Ruthie, the New Orleans bag lady on roller skates with a duck stuffed in her pocket. The real Ruthie skated in and out of the shop near Antoine's while we were snooping around. Now her replica is part of our wacky doll family.

At Christmas time, when they all come out, assembled on and about our tree, friends tease us with such remarks as "You're getting to look a lot like Gimbels," and expect to hear "It's a Small World" tunes from Disneyland boom out from our stereo. We really don't care what others think, for every yuletide these unique folk toys bring back marvelous memories of joyous journeys.

Now, on trips, we look for out-of-the-way doll museums and the area's legendary dollmakers. Recently, on a visit to Scandinavia, we met Sweden's delightful "doll lady," Charlotte Weibull, at her doll center in Malmo. For over 40 years, she has made dolls in the extraordinary folk dress of Swedish provinces. She traces it all to when a sister of her grandmother opened a shop for Swedish national costumes there in 1901. Tradition-proud, many a Swedish bride is married in an absolutely authentic costume of her home country, and on national folk days, parties and fairs, entire families turn out in stunning handmade traditional outfits. Mothers brought their daughters to order a costume there when Mrs. Weibull took over the shop in 1942. The girls brought along their favorite dollbabies and would ask Charlotte to make identical clothes for their doll children. With hundreds of patterns, material, ribbons, trimmings and helping hands among the local seamstresses, she started making her own dolls. Having grown up on a Scandian farm, Gamlegard in Borrby, during the 1920s, she remembered when lots of the traditions were still alive, so she fashioned many of her dolls after characters and customs she knew long ago...like a Grandma Moses of dolldom.

A world away from there in Hong Kong, we encountered two remarkable down-to-earth dollmakers. In fact, we met one of their "babies" gazing at us with soulful eyes from the window of a souvenir shop as we stepped off the ferry at Kowloon. A sign proclaimed that this little Chinese orphan attired in pajamas and coolie hat wanted desperately to be exported, and was ready to emigrate, complete with "authenticated" Hong Kong-British passport. These rice-paddy babies are Hong Kong's answer to the Cabbage Patch Kids.

We soon learned that a Missouri-born Hong-Kong resident, John Damron, was the proud papa. They were "born" when he couldn't acquire Cabbage Patch dolls to take home to his two nieces in America for Christmas. Rather than arrive empty-handed, he created these substitutes, uniquely Hong-Kongese, cuddly coolie kiddies craving to be adopted. Adopting one couldn't be easier. All that is required is to pay "Immigration" $230HK and the little darling is yours, passport and all. Each doll carries a mini-passport attached to its wrist. It reads: "The Government of Hong Kong requests and requires in the name of Her Majesty all those whom it may concern to allow the bearer to pass free without lot or hindrance and to afford the bearer such assistance as may be necessary." Our "orphan's" passport had an identification page with these vital statistics:

Name: Choi Fong Ho (Kitty)
Occupation: Immigrant
Height: One foot, six inches
Distinguishing marks: Beautiful
Date of Expiry: 1997.

Damron's dolls are keeping a whole army of seamstresses busy all over Hong Kong. each one of these stuffed-stocking sweeties is one-of-a-kind, made by hand and takes eight to ten hours to produce.

While John Damron is making his mark as doll dynamo of Hong Kong, another local dollmaker, Michael Lee, is celebrating in local museums and galleries. Lee makes Chinese babies, too, in authentic Hunan costumes. Some have queues curling down the neck. unlike Damron's orphan dolls, who appear to cry because they have been "neglected," Michael Lee's babies are happy as can be. And, so is Michael. His eyes beam like Christmas tree lights when he shows you his character dolls, charmers inspired by personalities who have struck his funny bone. He fashioned a baseball player who bears a striking resemblance to Richard Nixon. There's also a Jimmy Carter attired in a jogging suit with a U.S.A. emblem. Among his other favorites are Marcel Marceau's "Mr. Blip," Betty Boop and Santa Claus in his workshop clothes.

At age 80, character-doll maker Michael Lee has become one of Hong Kong's great "characters" himself. He looks the part of a kindly bearded Chinese philosopher as played by movie actor-producer John Huston in a sweat suit. Daily, visitors troop to his workshop at 117 Shanghai Street, a block away from the famed Canton Road jade market. They climb dark, tenement steps to his studio-home which resembles more of a hippie pad than a toy factory. Jumbled about are shelves bursting with doll samples, stacks of fabrics, boxes of buttons and baskets of trimmings. Several of his seamstress-es live on the spot and, while they sew, a few of their tod-dling children watch a TV set nearby. Michael, himself a refugee from Communist China, gave them refuge and a job when they escaped to Hong Kong.

When Lee fled from the Communist scourge of Shanghai in the '40s, he arrived in Hong Kong not knowing a soul. His only previous job had been as a physical training instructor, and he couldn't speak Cantonese. There were no jobs, no relief agencies. He kept alive on "care" parcels from church-es in America, and checks from time to time sent by mission-aries who had helped raise him as a boy. One day, just to chase away his homesickness, he made a little doll like one he had fashioned during his artist days in Shanghai. Lee still has that original doll, a tiny Hakka woman wearing a bamboo hat. English ladies who saw it, asked him to make copies for them. When he tired of making them himself, he put some of his homeless refugee friends to work, giving them shelter in his tenement workrooms. He slept in a corner by his sewing machine and cutting table. Then he created a new doll inspired by Hong Kong fisherwomen.

Word got around that Michael Lee's dolls were truly works of art. Eileen Kershaw featured them in her arts and antiques shop at the posh Peninsula Hotel. Hong Kong Arts Center and Macau's Meseu Luis de Camoes jointly held an exhibition of his work. His Australian tramp doll won first prize in the toy competition staged by Hong Kong Development Council. Yet he refused offers to "go commercial," believing that if he did, his dolls would lose the personal touch, looking like they came from a production line.

"My shop produces no more than two or three hundred dolls a month," Lee says. "That's enough to keep us happy."

Like a proud grandpapa, surrounded by his live-in seamstresses and smiling doll family, Michael Lee is, indeed, one happy fellow. Discovering such a national treasure is what makes dolly dallying on our journeys special delights.

THE PRESIDENT & DUCHESS OF PERU

I n 1980 we were invited to write about Peru—all expenses paid; personal guide and visit with Peru's President included.

Ever since I had read Thornton Wilder's BRIDGE OF SAN LUIS REY, Peru had been at the top of my list of places I wanted to visit.

There was so much to see: The Andes; llamas; vicuna; condors; islands of penguins; ravines deeper than our Grand Canyon; salt lakes with flocks of white flamingoes; Incas; ancient customs and costumes. Besides, an invitation to interview President Belaunde in Peru's Presidential Palace.

Of course we accepted with delight.

The President received us in his office on a Sunday afternoon when there was no one else in the huge rococco palace but Barbara, Belaunde and me. Uniformed guards stood grandly at the gates, but inside, we were alone, since the President had returned unexpectedly from his holiday in Arequipa, and had summoned us on the spur of the moment realizing this was the only time he could see us due to a busy schedule.

He couldn't have been more gracious. A courtly, Peruvian aristocrat, Belaunde had a Degree in Architecture from the University of Texas. He loved America, and had in fact adapted THE EYES OF TEXAS ARE UPON YOU for his campaign theme song.

President Belaunde was pointing out the window to a fig tree said to have been planted by Pizarro when he conquered Peru for Spain 400 years ago. "It still produces figs," he was telling us when his emergency phone began ringing, red buttons flashing URGENT!

He picked up the phone and gasped "Oh, no!" then turned to tell us, "Your President Reagan has been shot."

After that eerie incident, other unforgettable adventures took wing...and so did we, flying from Lima, below sea level, directly up—to Cuzco, 11,000 feet high.

President Belaunde had warned us to "Watch out for those heights," suggesting that we walk off the plane slowly; rest for an hour in the hotel; sip coca tea first thing after arrival. Then we might avoid suffering from altitude sickness.

Cuzco atop the Andes, looked much the way it must have appeared when Pizarro marched in with his Spanish troops four centuries earlier. Ponchoed Indians with llamas moved through cobblestone streets past walls of gigantic granite blocks that had been carved and fitted perfectly together by the Incas. Every woman seemed to wear a hat, some derbies, others flat as a Frisbee.

Men, heads covered by knitted helmets, sported braided jackets cut like Coco Chanels. Mama llamas, with babies along side, ran through town un-attended, as if being chased by a phantom. All, a bizarre street-ballet in blazing colors. Cuzco's sights, as well as heights, left me breathless.

In spite of following Belaunde's cautionary advice to a T, coca tea, I awoke at three in the morning gasping frantically for breath, drowning, speechless. I stumbled down dark halls, finally found the deserted lobby, banged on a bell at the reception desk and collapsed.

Since this sort of occurrence happened often here, the hotel had an oxygen tank handy, so I was quickly revived.

Our Hotel, Liberator on Calle San Agustin, had once been Cuzco's most famous mansion: The House of The Four Busts, home of Pizarro's descendants in 1571. Busts of four bearded brothers and their family-crest were carved above the entrance. Built in ancient Incan walls, its massive door stood only a step from the street.

Every morning the hotel dining room was abuzz with diners getting ready to either catch a plane or take the train to Machu Picchu 76 miles away. When we first glimpsed this Machu Picchu choo-choo it reminded us of THE LITTLE TRAIN THAT COULD.

As we chugged along, switching back and forth, views of the lush green Sacred Valley of The Incas kept us enthralled. Climbing over mountain after mountain looking like The China Wall far as the eye could see, were steps, terraces, battlements built miraculously as far back as 1200 AD. In this valley, on Sundays, Inca chiefs and village-mayors, carrying tall silver-tipped staffs-of-office assemble at Pisac for Mass, and to open a Sunday market selling superb handmade sweaters, rugs and folk art.

As our train gathered speed we passed ruins at Pacapucara, Sacsayhuaman, Tambomachay and Ollantaytamo.

The aged engine seemed to be trying to race the roaring Urabamba River on its 350-mile course from a height of 13,000 feet to its final destination: the mighty Amazon. One minute we were admiring immaculate fields of grain, only to shoot into the total blackness of miles-long tunnels, then to emerge to a patch of jungle ablaze with orchids and bromeliads.

We looked down into rapids splashing over rocks; Indians swinging across rushing streams on shakey suspension-ropes. Then, without warning, our train stopped at the bottom of a chasm with walls of granite reaching 2,000 feet up.

There was a hush, as all of the passengers craned their necks heavenward. Then, as if God swept back the clouds, the magical, mystical ruins of Machu Piccho came into view.

Certainly, Machu Picchu was the apex of our Peru experience. Yet there were memorable surprises to follow.

At Arequipa, midway between Cuzco and Lima, we set out to trace the paths of Tia Bates.

London had "The Duchess of Duke Street."

Latin America, Tia Bates.

In her day, the world's most famous landlady. Her elegant pension QUINTA BATES, nestled between three towering volcanoes in Arequipa, attracted luminaries from around the world for four decades.

Edward VII and George VI enjoyed her hospitality before either became King.

Film star Clark Gable once journeyed 1,000 miles out of his way just to stay there.

Thornton Wilder wrote parts of THE BRIDGE OF SAN LUIS REY on the rooftop. Later he made her the prototype of "Mrs. Wickersham" in his novel THE EIGHTH DAY.

There was no inn on earth like Quinta Bates.

Guests found it hard to leave. Two of them stayed for 16 years.

Noel Coward arrived for a few days visit and remained a month. He was so enchanted, he composed a three-page poem in octosyllabics, scrawled extravagantly in her guestbook. Quinta visitors found this passage particularly apt:

> The spirit of the place conserves
> An anodyne for jangled nerves.
> The water is hot, the beds are soft,
> The meals are many a time and oft,
> The flowers are sweet, the grass is green,
> The toilet is austerely clean,
> Which, in this ancient continent

Occasions vast astonishment.

Always, it seemed, reports from Tia's visitors were raves. But who was she? Where did she come from? How did she land in Arequipa, Peru? Why was her inn so special? What made Tia tick? Before all memory of her faded from this earth, we sought to find out.

First, we discovered that Tia wasn't South American at all. She was born Joanna Monteith in Rensselaer, NY on the Hudson. In 1876, at the age of 8, she moved with her family to Chile. Fortunes were being made there in mining. Her father had been appointed superintendent of a railway, lifeline to mines loaded with rich mineral deposits of gold, silver, copper and vanadium. Railroads were needed to remove the ores to international steamers by means other than the back of llamas. Or burros. Or Indians.

Young Ana grew up in Chile surrounded by Spanish-speaking servants and children. In no time at all she spoke like the rest of them. Endowed with an ebullient personality and natural inquisitiveness, she became quite popular with the international set there. So popular, in fact, that at sixteen she married a British mining engineer, John Bates. He had met her father, first, in the pursuit of business.

As a young bride, she accompanied her husband to make their home in Coro-Coro, Bolivia, a copper mining town so high in the Andes that the nearest neighbors were condors.

The place couldn't have been more remote. Treeless, and bitter cold, night and day. At an altitude almost two miles up, health problems were serious there. Plus that, she was the only white woman around...young, inexperienced and utterly bewildered by the customs and language of the Indian servants. Even though Ana understood and spoke Spanish like a native, the Bolivian Indians talked only in a dialect.

Ana had to depend upon the Indian women for help. Especially when she became pregnant. Because of the rarefied air, pneumonia was the dreaded disease there, and Ana lived in terror of catching cold. In such high altitudes, when pneumonia struck it killed...fast. So when her little girl was born, she had to give her more than ordinary care. With an Indian nurse for her baby, Ana learned the native dialect though sheer necessity.

Mrs. Bates did a great deal of entertaining. There was a steady flow of men to service the mines...civil, mechanical, electrical, hydraulic, mining engineers; accountants; metallurgists...from all parts of the world. They brought her books, newspapers and, most important, conversation. On such visits, she heard about the Peruvian city of Arequipa, a rest stop for many of the men coming down from the mines. The name "Arequipa" meant "Here we rest" in the Quechua Indian language. Although the town was refounded by Pizarro on the Day of the Assumption, 1540, it had been known for centuries as a rest station for Inca runners rushing to bring fresh fish to tables of their chieftains in their highland capital of Cuzco.

Situated nearly 8,000 feet above sea level, midway between Lima and Cuzco, Arequipa was blessed with a climate of eternal spring. Because of its-invigorating air, its accessibility to the mines and flourishing wool industry, the town had attracted an international group of residents. Towards the end of Spanish vice-royalty, Arequipa had the greatest white population of all South American cities under Spanish dominion. Its people had a special spirit...independent, intellectual, religious and patriotic. Arequipa sounded like a place Ana would like to visit some day.

Time passed. Other white women arrived at the mine with their husbands. Just 20, Ana was so established she was looked upon as a co-mother "co-madre," by Indians and prospectors as well. They called her affectionately "Tia," Spanish for "auntie." Indians turned to her for medical advice when their infants were near death. The newly-arrived white women sought her out to find how to deal with the servants. Lonely engineers and accountants came to her for a taste of civilization. It was apparent that Tia had an innate genius for giving comfort. This talent later served her well through bloody uprisings of the neighboring Coroccora tribes.

At Coro-Coro, in one presidential election, the Indians were given much firewater. They attacked the "foreigners." Whites were beaten to death with iron rods, their bodies left on the pampa for dogs to eat. For days white families hid in the mine, in deadly fear. Slowly starving, the manager of the mine and his wife went out, waving a white flag of truce hoping to negotiate for the safety of the others. Both were shot on sight. Finally one night in a torrential downpour, Tia and the group of whites escaped, fording a dangerous swollen river. Miserable and half frozen, they huddled together in the dark. When it got light, they suddenly broke into laughter. A woman's face had turned black. In the rain, the dye from her black hat had run, completely covering her face and neck.

Tia Bates was the first white woman to return to that copper mine when the troubles were over. The Indians welcomed her like their long-lost mother. She was invited to their day-long wedding festivities. She joined them in their sacrifices to the Sun God. There she watched Indian holy men cut out the hearts of llamas, goats, sheep and chickens and throw them with a bloody plop on the sacrificial altar.

As she was getting her Coro-Coro life back in order, her husband walked out on her. Being deserted by your husband, with a baby daughter, in a remote mining village nearly 15,000-feet in the Andes might have been devastating to some young women. But Ana was abundantly endowed with the moral fibre to survive. And with supportive friends to help. After all, she had come to their rescue when they needed her. Out of compassion, she had invited many of them to stay at her home when first they arrived there. They found her an extraordinary hostess. Some suggested she start an inn, and entertain travelers in a big way. They would back her financially.

The idea appealed to Ana. She enjoyed playing hostess, and knew she was naturally good at it. But Coro-Coro was not the place to bring up her daughter. She recalled the rest-stop-place visitors raved about...one with "the greatest climate in the world aristocratic...charming...Arequipa." This "white city of Peru" had by then become the first night's stop for railroad passengers on their way to Cuzco and the Indian empire. Thanks to a California adventurer, Henry Meigs, Peru now had the greatest railway system in South America. Meigs had confronted the most difficult engineering problem man ever tackled and built tracks where formerly only llamas had trod. "Anywhere the llama goes, I can take a train" Meigs promised the Peruvian government. And build the railroad he did. Not only overcoming the stubborn and treacherous obstacles of nature, but also the abysmal difficulties of untrained labor and a depleted government treasury. By the force of his dynamic personality, Meigs persuaded his railway workmen to keep on working for almost no wage. As a result, Ana and her daughter traveled to Arequipa on a railroad that rose to a height of over 15,800 feet, highest point of any standard gauge railroad in the world. The line passed through 61 mountain tunnels, over 41 bridges, and negotiated 13 switchbacks.

One bridge hung in the air like threads of a spider web, 530 feet long over a valley 250 feet below. Through tunnels, over bridges, along canyons, by the edge of yawning precipices, under cliffs, past rock slides and streams running wild, they chugged to Arequipa. As Tia Bates approached the city, they passed near a soda lake fringed with hundreds of flamingoes, flapping their feathers like so many fan dancers. All along the roadside entering town were long strings of llamas, a multitude of colors. Fawn. White. Chocolate. Pink. Looking at passersby with a haughty, lorgnette stare, they loped in a steady parade. Their backs were loaded with firewood from the mountains. Leading the llamas were Indian women topped by their ever-present derbies and wearing skirts over layers of petticoats, in hot pink, orange, magenta and turquoise. Men in multi-hued Inca helmets, were draped in ponchos of Andean brown and beige. And when the town itself loomed into view, white-white in the brilliant sun, the site was breathtaking. Streets were lined with regal, baroque Spanish colonial homes, all white, grey and ochre. Built of sillar, a volcanic stone, they had an ethereal quality...silvery as moonlight.

And surrounding this Garden of Allah-like valley of verdant fields and bubbling brooks were three dazzling snow-capped Fujiyamas-of-volcanoes: El Misti, Chichani and Pichu Pichu. Not one, but three, silhouetted against a luminous blue sky.

It seemed an ideal place for her inn. In those heights, trains did not travel at night. Arequipa was the first stop to and from the sierra. Plus that, trains rarely ran on schedule because of weather, landslides and any number of reasons. Travelers would often have to stay longer in Arequipa than planned. Here, too, were bountiful crops, fish, game and cattle. With its fine universities, British clubs and old-world ways, it seemed a nice place also, for bringing up a daughter.

Ana had written friends in Arequipa of her plan. They insisted she stay with them until finding a place to buy. Attractive, handsome and obviously well-bred, Ana was quickly accepted by the aristocratic Ariquepenos, said to be the friendliest latinos of all. Tia was charmed by their houses. Most of the architecture was a blend of Moorish, Spanish and Inca...a mix..."mestizo" the Peruvians called it. A style that flourished in Arequipa from the late 1600s. Mestizo buildings of the 18th Century abounded, block after block. Many mansions had ornately carved portals, with two stories-high, metal-studded double doors opening right from the sidewalks.

Most fascinating of all, however, lay behind high walls, covering a distance of five city blocks. There, existed another city. Its name: Santa Catalina. A cloistered town. A city of silence. Inhabited for four centuries solely by generations of contemplative nuns. An enchanting 16th century Moorish-Spanish village untouched by time. Winding alleys were bordered with Spanish-colonial architectural jewels. Its narrow streets, their original stone pavement intact, still bore the same names given them by the Spanish conquistadores: Seville, Granada, Burgos and Toledo. Avenues of awesome hues. One block, watermelon pink. A greenish-blue arcade led to a secluded garden with an apricot-orange wall. Arches, angles, shades and shadows...a casbah of colors. This nunnery was where wealthy Spanish ladies used to live as nuns, in absolute retreat from the world, yet surrounded by their servants, their fine china and other creature comforts. Tia was told that in the 1600s it was the custom for prosperous large families to send a son to the Army and a daughter to the Church. Moved by faith and devotion to dedicate themselves to a life of silence and prayer, many daughters begged their fathers to "buy" them a place in Santa Catalina. For a large sum of money a privileged daughter could be bought an apartment there, and retire to spend the rest of her life making prayers and penances, bringing along her personal maid and cook to attend her.

Santa Catalina was fascinating, mysterious, luring. The more Tia saw of Arequipa, the more determined she became to settle there. She especially liked the Arequipans. "Since we live in walls fashioned from the fruit of volcanoes," one of them confided, "we are more virile than the citizens of Lima. We are quick to flare into love, quick to hate, to forgive, to ridicule, to dance, to rebel, to take Holy Orders."

However, they were not quick at finding her a building suitable enough to convert into the kind of inn she had in mind. Location was most important in her plans. Guests should not have to travel far from the train station. She wanted to be near the town square, with its covered arcades, block-long balconies and towering cathedral.

One day after a fruitless search, she returned to her hostess, despondent. "I now know how Mary must have felt when they told her there was no room at the inn," she sighed. The remark kindled an idea. "My dear that's it!" her friend exclaimed. "Jerusalem! There's an abandoned priory on the Calle Jerusalem. Like Santa Catalina, it is completely surrounded by high walls. It's close to the middle of town and has a lovely garden..."

It was the garden that first won Tia's heart. Birds sang in the topmost branches of pine, mimosa and eucalyptus trees. Roses, lilies, bougainvillaea bordered flagstoned paths, and flaming vines climbed up the walls. Flora everywhere seemed to beg for her care. The garden was huge, more of a park. It was enclosed, peacefully private, behind a 10 ft.-high pink wall. At its center was an impressive fan-shaped entrance gate of wrought iron. Hovering over it all, like a magnificent white guardian angel was the snow-capped volcano El Misti, against the clearest blue sky she had ever seen,

The Monastery building itself was a different story. Adobe, abandoned, with row upon row of tiny cells. As she walked through the rambling structure, plans started to formulate. She would convert the wide brick verandah into an entrance lobby...knock down the walls and enlarge the monks' cells into comfortable rooms with adjoining baths. There would be windows everywhere for views of the garden and volcano. The chapel would become an elegant drawing room. She would enhance the adjoining dining hall with paintings, textiles and antiques from all over ancient Peru. She would call her place "Quinta Bates," quinta being Spanish for "house with a garden."

Thus began the most famous hostelry in South America. Tourists were usually settled in the big house, with its added second story and roof garden. She glassed-in the verandah and decorated it with antique Inca ceramics and ancient Spanish leather trunks, seemingly left behind by the gold-hungry Conquistadors.

In later years the inn was described as "a long rambling structure built high off the ground, with a dozen additions of rooms, nooks, sun parlors, baths, all on slightly different levels, and penthouses like cabins perched on the roof and reached by narrow flights of stairs appearing in unexpected places. In the wood-paneled dining room, one ate at tables for two or four or eight in a veritable museum of art treasures and paintings of the El Greco school. One had whiskey and soda in a den hung with priceless Inca tapestries...in the drawing room in the evenings one played bridge in an atmosphere warmed by a brazier and scented by an aroma of eucalyptus leaves simmering in a brass finger bowl.

Harassed businessmen. Dog-tired diplomats. Mining engineers almost crazed with cabin fever. Widowed society ladies. Exhausted tourists. All were soothed in body and spirit at Tia Bates'. Staying there was like being part of a gala house party in a fabled country mansion, with very special and fascinating guests.

Breakfast was served on a flower-bedecked roof so that guests were seated among the tree-tops in full view of the dazzling snow-covered summit of the nearby volcano. "You could unravel there," said one guest, "in a deck chair, luxuriating in an abandon of relaxation. The air was like dry champagne. At night you would doze into heavenly sleep, under soft, fawn-colored vicuna skins." Permanent guests were put in a cluster of little houses in one corner of the great garden. The occupants were mostly young, English, German, French, Dutch, Swiss or American gentlemen down from home on three-year contracts to serve in the consular corps, banking, mining or the wool business. To these young guests, Tia was "aunt" in every sense of the word. If they needed encouragement, she gave it to them in triple measure. If they needed scolding, she dressed them down like a top sergeant. Indeed, it was her peppery tongue that many guests later remembered most. When a stranger arrived to check in, she would clap-clap her hands and bark shrilly in the patois of the sierra for a houseboy: "Alesandro! Alesandro! Quick, quick." An Indian would come running. "Move these bags of Senor Schwartz to number nine damn-damn fast...and make the room perfect like paradise. When it's ready, carry hot water to the bath and come to me." Then she would tell the new guest: "Alesandro is your house boy. Look on him as your personal valet. But he's supposed to anticipate your wishes. Dinner is at nine. Jacket and tie. If you want a drink before dinner, be sure it is half strength. The first twenty-four hours after a descent are tricky. Now, won't you join me, while you wait, in my little get-together room for a cup of—coca tea...or perhaps a Cinzano before luncheon." Luncheon and other meals featured good American food. Also such local specialties as rocolo relleno (hot filled pepper); acopa Arequopena (potatoes with hot yellow sauce); camerones (sweet water prawns) and pollo chactado (barbecued chicken)...enough native dishes to remind guests that they were globetrotters. Tia equipped her beds with good mattresses imported from New York. She always made sure that there was plenty of hot water. "That's all I do," she insisted. "Misti does the rest. My guests go up on my roof garden, stretch out in deck chairs and look at the volcano. El Misti casts a spell over them."

And so did Tia Bates herself. Like a regal duchess with a hand-picked salon of the world's most fascinating personalities, she would reign over her "house party."

Guests often included lords, ladies, counts, countesses, ambassadors and ministers. Ex-premier Venezlos of Greece was there. General Pershing. Opera star, Grace Moore. Anthony Eden. Sumner Welles. Sculptor Jo Davidson. Dr. Korff, the Finnish nobleman scientist (they were all completely at home at Quinta Bates). For Tia would mix the guests and conversations as easily as she did her famed Pisco Sours. She was most particular about who stayed with her. Bores and boors were booted out "because of unforeseen circumstances," and rooms were found for them elsewhere. Somerset Maugham was turned away, furious, for Tia had found him grumpy.

Early in the 30's, the entire Quinta was taken over by the Prince of Wales, his brother Bertie, then Duke of York, and their entourage. They were on a mission of state. Arequipa's large British colony, which included wool and mining moguls, was agog. Everyone wanted to meet the royal visitors. It was settled that a reception would be held for them at the private Arequipa Club, in its elegant Belle Epoque Tiffany-domed ballroom. Everyone-who-was-anyone in town showed up in white tie, gloves and evening gown... except the guests of honor. The Prince and Duke appeared in their safari clothes.

Noel Coward was the next big super-guest to arrive, and

he couldn't bear to leave.   In the guest book he wrote:
"Of all the places I've been to yet,
This I shall leave with most regret."
And he stayed a month.

Tia made sure no one was bored. She sent her guests off to enjoy the delights of Arequipa...to the bull ring, the race track, the thermal Baths of Jesus on the slopes of Pichu Pichu, to the Harvard Observatory built on the side of Misti. Sightseeing was part of the fun. The Quinta crowd would make trips to the nearby villages of Yanaguras and Cayma, with their charming colonial churches and plazas. Tia would point out Yanaguras' stone archways.

Each was engraved with stanzas by the town's foremost poets singing praise to Arequipa. Climax of these were excursions exploring the Sistine Chapel of Arequipa's Compania Church. Here one saw a domed ceiling decorated with frescoes depicting the flora and fauna of the Amazon jungle, painted by returned missionaries. Tia would time the visit so that the sun would hit the ceiling paintings and turn them into a blaze of seemingly heaven-sent color.

Outside, on the town Plaza, she pointed out the unique Arequipan ice cream carts, each painted brilliantly with scenes of court folk at play. The vendor's carts were fashioned after 17th century sedan chairs, once imported by grandees to Arequipa for their wives and mistresses.

At Quinta Bates, one could spend days in complete *dolce far nientei*, basking in the sun on the roof-garden, watching hummingbirds dart like animated jewels from morning glory to morning glory in the garden, playing golf, or riding horseback at nearby clubs. Often Tia would take a guest along on her visits to see her "children" in the orphanages, or her former staff members in jail. There was a mutual fondness between Tia and the Indians.

Supposedly, Tia was Godmother to over 5,000 Indian

infants. "They choose me," she said, "because they believe I have the bueno mano, or lucky hand. The Indians think it's good fortune if their children die in infancy. They believe that then they go straight to heaven. In hard reality, these Indians reckon it's a blessing to escape life...their lot is pretty hard. Because the proportion of my Godchildren who died was great, they say I have a lucky touch. Too, as Godmother to a departed baby they expect me to provide a tiny shroud and a wooden coffin. Sometimes parents ask me to furnish a yard of white ribbon. They fasten it to the baby's shroud and let it hang out the coffin. That is to help pull me, the Godmother, up to heaven when my time comes. I hope it works."

Often guests would see Tia arrive at the Quinta after breakfast, dressed in an evening dress. "I have just returned from a wedding," she would explain, pointing to her black lace dinner gown and black lace mantilla. "Here, weddings of the poor take place at 4:30 a.m. Only at that hour will the church make honest women of them free of charge. I have to attend these occasions. My staff would have hurt feelings if I hadn't been there to give moral support."

Isabelle Hensel, wife of Struve Hensel, who served as Under-Secretary of the Navy with Forrestal visited the Quinta in 1940. "By then, Tia Bates was definitely the Grand Dame...literally Queen B," she says, "plump, white haired, Tia looked rather like pictures of Mary Cassatt. Her chauffeur would take us calling on the orphans at a convent. Sometimes we'd go to see her houseboy or gardener who had been locked in the local pokey. Tia had presents for all. Everyone adored her. At night she would hold court at the inn. Everyone dressed for dinner. Tia would sit by the fire, very chic in her dinner dress and jewels. Her dear bulldog Misti slept purring by her side. Tia would spark the conversation over very good brandy. We heard the most marvelous stories.

One of them came from a visiting ornithologist. A king condor had been sighted between Cuzco and Lake Titicaca. The bird reportedly had a wing-spread of 25-feet, the length of a good-sized living room. Since Lima's Museum of Natural History had no such specimen, the scientist set out to find it, shoot it and mount it for the Museum. But the ornithologist hadn't reckoned with the king condor's court. He and his Indian guides laid a trap, using fresh carcasses of llamas. Soon, the giant bird soared overhead, wings so large they cast a shadow over the clearing below. The condor flapped to the quarry with the hunters on the alert, hidden in a nearby cave. As king condor began his meal, the scientist shot it. But before the hunting party could reach their trophy, a flock of furious condors swooped down screaming from the sky. They kept circling and diving, keeping the party in the cave for two days. Then, as if on signal, the attacking condors flew away. When the hunting party ran to fetch their giant specimen, they discovered that the condor court had flown off with their king.

When Tia died in 1953, the end came in her quarters. At the Quinta, TIME magazine gave her a lengthy obituary, headed LEGENDARY INNKEEPER. "Arequipa came to think that Tia Bates was as monumental and enduring as the Misti," it said, "but last week she was dead of uremia and old age (almost 85)." Indians and whites crowded Quinta Bates to mourn. Said a weeping Quechua: "She was like charapa, the land turtle... tough outside tender inside."

And it quoted Noel Coward's verse from Quinta's guest book:

> "Her name is plainly Mrs. Bates,
> A strange capricious whim of fate's
> To crown with such banality
> So strong a personality."

What a privilege for us to visit her Arequia, and get first-hand, accounts of Tia before all those who knew her were gone. "Ah! Tia Bates!" sighed a friend of Tia's granddaughter Consuela. "She and her inn were our Camelot. Now they are just a legend. Only the Quinta's pink wall is left standing."

And, Arequipa?

Arequipa hadn't changed. Not one bit.

MEXICO'S BIG SECRET

There's a lollapalooza of a museum in Jalapa, the high in the sky "City of Flowers" half way between Veracruz and Puebla. Jalapa (pronounced "Hah-Loppa"), probably because it is slightly off the beaten tourist path, had been a well-kept secret until its Museum of Anthropology opened without international fanfare several years ago. It's another architectural gem by Edward Durell Stone Associates, the New York firm who gave us Manhattan's Museum of Modern Art and fifteen others, world-wide.

And according to architect Raymond V. Gomez, Executive Director of Edward Durell Stone Associates, who masterminded the project, it was a "building miracle"...thanks to the clout, vision and know-how of Governor Agustin Acosta Lagunes, who commissioned it to open before his term of office expired. A thousand people worked three shifts to complete construction within the fifteen-months deadline. Local mountains of volcanic stone were quarried; perfectly matched trees were transported across deserts in refrigerated trucks to landscape the project; roads and bridges were built into remote jungles in order to bring out giant multi-ton Olmec sculptures never before seen by the public. Governor Acosta long felt that here, in his state of Veracruz and along the Mexican Gulf Coast, Western civilization was born. But it was not until he took office that discoveries had been made to prove that, indeed, people existed in the Gulf Coastal regions of Veracruz and Tobasco as long ago as 5600 B.C., and that the Olmec culture was the mother culture of all Mesoamerica. It was a discovery as important as the discovery of Troy. Here were the Sumerians of America.

With such important artifacts recently unearthed, Acosta felt no time should be lost in providing a showplace of international importance. And showplace it is, a dream of a building rippling down a hillside of flowers, covering 15,000 square feet on 14.5 acres of land. It seems to be latticed entirely of rose cantera, a marvel of pinkish marble, with priceless pieces displayed in dramatically planted atriums. Tropical landscaping and soft lighting add a special magic, with ever-changing shadows and reflections touching natural motion to exquisite still objects...a happy feeling of past becoming alive in the present. Especially so, the smiling Totonac gods of gaiety, representing dance, music and the joy of living, some made in 1 B.C.

Unlike any other museum in the world, this Anthropology Museum of Jalapa exudes an air of light and spaciousness. On entering, one looks down level after level of civilization's artwork, seemingly, an infinity of cultures...Olmec, Haustec (a branch of the Mayas) and Totonac, the classic periods of the Gulf Coast. The Olmec are believed to be the earliest organized society in the New World and are compared to the Sumerians of Mesopotamia for their influence and contributions. "They constantly remind us," says Acosta, "what we were capable of doing before anyone else. The Olmecs converted the rain to harvests, cotton to fabric, stone to sculpture, the sun to a calendar."

Olmec Head #8, a recent find from the Olmec site of San Lorenzo, greets you head-on. Eight-foot tall, in almost perfect condition, it literally is so majestic it stops you in your tracks. "Of all the San Lorenzo heads, and Governor Acosta brought in three of them for this museum, this one alone was found pure, unscathed," according to cultural anthropologist S. Jeffrey K . Wilkerson, an advisor on museum content and display. "We're seeing it exactly as the Olmecs saw it."

It's just one of many giant sculptures, some exhibited in atriums magnificently planted with the flora of where the pieces originated. By an ingenious use of glass walls to separate atriums from the six exhibition rooms, visitors leave one area and move to another without being cut off from the sculptures and jungle landscaping around them. A 600-foot, 18-level orientation corridor leads to the areas of the culture represented adjacently. Time sequence charts put the Olmecs, Huastecs and Totonacs and their artifacts in context. Models of their sites: El Tajin, Zempoala and Castillo de Teayo...indicate the magnificence of their pyramids and cities. (El Tajin, a four-hour drive north of the museum, near Papantla, played a major role on the Gulf Coast between 300 and 1199 A.D. Its famous Pyramid of the Niches is considered one of the most beautiful ancient structures in all of the Americas. Like Zempoala, near the city of Veracruz, it's a site that can be studied within driving distance from the Museum.)

One of the most riveting life-size statues on display is the "stripped man" of Madereros, Xipe Totec. Not your everyday nude a la David, he represents a sacrificial victim who was completely be-clothed of his outer SKIN. Scales of his raw flesh are represented like a union suit of chain mail. The Museum's director, Mtro. Fernando Winfield Captaine, points out that a priest wore the skin like a cape in later ceremonies, and shows a huge stone figure of one wearing such, arms over his arms, legs over his legs, dangling like his own double appendages.

There are stone jaguars, jadeite gods and goddesses of fertility, a whole roomful of them, hauntingly displayed, all big as life, seemingly screaming out into eternity. All of the El Zabotal goddesses date back to the sixth and ninth centuries. They represent women who died in childbirth. All wear belts in the form of serpents, which are associated with giving birth and the life force. These figures from El Zabotal, excavated by Manuel Torres Guzman, head archeologist at Jalapa's University of Veracruz, are considered the height of the pottery art form in all the Americas. They, like the Totonac smiling gods, stone-carved ball game yokes, Olmec heads and Haustec material represent "the largest collection in the world of their various types of art," according to Director Winfield.

Edward Durell Stone-architect Gomez gives Agustin Acosta full credit for his art-museum approach: placing objects on individual marble or cantera pedestals, and in settings landscaped to suggest the original sites from which the sculptures originated. The spectacular landscaping in and out, with over 16,000 native plants; the marble floors; wheelchair ramps; splashing fountains by each of two entrance ways and natural lighting effects are all attributed to the ex-Governor's personal contributions, not to mention the many prize objects he gathered personally from private collections both in Europe and the Americas, plus important Sotheby auctions. "Thanks to Acosta's vision, taste and authority, the important pieces of Gulf Coast culture, from 3000 B.C. on, can be seen all in one place," states Gomez. "This Museum can't be compared to the National Museum at all. If you want to see Gulf Coast cultures in their entirety, you must come to Jalapa. There is just nothing to compare with this Museum of Anthropology anywhere else." There's no other city in Mexico that can compare with Jalapa, either. Like San Francisco, all its streets run at steep inclines. Totonac Indians settled in the area around 1350 A.D. Throughout, there are charming parks, gardens, lakes and vistas. On a clear day, you can see Mt. Orizaba; at 18,855 feet, it's the third highest mountain in North America.

Capital of the rich agricultural state of Veracruz, you find more poets, philosophers and painters here than peasants. This is where the University of Veracruz is located, and its 100-piece symphony orchestra is considered among the best in all Mexico, as well as its Ballet Folkorico.

Walking along the lakes in Los Lagos park, with its Victorian iron-filigree white benches, you are surrounded by trees, flowers, birds and courting couples. Since the city is located near magnificent ranches, fincas, mountain streams as well as the abundant seafood from the nearby Gulf of Mexico, food is delightfully fresh and meals reasonable. Best restaurants: La Pergola, overlooking the University, where marvelous beef is cooked at your table; La Casa de Mama; the very modern Hotel Jalapa; La Estancia and La Bamba, for seafood. Jalapa is also known for its coffee, and the Baalbeck, next to Hotel Maria Victoria, is a good place for coffee drinks and people watching. The Government Palace is a block-long colonial style building on the main square, opposite a massive cathedral, begun in 1773 and never finished (they like it that way). For plant lovers, there's a botanical garden covering 18 acres, surrounded by thousands of coffee trees. It's located on the road to Coatepec, a charming unmodern-ized colonial town where the rich coffee growers reside. Fifteen minutes beyond Coatepec, is Xico (Hee-co), site of Cascades de Texolo (Teh-SO-lo), a waterfall 130-feet high, where Michael Douglas filmed ROMANCING THE STONE.

However, the must-see in Jalapa, other than the superb Museum of Anthropology, is the hacienda of General Santa Ana on the outskirts of town. Another project of Acosta's while he was Governor, this refurbished, re-gardened estate is one of the most charming in all Latin America. The

167

Acostas searched all the way to Texas to round-up the right colonial antiques, and visitors can have coffee on the verandah overlooking spectacular gardens with a swan lake, to boot.

For a peek at where the well-to-do Jalapans live, we drove to the Las Animas residential area, along its Paseo de la Palmas. While there, we payed a visit to the lovely private Chapel of Our Lady of Guadeloupe.

Jalapa is a five-hour drive from Mexico City via the historic city of Puebla. The drive between Puebla and Jalapa is pure cows-in-the-meadow-sheep-in-the-corn scenic, good roads among hills pillowed in worlds of clouds, past tiny chapels in valleys, rumble-tumble towns with stray chickens and squealing pigs, trucks en route to market, each piled high with produce...a smooth, soothing drive, all open country, no billboards to mar the paradisical vistas.

In Jalapa, we enjoyed our stay at the very modern, government-owned Hotel Jalapa. Since the town is 4,300 feet above sea level, we toured by taxi. Most inexpensive. Also, we brought along an umbrella. There's usually an afternoon drizzle, called the "chipichipi." Jalapa is a friendly city, unused to tourists...we didn't see a visiting American, Japanese or German there, but the new museum should make Jalapa Mexico's new place-to-go.

A DAY WITH BERYL MARKHAM

Before we left for Kenya we had a surprise phone call:

"Hugh! Do we have a Scoop for you! An exclusive interview with Beryl Markham! At her cottage on the grounds of Nairobi Jockey Club!"

Our Palm Springs pals, Nona and Jim Lantz, had arranged it with friends who had known her at Paramount Studios, where Beryl served as advisor on the movie SAFARI starring Douglas Fairbanks, Jr. back in the 30s.

Beryl Markham was hot copy at the time. VANITY FAIR had just published a sensational story about her headed: THE BERYL MARKHAM MYSTERY. It's subhead read: QUESTIONS BUZZ AROUND BERYL MARKHAM LIKE DEMENTED TSETSE FLIES. DID SHE BREAK UP ISAK DINESEN'S GREAT LOVE AFFAIR? HOW WAS SHE CONNECTED WITH THE BRITISH ROYAL FAMILY? WAS SHE THE SOLE AUTHOR OF "WEST WITH THE NIGHT," THE MEMOIR THAT MADE HEMINGWAY GUSH?

We were told that Beryl, at 82, lived alone, impoverished, in a bungalow of the Nairobi Jockey Club, where she once had the strongest training stable in Kenya.

"You'll be shocked when you see her," we were warned. "We hear she has fallen on hard times, been robbed, badly beaten-up and nearly killed during an attempted coup when a soldier fired on her Mercedes. She was late for luncheon at the Muthaiga Club and refused to stop at a barricade."

Checking into our Nairobi hotel, we found a note from Beryl's friend, Paddy Migdoll, saying she would take Jim and me to Beryl early the next day. "It's better to interview her in the morning, "Paddy wrote, "for she thinks clearer before lunch. She was thrilled when George Gutekunst phoned from Sausalito and announced that you were coming especially to see her."

George Gutekunst was the moving force in having Beryl's 1942 WEST WITH THE NIGHT republished forty years later, to become a sensational best-seller. A bigger-than-life character, Gutekunst ran Sausalito's Ondine Restaurant across the Golden Gate Bridge in San Francisco, and "knew everybody." It was through his connections that our private visit was set-up.

Paddy Migdoll arrived slightly late for she had been exercising her own horses at the Jockey Club's racecourse. A very attractive Vivian Leigh type, she looked great in her "stable clothes." Like Beryl, she trained her own racehorses, naming them for Cole Porter songs. We later were privileged to stop by her stable and meet such thoroughbreds as "Night and Day"; "Let's Do It"; "Begin Beguin"; "Rosalie," "Love For Sale" and "Kiss Me Kate."

"I wish you had seen Beryl when I first met her 35 years ago," Mrs. Migdoll said as we sped to Beryl's bungalow. "She had a soignée glamour; great blonde hair; bluest eyes ever—looked like a British Garbo in her slim slacks and open silk shirt. Men went mad about her."

"We understand she stole Denys Finch Hatton from Karen Blixen. And is it true that she had a son by the Duke of Gloucester, as VANITY FAIR implied?" I asked.

Paddy laughed: "Oh that has never been proven. But I do know that ever since her son was born in England, she received a monthly check from the royals. She met the Duke,

Prince Henry at a dinner party given by Karen for the Prince of Wales when he was here on safari. I understand they had quite a run-around, lived openly while she was still married, to the Throne's dismay."

"Then what happened to her child?," Jim countered.

"He was raised by her mother-in-law, Lady Markham, in London. Beryl just was not a mother-type," Paddy replied as we rolled to a stop before what looked to us like a 1930s motel. "Here we are at Beryl's bungalow, I'll leave you two handsome men alone with her for I have errands to do, but don't accept her offer of a vodka. She has a wee drinking problem."

We walked past Beryl's beat-up old Mercedes parked in an open shed, and were met by her barefoot Swahili maid-servant, Odhimabo, who didn't say a word or smile, just opened the door to let us in. Shades were down inside a darkened room.

"Come in, come in" Beryl purred gaily "How delightful of you to come" holding out both of her arms in greeting. "Excuse my not getting up, but I've been badly injured, you might have heard." Her voice soft, very English upper-class.

We certainly had heard, from Paddy, that five Africans had bound her wrists and ankles, hit her repeatedly and left her to die after taking everything she owned. That's why her room looked so barren and thrift-shop furnished. However, her personality glowed like a flame and we both were won over by her charm. At age 82, crippled, withered, chair-bound, there was still something very alluring about her. The way she looked at us we could tell she certainly liked men.

No wonder she had so many famous lovers. Besides Finch-Hatton and the Duke, there was Leopold Stokowski; Antoine de Saint-Exupery; Karen's husband, Bror Blixen; and Tom Black. People thought that her solo flight from

England to North America was to impress Tom, her great love. He had taught her to fly. On a dare she took off in a little single-seater plane with no navigational aids other than a compass; without a radio, heating or sanitary arrangement; alone in a cockpit dependent on one piston engine, she flew against strong prevailing headwinds over a cold and merciless ocean.

We asked Beryl to tell us about her flight. We noticed a picture of her being congratulated by New York Mayor Fiorello Laguardia after a triumphant ticker-tape parade in her honor.

This and other photographs were the room's only decorations. They also helped enormously in spurring conversation as we pointed to each with a "What happened here?" or "Who is that?"

An enlarged snapshot of a smiling gent wearing a felt fedora turned out to be Charles Clutterbuck her father who trained thoroughbreds in British East Africa. He raised her in the bush, having been deserted by his wife. Beryl grew up with her only playmates being sons of Nandi warriors. They taught her to hunt lions with spears; track game by spoor and scent; speak the languages of Africa. Growing up wild and motherless, she learned survival skills of a young male warrior.

Abandoned by her mother before she was five, she made a childhood career of being her father's stable-assistant; breaking-in savage thoroughbreds; learning the tricks of the racetrack. By the time she was 18, she trained champions herself and went on to be one of the most outstanding trainers on the turf in Kenya. She won one classic race after another, with six derby winners to her credit.

It was flying, however, that brought her world-fame. She was Africa's first female bush pilot; spotting elephant for the great white hunters; rescuing the lost; rushing medicine to the dying; delivering mail in the remotest areas.

Through piloting planes, she became involved with Karen Blixen's lover, Denys Finch Hatton (played by Robert Redford in the film OUT OF AFRICA). She worshipped Finch Hatton, and he obviously was smitten with her. It was Beryl, rather than Karen Blixen, that Denys invited to fly with him in his Gypsy Moth across Africa. She had to refuse for she couldn't miss a flying lesson permitting her to fly solo. Having seen the movie, we knew Deny's Gypsy Moth had crashed, killing Denys and his servant in a blazing inferno.

"Tom Black dissuaded me from going," she whispered. "Denys was a dear friend, but so, of course, was Tom."

She didn't seem to dwell on her past. Jim told her about my recent book, DEBRETT'S TEXAS PEERAGE which I had brought along as a gift. She seemed most impressed by my having been commissioned by Debrett to write their first series on American "nobles" for she had been presented at Court, hobnobbed with the Prince of Wales, Duke of Gloucester, top titled, and the glamorous of two continents. She seemed most pleased when I handed her my book, and asked me to autograph it.

While I did so, she shouted "Open the trunk! I have something for you!"

Jim opened the lid as I slid her chair across the floor. She began pulling out mementos: press clippings; air charts used on her flights; trophies; medals; but most important to us — her original WEST WITH THE NIGHT manuscript. There was no doubt she wrote it herself. Then with a triumphant gesture she handed me a glossy photograph picturing her in flight helmet and goggles, cover photo for WEST WITH THE NIGHT.

"This is for you," she said, scratching an indecipherable dedication with her frail, shakey hand.

Noon was fast approaching. Vodka time! We knew we

had better go before we all got into trouble.

We promised to reunion with her in San Francisco when her bio-documentary WORLD WITHOUT WALLS made its PBS world premiere. "This has been one unforgettable day" said Jim, leaning over to kiss her goodbye.

I followed suit, and she kissed me full on the lips, looking deep into my eyes.

Then pulled me closer with a gusty request for "Another!"

We couldn't leave Nairobi without making a pilgrimage to the home of Karen Blixen, immortalized in her classic OUT OF AFRICA. It looked exactly as we remembered from the Academy-winning movie. We saw that cuckoo clock which so fascinated those little Kikuyu boys watching its performance every hour. There, too, were the two old ship lanterns she had brought from her sea-faring country of Denmark. She lighted them at night to signal Denys that she was home waiting for him.

Her rooms had a warm comfortable, English country-house look. We visited the kitchen where her cook Kamante created his greatest triumph for Karen's dinner party honoring the Prince of Wales; her bedroom with its white-painted 18th-century bedroom furniture brought from her girlhood home; the gramophone and books both she and Denys held dear.

We could see why Eton-educated, aesthetic Denis Finch Hatton was deeply attracted to the life Karen created in her house. It must have seemed an oasis of cool, quiet, civilization where he could relax, make conversation with an admiring, indulgent, fascinating woman.

Her house was miles different from Beryl Markham's. Baroness Karen von Blitzen lived like a baroness. Beryl like the wild-one she was, a woman who couldn't care less for convention. They each had fallen deeply in love with

Denys Finch Hatton's blinding charm. Once we visited Eton and saw that he was still worshipped there, 50 years after. There was a monument to him on the campus, not for anything he had done, just because he was such an outstanding individual, a man who seemed to enjoy every experience life had to offer. With Karen Blixen, it was intellectual. With Beryl, sensual.

The National Museum of Kenya restored Karen's home not only for visitors like us who greatly admired her spirit and writings, but for Kenyans to have a glimpse of the past that's part of their history. After Karen became ill, lost both Denys and her coffee plantation, she had to go back to her family in Denmark. Before departing, there was a huge house-sale, her furnishings snapped-up by many local friends. Most of those affects were gathered back to make this house-museum as authentic as possible. Now the area around it is named "Karen" and has become an exclusive residential suburb of Nairobi.

Thus, Africa will always remember Karen.

Certainly, Karen never forgot Africa. Years later, when her great nephew took us to her home RUNGSTEDLUND, on the sea 15 miles north of Copenhagen, we saw she had brought Africa with her. On the walls were crossed tribal spears, shields and marvelous portraits she had painted of her beloved black house-servants in their best tribal finery.

PALM SPRINGS, PUSHBUTTONS
& THE ANNENBERGS

P alm Springs has always been a happy hunting ground for us.

Researching our biography of Rancho Mirage's legendary Thunderbird Country Club gave us a grand opportunity to interview such legends as Bob Hope, Ginger Rogers, President Gerald Ford, Charles "Buddy" Rogers, Phil Harris and Alice Faye. Also, to get inside some unforgettable residences. Like the mechanical house of Thunderbird-member Corwin Denney.

Denney's domicile came to our attention because of its submerged tennis court adjoining the golf club's #15 fairway. Yes, SUBMERGED — sunk deep in the ground, a regulation-size tennis court, air-conditioned and lighted for night play. Adjacent to it, on ground level, stood a velvety-grass croquet court which could be illuminated at dark. By pushing a button lights for it arose out of the earth on twenty-foot poles.

It seemed that almost everything inside the house was electronically operated, too. Its lavish bar took our order automatically. We just pushed the VODKA button and an iced bottle of Absolut ascended from the cellar below. We poked another button and presto! out from the wall came a drawer containing iced glasses right for any requested drink. Curtains, blinds, doors, sliding windows, all were operated by push-button. A wall of gauges reported outside wind velocity, as well as temperature of the weather, in each room and swimming pool.

Near the pool, Corwin and his wife had a sunbathing "lazy Susan" with seven full-length pads for sunning. This giant circular platform revolved automatically with the sun, assuring even tans.

On his sun deck, Denney and guests could play chess on a giant chessboard with fireplug-size chessmen, so big they had to be shoved in play.

Fortunately, Corwin and his wife Nanci could handle all the controls, since both flew their own Lear jets and his-and-hers helicopters. We saw them parked with Corwin's seven or eight other planes in his private hangar near Palm Springs Airport. All were serviced by a fleet of mechanics in matching coveralls labeled Corwin Denney Enterprises.

Wonderful what one can do when he has 3% of Kansas under lease for oil drilling.

Most privileged of our Palm Springs house-peeking was a visit with the Walter Annenbergs at their desert barony, Sunnylands. Ambassador Annenberg, perfect host and gentleman, gave us a personally-conducted tour of the premises, one that Queen Elizabeth, presidents, prime ministers, princes and the Shah had experienced before us.

We were there to see and write about the Annenbergs' collection of Van Goghs, Gauguins, Renoirs, Monets, Cezannes and other masterpieces of Impressionism and Post-Impressionism, considered America's finest assemblage of 19th century French paintings in private hands.

We found Sunnylands was a masterpiece in itself.

"One of the things I like about this property is that the outside works so beautifully with the inside," Ambassador Annenberg told us, looking out his shaded-glass wall onto acres of rolling lawn with its perfectly placed trees, pools, flowers and private golf course — a Garden of Eden.

The Annenbergs not only have the money to amass their

art collection, they have imagination and exquisite taste. Not just any old estate for Walter Annenberg. He decided to build the penultimate oasis right in the heart of the Palm Springs desert. At the time, 1964, all you could see on his property was scrub, cacti and sand, bone-dry nothing. He envisioned turning those acres into an Eden on a scale so magnificent that even his friend the Shah would be dazzled. He summoned California's top talents in desert-house design to pull out all the stops and create his "miracle in the desert." T. Quincy Jones, University of California's dean of the school of architecture, took on the job of executing a private world in total harmony with the environment. To do so, he worked closely with noted Beverly Hills interior designers Ted Graber and William Haines, who played a major role in the total concept. No doubt Graber could have been inspired by Sam Coleridge's "In Xanadu did Kublai Khan a stately pleasure dome decree," for he suggested a house that spread across the desert like a great sheik's tent. So when we arrived at Sunnylands, we entered a 6,400-square foot living room with a tentlike, skylit ceiling that rises to 38 feet at its center. Sunnylands' total living area is said to be 32,000 square feet. There are guest houses literally "fit for a queen" along with servants' quarters which are discreetly tucked away near the swimming pool, hothouses, two tennis courts and garages storing golf carts for the private golf course. It's only 9 holes, but no worry, it's laid out so that it can be played as twenty-seven. Prince Charles, no golfer, was seen buzzing around the course in one of the golf carts swinging his polo mallet right and left, chasing a ball, when he visited the Annenbergs.

We had heard about all this from friends who had spent weekends and New Years Eves there. But we weren't prepared for what we saw since it, truly, is indescribable. "Do you know how to get here?" Annenberg's secretary asked us.

"Just come down Bob Hope Drive and turn at Frank Sinatra. You'll see a high wall and then come to the gate. They'll be expecting you."

Well, that high wall covers a square mile of Rancho Mirage real estate, most exclusive on the Desert. An electric gate is so subtly placed you could drive right by it and not know this was the entrance. We passed muster with the uniformed guard, and swept up a half mile driveway through a private world of such great beauty and tranquillity we wondered if Heaven could be like this — and certainly hoped so.

In the center of the huge circular driveway before Sunnylands' massive front doors looms a 30-foot Mayan column, similar to the one fronting Mexico City's National Museum of Anthropology, only this one seems somewhat bigger. As we parked our car, we were met by a butler in livery consisting of a well-cut buff blazer and chocolate brown trousers, one of fifty servants, groundskeepers and guards who keep the estate so perfectly.

Never have we seen an interior so serene. Sunlight streamed down from the 38-foot apex of domed ceiling on cool marble-floored living areas in pale pinks, yellows, whites and celadon green — muted colors and furnishings that blend subtly, comfortable with the Monets and Gauguins that abound. Virtually every wall glows with masterpiece after masterpiece. On very first glimpse of the entry area, you see a wall of cocoa-toned Mexican volcanic stone paved in cubes, mounted with paintings that most museums would kill for. There's Van Gogh's OLIVE TREES alongside Gauguin's THREE TAHITIANS and STILL LIFE WITH FRUIT, both small and hanging one over the other. In the center of this wall grouping: Gauguin's soothing LA SIESTE. Next: Cezanne's STILL LIFE WITH MELON AND POMEGRANATES hanging over his slightly larger LE PLAT DE POMMES. Then, to balance with the first Van Gogh

OLIVE TREES is another olive-orchard scene, Van Gogh's THE OLIVE PICKERS. That's just the first wall.

Here and there, exquisitely placed, we noted Chinese-export porcelains, orchids from their greenhouse, Rodins, Giacomettis and a unique torso by Arp. "Jean Arp gave it to me," Annenberg told us as he demonstrated how the sculpture of a girl could be called "Before & After." When turned around, she becomes pregnant.

Nearby, on a pale green wall, he had hung Renoir's monumental (63" x 51 ") DAUGHTERS OF CATULLE MENDES, a portrait of three charming adolescent redheads. When we commented how sweet they looked, he answered, "Actually, I've heard they were little devils."

Van Gogh's most tranquil painting, ROSES, white roses in a blue vase against a pale jade wall, reigned center stage between his THE CRADLE and Gauguin's double portrait of a Polynesian girl and her grandmother.

Pointing to the Gauguin: "Look at those two faces," said Mr. Annenberg. "One so young, so innocent, she will believe anything. The older so cynical, she believes nothing. Here Gauguin depicts the cycle of life. It's a superb example of Gauguin in his second phase, after he moved out to sea from Tahiti to the less crowded Marquesas Islands. Here he shows very real people in a more humanly penetrating mood."

His side comments on the Van Goghs were also very revealing. "ROSES is one of Vincent's largest paintings, and certainly one of his greatest," said our host. "He created it while recuperating in the St. Remy sanitarium when, for a two-month period, he seemed to paint in a state of grace — pursuing a different response to nature — turning to natural beauty in a way he never had before." We were told that this was Lee Annenberg's favorite. When we asked to photograph the Ambassador and his wife in front of it, she excused herself and returned in a smashing "compatible green" dress.

Van Gogh's portrait of a woman holding a rope and rocking a cradle was painted shortly before he cut off his ear. Gazing at it, Ambassador Annenberg pointed out: "This is the wife of Roulin, Van Gogh's postman friend in Arles, where he painted some of his most memorable works. He persuaded Mrs. Roulin to pose for him just after she had borne a child. He did five such portraits of her, but this is the one she chose to keep for herself, so she must have considered it the best. She had no sympathy for Van Gogh... didn't realize he was mentally disturbed...just thought he was a hard person. You can see the sensitivity of the artist by the way he shows her disdain for him. Her gesture suggests she might be smelling a limburger cheese!"

Hanging these Vincent Van Goghs with the Paul Gauguin underscored Vincent's strong attachment to Paul, whose sudden departure to the South Seas literally drove Vincent insane.

There were historic connections like this throughout the Annenberg's house. They all seemed to knit together. Seurat's pale colored GRAY WEATHER, GRAND JATTE paired with a Monet, to show Monet's influence as father of Impressionism.

Monet loomed large in the Annenberg Collection, starting with a picture of Monet's wife sitting on a bench in their garden. It's a landmark Monet. For the first time, figures and light were combined with a psychological narrative.

Monet's WATERLILIES (Nymphées) occupied a whole wall at Sunnylands. It seemed very similar to those we had seen in the Orangerie at the Louvre in Paris. The Annenbergs had this painting on the walls of the U.S. Embassy in London, when he served as our Ambassador to the Court of St. James's. We remembered that our friend Robert Montgomery Scott, who served as Annenberg's Special

Assistant during his 5-year stint there, had told us about how this Monet had created an "incident" when it was thought to be a "missing Monet." One morning a reporter from the London Sunday Times called and asked: "Does the Ambassador have a painting by Monet called NYMPHEES?" When told that he did, the reporter replied "Are you aware one was stolen in France two years ago and that the Ambassador may have that stolen painting?" Scott told him that he doubted it, but would check. Doing so he found that Annenberg had acquired his paintings years before the robbery. "Besides " he told the reporter, "Monet painted scores of paintings all called NYMPHEES, which is the French word for waterlilies. "The eager reporter signed: "Oh well. It was a dull Saturday, anyway."

Along with the landmark Monets, Mr. and Mrs. Annenberg owned seven superb Cezannes. Besides the monumental VIEW OF MONT SAINTE VICTOIRE, two of the most intriguing are Cezanne's CRACKED HOUSE and UNCLE DOMINICK DRESSED AS A MONK. The young Cezanne painted many portraits of his family and his Uncle Dominick was one of his great boosters. "But he wasn't a Catholic monk at all," Mr. Annenberg chuckled. "He just liked to dress as one."

CRACKED HOUSE, one of Cezanne's greatest works, shows a house divided, literally — either from an earthquake or from old age and neglect. A huge stone cliff in the background reminds that the world of nature withstands age, and budding trees convey that nature renews itself — telling us that nothing made by man is permanent.

Any student of Cezanne will be enthralled with the range of his career represented in Annenberg's collection, including Cezanne's sketch book drawings. In fact, though the Annenbergs may not have set out to assemble such, their collection provides a complete history of Impressionism. We

185

could see that the Annenberg Collection contained central masterpieces of all the great Impressionists, the most beautiful painting in almost every category — the very best Monet, Cezanne, Renoir, of each stage in the artists' development. There were marvelous nudes by Matisse, Renoir, Toulouse Lautrec. Plus, Degas' masterpiece of a masterpiece, AT THE MILLINER'S, created in pastel on five pieces of paper in 1885 and glued to canvas.

Sunnylands' dining room seemed like an enchanted chamber thanks to a huge painting, THE ALBUM by Vuillard. Completed in 1895, it shows seven women in various poses looking at an album in a library. On opposite walls were THE PINK DRESS, painted by Berthe Morisot in 1873, and the earliest painting in the collection, LITTLE CURIOUS GIRL, one of Corot's rare figures, painted between 1850 and 1960. We learned that Corot had a great influence on Morisot and dined with her family every Tuesday.

Another "prized treasure" that Mr. Annenberg loved was a stunning stone statue of a narwhal given to him by his daughter. It was the only truly personal piece we had encountered, until he took us into his own very private "room of memories," a veritable museum of the great and near great that had touched his life.

Here, along with pictures of his beloved mother, Sadie, were signed photographs from British royal family members and prime ministers from Winston Churchill on. Every year the Queen Mother had sent them a Christmas card by special post, and the Annenbergs had framed them all.

Prince Andrew and his Duchess Sarah had been royal visitors there the week before we arrived.

"Sarah Ferguson has the most marvelous personality," he told us. "When she and the Prince came for a weekend, I had a high tea ordered — finger sandwiches, cakes, the works. When served, she smiled sweetly and asked,

'Ambassador, do you have any bangers?' So I asked the butler to have the chef grill a dozen sausages. She thanked me graciously and called after him, 'And plenty of ketchup!'"

Dominating his "memories" room was a spectacular portrait of Annenberg by his friend Andrew Wyeth. It's a stunner, but we couldn't understand what the Ambassador was wearing in it.

"Ha! Andy wanted me to wear his fencing jacket," he explained. "But I'm a bit too beefy in the chest and shoulders for it to fit. So instead I am wearing, of all things, a choir robe. Visiting Ely Cathedral in East Anglia, I was most impressed with the cut and color of the choristers' robes. So I went to Whipple in London and had them make me several. Sometimes when we are at home for dinner, I wear one of them with my shorts and velvet slippers. So that's how Andy painted me. He also did something he has never done on his pictures. He painted in the top corner "To Walter Annenberg by his friend Andrew Wyeth.'"

On the wall next to it are a group of pictures taken year after year of their New Year's Eve guests, Nancy and Ronald Reagan being prominent in most of them. There are autographed pictures from the astronauts and the men raising the flag on Iwo Jima. Most haunting is a photograph of Annenberg as a foreign correspondent looking out over Hitler's bombed Berchtesgarten. He appeared to be gazing hopefully toward a future that would return joy to the world, not destruction. That's the world his collection brings us — joy — captured in full bloom for all time. As we drove out from Sunnylands, we remarked "That's the happiest billionaire in the world!"

THE QUEEN & I

Our fascination with Bangkok began with a Main Line murder, a man who vanished mysteriously, a hotel, and Yul Brynner's THE KING & I.

First came THE KING & I. For a big anniversary, we splurged and attended its opening performance starring Gertrude Lawrence on Broadway. Never had we seen such splendid exotica...costumes, setting, dancing and a most memorable King.

Then and there we determined that some day we would go to Bangkok. Later we discovered, to our amazement, that today's King of Siam (now Thailand) is the only monarch ever born on United States soil.

Thailand's King Bhumibol started life in Cambridge Massachusetts while his father was studying medicine at Harvard and his mother, nursing, at Massachusetts General Hospital.

As a boy, Prince Bhumibol was schooled in Switzerland, where he studied law as well as science. He also pursued such American hobbies as jazz and fast cars. An automobile accident cost him his right eye, and during his convalescence he fell in love with a ravishingly beautiful daughter of a titled diplomat. Also while recovering from his accident, the untimely deaths of his father and then of his older brother, brought the Prince and his young bride, Sirikit, back to

Thailand.

We learned too, that he had taken clarinet lessons from Benny Goodman, played in a weekly jam session on Thai TV, and asked his male subjects to have vasectomies in honor of his birthday. One year, more than 1,190 men underwent vasectomies as a birthday present to him, setting a world record as 5 doctors with 85 nurses completed nearly two vasectomies per minute, some on dining room tables, while a rock band sang the virtues of birth control. Within ten years, Thailand's birthrate dropped from 3.3 children per family to 1.6, "the most dramatic drop in population growth in the world."

Once again, we determined to go to Bangkok, and perhaps write Bhumibol's biography.

Worldly pals, who had been everywhere twice, insisted that we stay at the legendary Oriental Hotel. Greeting us at the airport was the Oriental's assistant manager, attired in formal morning suit, striped pants and all. He whisked through the teeming traffic of Bangkok in the Hotel's Rolls Royce.

At The Oriental's entrance we were helped from the Rolls by a smiling, boyish doorman wearing white gloves and traditional jongkrablen knickers.

A string trio in native costume oozed Mozart music as we entered an elegantly informal lobby with huge bell-like chandeliers. There was no need to register; all attendants welcomed us by name; and as we walked into an enchanting atrium a-bloom in tropical plants, white wicker and colorful cottons, our greeter explained: "This is the Author's Lounge, part of The Oriental's 1886 building. We converted it to The Author's Resident with four suites, each named for Somerset Maugham, Joseph Conrad, James Michener and Noel Coward, all of whom stayed here several times. Since you are an author (our Texas book was in the Hotel's library), we thought you would enjoy The Noel Coward Suite."

ENJOY was hardly the word. ECSTATIC was more like it.

A double stairway entwined with blooming golden orchids swooped up to our secluded wing on the second floor. Double doors opened and our private butler, Wot, bowed with folded hands and bid us welcome.

"I am here to serve you any time, day or night," he smiled, handing us his engraved calling card. "Since you might have difficulty pronouncing my name, just call Wot, and I will come with happiness."

Our luggage had mysteriously arrived before us, so efficiently that we had forgotten all about it. We discovered later that luggage is NEVER carried through the Oriental Lobby. Here, there's no fumbling to "tip the busboy." Nonpareil service (not OVER-service) by a fiercely proud, friendly staff, is what gives The Oriental its reputation as "Best Hotel In The World."

Our Noel Coward suite had it all: understated luxury with Thai antiques, rare fabrics, Chinese ceramics and comfy furniture. Brilliant historic-paintings of the Ratannakosin period graced our living room walls. An airy bay window looked over a tropical garden and the River of the Kings, a floating city of sampans, houseboats and barges bulging with flowers, fruits and merchandise.

A handsome basket of native fruits awaited us on our dining table, with a gracious note from the General Manager, Kurt Wachtveitlk, wishing us a happy stay. With it was a chart describing each piece of fruit, how it would taste and the way it should be eaten.

The parlor had a lived-in feel, with its abundance of fresh lacy orchids and Noel Coward books stacked on the table-desk. Framed informal photographs of Noel made it like visiting the great wit-playwright-actor-bon vivant in his private digs.

SUMPTUOUS best describes our bedroom, with its wall-paper designed in goldleaf peacock feathers. Twin four poster beds had spreads of peacock-blue Thai silk. Lotus-shape lamps cast a low glow by the bedside table, with a fresh arrangement of orchids changed daily.

At night, champagne-silk kimonos were awaiting on each bed, seductively folded. Quilted blue-silk bed slippers were parked in the ready position. Come bedtime, we would find atop our pillows, a tiny Thai-straw basket holding a freshly handmade chocolate truffle.

And the dressing room! An entire wall lined with carved teak doors; marble floor; star dressing room mirrors; 22 plump monogrammed towels. Fixtures in our marbled and mirrored bathroom were of polished brass.

A soft knock, and butler Wot appeared in his celadon-green short sleeve Nehru-style uniform. "May I make reservations for dining this evening?" he offered. "Since all of our dining rooms are very popular, we want to make sure our guests have priority, so its good to make arrangements ahead of time for each night of your visit."

"What do you suggest?" we asked, reminding that we would be there only five days.

"For your first night it would be quite lovely to dine on our terrace and watch the boats ply by in the moonlight. Here, meats are grilled to your taste and there is a bountiful buffet. All most informal, with happy music, too."

That sounded perfect... and it was.

In fact, every night we dined in a different restaurant without leaving our hotel. Very nautical was LORD JIM'S, named after Joseph Conrad's seagoing hero. It resembled the afterdeck of a very well appointed ocean-going yacht, offering a spectacular gull's-eye view of the river twinkling with reflections of boat lights and lanterns. Informal, fun, LORD JIM'S menu listed over 40 dishes... Chinese,

Continental, Japanese or Thai, with fish bought fresh from boats at the morning market.

On Wednesday night we had a candle-lit dinner gliding down the Chao Phya on The Oriental's private cruiser, serenaded by musicians. For dining formally, we went to the hotel's penthouse-perched Normandie Grill, offering cuisine worthy of the best 3-star restaurants in France.

One day we visited Jim Thompson's House On The Klong. Jim Thompson, we were told, is a "Bangkok legend."

Born near Wilmington, Delaware; educated at Princeton and the University of Pennsylvania, James H.W. Thompson had cut quite a swath in East Coast social circles. A year before Pearl Harbor, he dropped his thriving architectural practice to enlist in the U.S. Army, later serving as a Captain in the OSS stationed in Bangkok.

He fell in love with Bangkok with all its exoticism and Arabian Nights dazzle, and decided to settle there after the War. He became active in reorganizing the Oriental Hotel, which had been taken over by the Japanese army during the occupation of Thailand. At the same time, sensing the commercial possibilities of Thai handwoven silk, he revived Thailand's silk industry. With its smooth texture and brilliant colors, Thai silk was unique, once produced in quantity as a cottage industry by family after family up and down the klongs, those canals that weave in and out of the city which gave Bangkok its reputation as "The Venice of the Orient." This cottage industry had long been displaced by cheap machine-made goods until Thompson stepped in.

He took samples of Thailand's shimmering silks to Edna Woolman Chase, editor of VOGUE, in New York. She agreed Thai silk would be a hit in the post-war fashion world, hungry for luxury and color after drab war years. She featured it in a designer dress commissioned exclusively for VOGUE, and from then on Thai silk took off, encouraging

Thompson to start The Thai Silk Company and open a chic shop featuring custom made fashions on Bangkok's Surawong Road.

In the 1940s, Bangkok was a happy-hunting ground for lovers of Southeast Asian antiquities. Jim Thompson, with his eye for beauty, began acquiring the best Buddha images, Chinese porcelains, fragments of temple statuary, textiles, miniature Indo-Chinese paintings, oriental cabinets, tables, screens and chairs. As his business grew, so did his collections. To house them, he built his famed House On The Klong.

Jim Thompson's house was actually a melding of six classic Siamese country houses joined as one romantic residence. Built right on the water, it seemed an enchanting fairy-tale palace. Here he entertained visiting celebrities and friends in such a memorable way that Jim Thompson's House On The Klong became a desired destination for sophisticated travelers.

In 1967, on Easter weekend, Thompson disappeared. While on holiday in the Malaysian highlands, he went out for an after-lunch walk and was never seen again.

While we were enjoying the riches of The Orient, King Bhumibol's Head of Security, General Vasit, had to attend a whole weekend of wakes. He couldn't meet with us for three days since it was "The Time of Cremations," when families have elaborate "cremation parties" honoring members who had died the previous year but "funeraled" at this annual event.

"You fortunately are here in time to see the Queen Mother before she has her Royal Cremation," he smiled.

"Oh—we hadn't heard that King Bhumibol's mother had died," I said in my softest, sympathetic voice.

"Not King Bhumibol's MOTHER, his GRANDmother," General Vasit explained. "She died in Paris several months ago. Would you like to attend her viewing?"

Hearing that she had been preserved in a huge glass jar, until "cremation time," we offered sincere excuses.

Because of interruptions like this, our Royal Visit would have to be postponed for another week. We couldn't afford to wait, so had to leave without meeting the King personally.

However, His Majesty sent us a lavish farewell gift with his apology: 13 handsomely-bound books on Thailand and his kingship.

A year later, I received a telephone call from Queen Sirikit's principal lady-in-waiting asking Mrs. Best and me to join Queen Sirikit for dinner at The Helmsley Palace Hotel in New York. She said that Her Majesty was at that time visiting in Palm Beach, but would be coming on to Manhattan to see a few friends. Could we join them?

OF COURSE, we could!

We had never dined with a Queen before, and her Royal Dinner outdid THE KING AND I in glamour.

The Thai Ambassador to the U.S. greeted us by name as we entered the Helmsley Palace's exquisite Library for champagne and caviar before Her Majesty's arrival. The room was filled with varieties of lotus and orchids flown-in from Thailand for the occasion. Acting as hostesses were the Queen's gracious ladies-in-waiting, each attired in a stunning Thai-brocade sari made by Balmain, of Paris. Soon we were joined by such fellow guests as Mrs. Douglas MacArthur; the Cornelius Vanderbilt Whitneys; the Kissingers; Ex-New York Mayor and Mrs. John Lindsey; Baron von Krupp; Bulgari, the Italian jeweler; CEOs of TIME, FORBES, IBM, and on and on and on. "Everyone" was there.

We formed a receiving line to meet the most gorgeous Queen imaginable with her dazzling Thai smile, and subtly dazzling diamonds.

THE SPIRIT OF NAKASHIMA

Strange can be the serendipities of life.

Such was the case of my friendship with George Nakashima, woodworker, architect, philosopher.

I first met George when I made a wrong turn looking for a friend's farm outside New Hope, Pennsylvania. Driving down a leaf-dappled road, I found myself entering into a woodland Shangri-La. There was a Teahouse-of-the-August Moon quality about the place. Serenity. Pebbles and ponds. Bamboo shoots reflected in water.

Ten low buildings stood silently in the woods, six of them with wing-spread roofs graceful as gull's wings.

I had lost my way, but found the compound of Nakashima. Later I learned that Nakashima-furniture collectors came there from all over the world. Some jetted-in from as far as Tokyo, placed their order and flew right out again. Nelson Rockefeller arrived in his private helicopter. His house in Pocantico Hills was furnished entirely with sleek, ebony-smooth pieces by Nakashima.

Names associated with great modern art—Ben Shahn, Morris Graves, Harry Bertoia, Charles Coiner—had early recognized George's genius. His pure, timeless design contemporizing Pennsylvania-colonial with Ancient Japanese appealed to both traditional and modern tastes. Our friend

Frances Wainwright, a long-time Nakashima collector, mixed his pieces with fine 18th-century furnishings throughout her Georgian manse. To her, Nakashima furniture was more than just tables, chairs or chests. It was sculpture. Wood with a soul. Her Nakashima treasures brought peace and harmony to a room.

This spirit of meditation, even mysticism, that Nakashima instilled in his work was first sparked in a monastery, when he was in his late twenties. I learned all about it one night when George and I were stranded in a car, and had a long chat until rescued.

He was born and raised in Seattle, graduated as an architect from M.I.T., and when he worked for an American architectural firm with offices in Tokyo, was commissioned to design the dormitory for a Hindu ashram outside Pondicherry, in India.

"At Pondicherry, with the great Indian spiritual leader Sri Aurobindo, I found the inner peace I had been searching for, subconsciously, all my life," he related. "I stayed there two years, living the life of a monk, and given the Hindu name Sundarandanda, which means Beautiful Joy."

Here he first began to find the ways to work with wood. George not only designed and helped to build the dormitory, but all the furniture in it. When he returned to the main office in Tokyo, he became even more fascinated with traditional Japanese techniques of carpentry. The Japanese reverence for wood and deep concern for materials and craftsmanship impressed him mightily.

One day he visited a temple garden and there, luring him like a Lorelei, was an ancient Keiyaki tree over 1,200-years old, and 10 feet thick. One small part of it was still living. Then and there, Nakashima promised himself that if the tree died, he would come back and try to buy it. He wouldn't let it decay and return to the soil. He would give it a second life.

In furniture.

In his book THE SOUL OF A TREE, Nakashima wrote: "A tree is perhaps our most intimate contact with nature. There are even specimens which in a single life have spanned the entire history of civilized man as we know him. It is a sad destiny that some of these noble trees, some of the cathedrals of all time, are debauched by the greed, insentiveness and gaucheries of man."

Making furniture from rare roots and ancient trees became Nakishima's life work. In his hands, a tree given up for dead became alive again as an exciting table, chest or chair—wood grain, knots and all.

However, Nakashima didn't fashion furniture out of just any tree. He probably cornered the market on the world's choicest wood trophies...zebra wood from Africa; exotic rosewood, teak and laurel found in Kerala, India; incomparable walnut from forests planted by Queen Elizabeth I after Britain's trees had been cut down to build ships to combat the Spanish Armada.

All over the globe, foremen of logging operations kept an eye out for odd-sized, uniquely grained, weather-worn specimens that might appeal to Nakashima. Such finds were sometimes costly. He once paid $8,000 for a log measuring 12 x 512 feet. He said at the time "I don't have any call for it. Our storage buildings are stocked with rare woods. But when something this fine is brought to me, I can't resist. I have no idea what it will become. But one day, inwardly, the log will tell me. I listen to the cries of wood."

He believed each tree had its own special character and tried to catch the spirit of it. For Nakashima, the shape, color and grain determined whether it would become a desk or a door. Having wood's natural edges and knots become a part of a piece became his hallmark.

George pointed out, however that retaining the deformities in a plank required the discipline of a diamond cutter.

"The direction and thickness-of-cut are very important," he stressed. "Cut one way, you get something good. Cut another and you lose it. Every board brings a big surprise. Each is unique. A tree's history of a hundred, a thousand years; the joy, diasters and unspeakable pain. is told in its markings. A storm in a particular year might leave an unexpected touch of color. Growth lines of winter, when the tree grows slowly, give it bands of darker, harder wood. Summer growth stripes are wider, softer.

Nakashima and his woodworkers developed a special technique to bring out that exceptional character. They could part a thick, wide slab like an open book, so the two matching sides formed a huge table top. Butterfly insets of contrasting wood connected their two pieces and became a fascinating part of the design.

During the Depression in the 1930s, after he received his architectural degree, Nakashima moved away from the mob. Then, his most interesting commission was building bathhouses on New York's Jones Beach for the WPA. The Depression was at its depth. To George, American architecture and design, along with the philosophy behind it, was even more depressing. So he took the $600 his family gave him as a graduation present and traveled around the world on freighters, getting off at different ports to take odd jobs for income.

In Paris, an exiled Russian prince and his princess took the young George under their wing and found him work as a draftsman for architects. Also, with his skill at calligraphy, he transposed music sheets for such music hall performers as Mistinguett and Maurice Chevalier.

There, he observed Le Corbusier's Pavillion Suisse being built, and became swept up in the activities of Ozenfant and his studio. He studied at Fontainebleu and later joined forces with Czech-born architect Antonin Raymond in Tokyo, where he worked for five years.

During this period, he designed The Church For Christ The King near Kyoto; St. Paul's Church in Karwizawa, north of Tokyo and the ashram dormitory in India. In Tokyo, he met Marion a lovely Japanese-American school teacher. Renewed and inspired, George came back to the United States in 1941. He and Marion married, moved back to their native Seattle and started a family. Ten months later, Japan attacked Pearl Harbor. With thousands of other Japanese-Americans, the Nakashimas and their newborn baby, Mira, were herded off to a concentration camp.

It was a horrifying and humiliating experience for these born and bred Americans who loved their country, and it changed the course of their lives.

During their year of internment, Nakashima met a Japanese carpenter who was traditionally trained. George worked with him daily, learning the skills and tools for fine Japanese woodworking. So great was his joy in working with wood, that he put thought of continuing architecture aside and began making furniture seriously, fashioning it entirely by hand.

His old boss Antonin Raymond, who was living on a farm in Pennsylvania, worked for their release. Once they were freed, George, Marion and baby Mira left the West Coast to work for Raymond on his farm. Conditions there could not have been more primitive. Living in a waterless shack, they bathed in the rain and toileted in the woods. Their job was tending chickens, scarcely something an M.I.T. architect and an English teacher knew much about.

When they were offered $300 as a down payment to move out of the shack so someone else could move in, they took the money and ran, right across the fields to a beautiful wooded site on a hill. George discovered that his Pennsylvania surroundings provided a treasure trove of trees, including black walnut, ideal for his woodworking. He wanted to buy his own woodland and build his own business.

They used the $300 as a down payment on ten acres and while building their woodworking shop, the family lived in a tent. Snow would fall on his workbench. But the cold and discomfort didn't hold him back from turning out furniture with a poetry and vigor that won him immediate reknown with a small but influential group.

Patrons beat a path to his door. Orders stacked up for months ahead. Helpers had to be added, and more workshops to accomodate them.

To house his growing business, Nakashima put his architectural skills to work again, this time for himself. He designed first a workshop, then a house and next a storage building for rare woods needed for his furniture making. Later he added a larger workshop and also a handsome sales pavilion with a Ben Shahn mural and a volcanic-rock sculpture by Masauki Nagare.

His work was heralded around the world, and he was considered a national treasure. The American Institute of Architects (AIA) awarded him its Gold Medal, calling his Monastery Of Christ In The Desert near Abiqui, New Mexico "an achitectural masterpiece, perfect expression in adobe and plaster of the monastic spirit."

George's dream was to build an Altar Of Peace, around which "some will lay flowers, some will sing songs; and others may simply pray." Before he died, his dream came true. He found a phenomenal great Walnut tree, 300 years old, 125 feet high and weighing 10 tons. Out of it he fashioned a tangible shrine, installed in The Cathedral Church of St. John The Divine in New York. He saw it installed in the center of the Cathedral's great nave near the front entrance.

On New Years Eve, 1986, it was dedicated during a

Concert for Peace, with Leonard Bernstein as guest conductor Isaac Stern, guest soloist, and Nakashima guest of honor.

I attended George's memorial service at The Cathedral June 28, 1990. George's grandchildren welcomed guests outside bearing huge bouquets of big chrysanthemums. They handed each of us a pom pom "to place on the Altar of Peace and touch wood in communion farewell to George."

Steven Rockefeller, who sat next to me, gave a tribute along with representatives from Metropolitan Museum of Art, American Craft Museum and others. A procession led by The Very Reverend James Parks Morton, Dean of The Cathedral, came down one aisle to be met by a group of brilliantly robed Buddhist monks, there to make a Zen meditation. As the memorial service began, Nakashima's daughter Mira, now a graduate of Radcliffe, played a lovely flute solo. Prayers were said, we were asked that on leaving we would form a line and file by The Altar of Peace, place our flower there, then rub the smooth wood and make a silent prayer for George...and for peace.

It was a touching farewell in more ways than one as we all glided our fingers over George's most beautiful table, singing softly together;

> "Let there be peace on earth,
> and let it begin with me.
> Let there be peace on earth,
> the peace that was meant to be.
> With God as our Father, we are family
> Let us walk with each other
> in perfect harmony."

After retiring from advertising/publishing, Barbara and I became "travel writers," satisfying our passion for experiencing the best places on earth, with our reports from the field appearing in MAIN LINE Magazine, and MAIN LINE LIFE, voted Best Suburban Newspaper In The Nation.

On the following pages is a roundup of our travel articles published during the 1990s...

Ballooning Safari in Kenya

BALLOONING SAFARI IN KENYA

In OUT OF AFRICA, one of the most memorable scenes is when Denys Finch-Hatton takes Karen Blixen for her first flight in an airplane. In the open cockpit of his Gypsy Moth, they soar over the Rift Valley and the volcanoes of Suswa and Longonot to "the lands on the other side of the moon," flying low enough to see the animals in all directions, feeling towards them as God might have after creating them, and before He commissioned Adam to give them names.

In AROUND THE WORLD IN 80 DAYS, the solace and peace of ballooning instilled in us an urgent desire to travel like Passepartout, up, up and away, with that tune of The 5th Dimension in our heads and a bottle of cold Moet in hand.

So, when we heard that on our safari in Kenya it might— just might—be possible to glide silently over the Masai Mara plains in a passenger balloon, we just had to do it. Other than dying, it would be our ultimate trip.

"But what happens if you fall right into the middle of a pride of lions? Or hungry jackals, or charging rhinos, or a river full of hippos and crocodiles? How will you get help? Isn't it just a bit risky?" we were asked by family and friends. Also, we were told by "old African safari hands" that one has to be in the right place at the right time in exactly the right weather conditions in order to assure such a flight. (The

Philadelphia Zoo people sponsoring our adventure offered to help us take this side trip, but emphasized that they were not responsible, and couldn't hold up or inconvenience others along just for us. So be it, we said. We'll just have to see what happens. But it MUST happen!)

Preparing for our passage into the wilds of Kenya was part of the fun, especially delving into Banana Republic for our very special bush jackets and khakis. We made sure to take our shots for cholera and black water fever and to pack repellent to ward off the tsetse flies whose bite could render us brain-dead or blind. We brushed up on our Swahili, remembering only the greeting "Jambo" which can mean "hello," "good morning," "how are you?," "glad to see you" or "goodbye." It is a word you can use for just about any occasion. We also took along a box of surgical masks to keep the fierce red dust from clogging our lungs.

Then we were off—goodbye good old USA, hello Ernest Hemingway, Tarzan, Teddy Roosevelt, Stanley "Dr. Livingston, I presume"-land. We recalled all those past African adventurers as we approached Kilimanjaro and WHITE MISCHIEF country, touching ground in Nairobi.

To get there, we traveled from Philadelphia, with a rest stop in London, then on a British Airways 747 non-stop over the French Alps, Rome, the Mediterranean Sea, Alexandria, Khartoum, Egypt's vast Sahara Desert, arriving 9 hours and 4,000 miles later at Nairobi Airport, greeted by an orange-pink blazing sunrise across the sky.

Almost all comings and goings into the African bush begin and end in Nairobi. Driving into town from the airport, we passed the edge of a wildlife preserve peppered with prancing ostrich and wandering wildebeest. This, on the outskirts of the city.

Nairobi itself proved to be a delightful surprise, fascinating and festive, abuzz with khaki-clad visitors talking excitedly to guides and white-hunter types looking as if they had just stepped out of an old Stewart Granger movie. Safarists crowded at tables by the pool at The Intercontinental and on the wide verandah of historic Norfolk Hotel, a gathering spot since the days of Bror Blixen, Isak Dinesen and Lord Delamere. On the streets, inter-mingled among tee-shirted tourists and business-suited locals, turbaned togaed, saried and shukaed natives added a touch of the exotic.

Before we left for the bush at dawn the next morning, we inquired about that balloon flight. Again, the answer was "maybe."

Our group departed immediately after breakfast since the best game-viewing is shortly after sunrise. As we drove out of town, both sides of the road were lined with blacks in boldly patterned tribal dress. They contrasted dramatically with troops of black children in spotless preppy blazers, en route to class in ultra-modern school buildings.

Six of us, plus our driver, were comfortably ensconced in a Nissan van. Built specially for tracking animals in the wilds, it featured a pop-up top, enabling us to stand, look out and photograph whenever the occasion arose (which was quite often). Carrying all our luggage, fuel cans and extra tires in the rear, these intrepid landrovers tackle potholed plains, stone-jagged mountains and dust-blinding deserts with equal ease.

Our caravan drove from Nairobi at approximately 5,500 feet, to a height of 7,000 feet before descending into the awesome Rift Valley. We stopped in our tracks as we first sighted this vast, verdant expanse, bordered on three sides by towering mountains. Standing on a high promontory to take it all in, we couldn't help but wonder what adventures were awaiting us beyond those mountains on the moon-type landscapes below.

Would we be able to make contact with a balloon camp

when we arrived at our first overnight stop, Masai Serena Lodge? And if the balloonists could take us aloft, what WOULD happen if we landed right in the midst of hungry lions or stampeding water buffalo?

What would we do this very night if we came face to face with a leopard en route to the privy?

These wonderments were still on our minds as we bumped through The Rift, then they fast disappeared as we spotted our first giraffe—then zebra, topi, and whole plains of buffalo.

"Look!" shouted a companion. "Masai!"

Sure enough, striding gracefully across the valley with their sharp spears and shields, Masai warriors added dash to the scene, their sleek ebony bodies loosely draped in what appeared to be—tablecloths. Decorated with red earth, plaited corn-rowed hair and bibs of brilliant beads, skin tattooed with ceremonial scars, they seemed at one with the animals. Totally independent, they paid no more attention to us than the grazing and leaping gazelles nearby.

We cut off the main road to jostle amidst the wild ones and, after a 185-mile bone-rattling ride, we arrived at Masai Serena Lodge in time for lunch. The Lodge, built like a series of Masai mudhuts, hugs a high hillside overlooking great sections of exceptional grazing land. It is ideal for observing animals in their natural habitat. There are no boundaries to the Reserve, so the animals roam at will in all directions. From our room window we trained our binoculars on a herd of elephant heading for a tree-fringed hill. That night we heard a lion splashing in a water-hole just below us. Or, was it a leopard? All we could make out in the shadows was the shape of a cat-like creature, a big cat-like creature. Certainly it wasn't a hippo. Hippos we encountered at daybreak the next morn, as they bobbed up and down in a mossy river, still yawning widely.

On our very first game-run, we came upon regally relaxing lions and their rough-housing cubs. Our van seemed only a paws-length away from these lounging Leos, but they paid us no mind, whatsoever. Our next lion encounter was something of a stomach-turner—our first close-up of a kill. Tawny twin lionesses had tackled one of liondoms greatest delicacies: a sweet, juicy warthog. Their equivalent, perhaps, of our Virginia ham. We came upon them engaged in a very strenuous struggle to make certain that each got an equal share, or, hopefully, whole-hog. Both had a firm grip on the freshly-killed piglet, neither giving an inch. All this gore took place less than a few feet from our van of shameless voyeurs, snapping pictures of the action as if this was our last chance on earth.

Our driver told us that we were observing a most unusual sight. He had never seen lions in a tug-o-war over something so tiny as a warthog. Excitement never stops on such a safari. When you think you have seen every animal in the alphabet, others emerge—gazelles, caution-frozen, standing stiff as stone, their tiny black tails moving like inverted hands of metronomes. Warthogs jounce prissily along with their tails stuck up as a car antenna. Over there, wildebeests browse shoulder to shoulder. Nearby, an imperious male impala with backward-curving horns rounded up his harem of oriental-eyed does. Darting from under a thornbush, two dik-dik appeared, teenie as toy Bambis. We passed carousing monkeys, and a baby baboon hitching a ride on its mother's underbelly. We stared mesmerized, armed with curiosity and cameras, with a great desire to capture in our memories this planet's last great natural spectacle.

That night, as dancing Masai tribesmen entertained gin-and-toniced guests, we received word that we could take off in our balloon at dawn. Suddenly, all our insides seemed aflutter with anticipation and tingling nerves. We would have to drive through deep country in darkest night - with all those staring eyes reflected in the flash of our headlights and glow of the huge African moon. Did John Glenn feel like this in his last hours before taking off? Later, en route to our balloon departure point, we understood the meaning of "darkest Africa." Would we find our way through this total velvet-black night? Then suddenly, as if in a cinemascopic dream, giant rainbows seemed to be rising before us, sky-high colors emerging from the flare of flames inflating massive hot-air balloons, one after another. We hadn't expected so many, or ones so gigantic. We counted at least six.

We were at Governor's Camp, being greeted by the captain, as British and James Bondish as any casting agent could possibly muster. Epaulets on his zippered flying suit were much grander than those sported long ago by Errol Flynn and David Niven. We discovered that our balloonists were part of Buddy Bombard's bunch of Burgundy fame. Our pilot, in fact, was the very same who had taken our traveling companion ballooning over chateaux country in France. Scurrying in and out of a sea of tents, a busy ground crew hop-toed to ready our rapidly inflating airship. In soft, Oxfordian tones, an attendant in splendid overalls suggested we use the loo: "Lawst chawnce" before going aloft. What would happen if we were gripped by a sudden attack of turista dangling in a balloon basket over Kenya!!!

As if on signal with The Man Up There, dawn lifted like a world-encircling windowshade—and then there was light. The mist began to rise, and so did we, seven of us, the captain's daughter on a visit from London, and our Buddy Bombard balloonist. We were standing hip-to-hip in our basket as the sun slowly rose across the boundless, dewy plain. Wordsworth's words came to mind as we "wandered lonely as a cloud...that floats on high o'er vales and hills"—when all at once we saw a crowd of, not daffodils, but giraffe.

Grant's gazelle, gemsbok and gerenuk. Here we were floating silently, smoothly almost touching treetops, casting our giant shadow over streams of hippopotami beginning their day. We glided over an endless meadow bathed in the dew of dawn. Below us, the Lord's animal kingdom at breakfast, an all star cast of African beasts and their supporting players, from Secretary Birds to bongos. A lion family had already made their kill, gorging themselves on a freshly-blooded carcass of a topi.

As far as the eye could see: giraffe, elephant, rhino, ostrich, zebra, Cape buffalo, lion, all grazing silently, seemingly oblivious to the other—each minding their own business. Shrill squeals ripped the air like a surprise lightning bolt, as a pack of hungry hyenas dashed at full speed to encircle a frantic terrified warthog, beating hell-to-leather towards the safety of a ground hole.

Everywhere, creatures great and small roamed free. Elephants paraded their baby Babars across the landscape. Nonchalant zebras nibbled grass. Giraffe necks poked up like periscopes from a crumpet of trees.

On the border of Tanzania, we began to descend. We watched as other balloons touched the ground on a treeless plain. Scout cars suddenly appeared to greet them.

"Brace for landing!" came a shout. "We're going to tilt!" We held oh-so-tight to our basket as we skirted across the ground, landing on our side. None seemed hurt as we scampered out on our bellies. We stood up, elated.

We felt like roaring out a Tarzan yell. We had made it!

KATMANDU & TIGER TOPS, TOO

Marco Polo Meets Indiana Jones! That was our first thought as we jammed through the exotic crowds in Katmandu's Durbar Square.

Katmandu! Largest city in the Kingdom of Nepal, closest place on earth to the remotest place on earth.

Rickshaws skirted around ancient Shangri La-type pagodas that appeared unchanged in a thousand years. There must be more temples lining Katmandu's crooked cobbled streets than anywhere in this universe. And here we were, caught in its whirlpool of humanity — Hindu holy men, Fu Manchus, Sherpas, Gurkhas, Tibetans, Tamangs, monks, Mongols, Newars, Thakalis, Burmese, Buddhists, Tauris, Garungs — women in saris, men in flowing robes — faces and costumes of Nepal's 70 different languages — jabbering dialects we had never heard before. This was like being in an ever-changing kaleidoscope, not knowing what would be happening next.

Why were we here, smack in the midst of earth's mightiest mountains, Himalayas, where gods are said to mingle with men?

What was the magnet that drew us over thousands of miles of oceans, an infinity of frozen steppes and endless Afghanistan deserts to this remote kingdom bordered by Tibet, India and Sikim?

The answer: Mt. Everest, ultimate of mountain peaks.

Actually, dreams of this adventure began in the early 1950's when we met Sir Edmund Hillary at the University Club in Chicago. Hillary and Sir John Hunt were there to give a slide talk promoting their book and film, THE CONQUEST OF EVEREST. On May 28, 1953, Edmund Hillary and his Nepalese guide, Tenzing Norkay, had been the first to scale this 29,028 ft. pinnacle. We were lucky enough to hear Hillary tell us about it personally. During his talk we happened to be standing next to him in the back of the room as he clicked slide after slide picturing his expedition's mind-boggling feat. Even our kidneys became thrilled as we saw scenes of their trekking through fierce winds and snowstorms as they reached the summit in sub-zero maelstroms. We wondered "What did they do about going to the bathroom?" So we asked him.

At first, Hillary, who reminded us somewhat of a genial cockney Lindbergh, didn't understand what we meant. But, when he did, the ice was broken and we had quite a chat. After that encounter with Sir Edmund, Mt. Everest became one of our "must" destinations. However, almost forty years later, we certainly didn't desire to climb it. We intended to *fly* over Mt. Everest and the Annapurnas if weather conditions permitted. Back in 1932, travel writer Richard Halliburton had hoped to do so, but planes weren't equipped for that altitude. Today, we understood, one could sightsee the very tip-top of the world in comparative comfort. However, shortly after checking into Soaltee Oberoi Hotel, the Katmandu airport and entire valley seemed lost in fog. We had come all this way, yet we couldn't even SEE the Himalayas. So what does one do in Katmandu until the fog lifts?

Our hotel host suggested: "Why don't you hire a guide to take you to see the Kumari Devi, Nepal's living goddess!"

We learned that even though the Nepalese honor thousands of gods and goddesses, there is only one that is a living human being, and she is a 9-year old girl sequestered in the upper floors of a small stone palace, the Kumari Bahal, in the middle of town. Millions of devout Nepalese consider her the goddess who came to life, a divine of great spiritual power. Even the king comes to her once a year to receive her blessing. Legend has it that two centuries ago, another king there had wished for a girl or goddess and that the gods granted his wish, allowing him to choose an eternal virgin goddess, one who would be a virgin and physically perfect. It was decreed that she must never bleed, even from so much as a pinprick. So when she menstruates, she is replaced, pronto, by another.

Our guide explained that the goddess we hoped to see had been selected from several 5-year old girls who had to pass a test of courage. Many girls were carefully screened to determine if the spirit of the Kumari Devi lived with them. The chosen ones are then herded into a dark, cavernous room to spend the night being observed by an astrologer and several Goddess-committee big-wigs. A hundred water buffalo are slaughtered, their heads chopped off and placed under eerie lights around the darkened room, along with frightening masks and candle-lit skulls. Through the night, choruses outside moan, wail and scream to frighten the little girls even more. The tot who emerges from this ordeal least scared-out-of-her wits and showing the greatest calm is crowned the new "living goddess" cloistered immediately in the Kumari palace. Such has been the custom for centuries. Crowds assemble under her gaudily carved windows hoping to get a glimpse of her, for luck. She allows herself to be seen for a few seconds, so one has to watch closely playing this game of "I Spy." We waited patiently for her to peek-a-boo.

Suddenly her face appeared, as heavily painted as a

217

Kabuki dancer, her eyes outlined in thick black kohl from her lashes to her ears. Her entire forehead was painted lipstick red, with an oblong "eye" in the center. We were yet to see the Himalaya peaks, but at least we had been privileged to peek at the Himalaya's Living Goddess.

We encountered another little girl every bit as memorable shortly afterwards, one about two years older than the Kumari Devi. She seemed to be the sole proprietress of a rather chic boutique selling colorful handmade women's cotton jackets, soft woolen scarves and such. In our country she may have been old enough to join a Brownie troop but, here in Katmandu, she was running a flourishing shop single-handedly, seeing that a horde of customers were taken care of, speaking perfect English, all the while babysitting for her 5-year old brother. On the side, she also designed and sewed after closing time.

Another store, next door to this 12-year old wonder, displayed charming naive paintings featuring landscapes, major temples, farms, city squares, people and palaces of the Katmandu Valley. Such painting is considered very rare, for until this century, Nepalese art represented only religious figures and symbols, scroll painting, illustration for religious manuscripts, icons for meditation. Every detail in the art followed religious guidelines set centuries ago, so there were no "original" paintings, nothing to represent personal expression. Since the 5th century A.D., the object of art in Nepal has been strictly for worship and devotion.

Only when artists were commissioned to paint frescoes on the walls of palaces and monasteries did the painters "do their own thing." We were told that Nepalese craftsmen decorated courts of Kublai Khan in Northern China and monasteries of the Dalai Lama in nearby Tibet. Today, Nepali artists depict life as they see it.

Now hundreds of refugees from Tibet can be seen throughout the Katmandu Valley. Near Patan, an ancient town an hour away, we bussed to a Tibetan refugee camp where these disciples of the Dalai Lama were practicing their art of rug weaving. Patan must have looked the same in Kublai Khan's day for, thanks to German archaeologists, its architecture is being preserved. Unfortunately, this is not so in Katmandu.

As we waited for an all clear signal to fly over Everest, we observed decaying holy temples sporting pairs of eyes painted on four sides of their steeples, eyes of four meditating Buddhas depicting awareness inherent in the "enlightened mind."

Buddhist monasteries abound in the valley and high elevations, and everywhere one sees parades of Buddhist monks in saffron robes. Here it is considered an honor for a family to have a son as a Buddhist monk.

This blend of Hinduism and Buddhism has contributed a unique fusion of art and architecture, plus a strange sense of peace among the people. Most holy of sites in Nepal, perhaps, is the Hindu temple of Pashupatinat where thousands of "holy men" and pilgrims gather each winter to honor the Lord Shiva. These Hindu holy men, called saddhus, look more like wild men, with their freakish flowing beards, swirling manes, flashing forked staffs, or tridents. Unkempt describes their demeanor — a far cry from the appearance of Nepal's famed fighting men, the Gurkhas, the epitome of "spit and polish." Their prowess as soldiers came to the fore in 1814 when the British were at war in India. The Brits were so impressed with the Gurkhas that a special treaty was created allowing Britain to recruit these exceptional soldiers, the first foreign mercenaries to be stationed on English soil. They also serve in the Indian army and cut quite a figure in their slant campaign hats guarding a temple gate in Durbar Square.

Gurkhas, holy men, Living Goddess, flamboyant temples and pagodas made waiting for our flight to Everest far from boring. But nothing compared to our first sight of that world of ice, the Himalayan range, seen from the air. Somehow we expected our plane to be rather pre-War and dangerous. Instead, it seemed comfortable as a parlor car. A steward served coffee, then invited us to come one-by-one to visit the cockpit and see Everest and Anapurna's towering peaks close-up.

We couldn't help but wonder if we would be sucked down into the hungry jaws of those frozen ravines below.

We felt confidant, however, that we would survive this awesome flight for, after all, having had The Living Goddess stare at us full-face assured that good luck would follow.

And it did, later when we were riding elephant at Tiger Tops and had an encounter with a charging one-horned rhino.

Have you ever been attacked by a one-horned rhino, charging at you, head on?

Well, we were.

Peg Vick, my wife and I were crashing through the high grass on elephant back, tracking tigers in the jungles of Nepal when... Wait a minute! What were we three greenhorns doing riding elephants looking for tiger? The answer is simple: we LOVE elephants.

So, when we heard that a maharajah's former hunting preserve had been turned into a National Game Preserve just loaded with endangered species like Bengal tigers, Asian elephant and long-snout crocodiles, we figured we'd takeoff for the camp at Tiger Tops before we became extinct, too.

To get there we took a puddle-jumper plane, flying seventy-five air miles south from Katmandu to the site of Tiger Tops Jungle Lodge, nestled right in the heart of Royal Chitwan National Park, 360 square miles of tall grasslands

220

and forests with flora and fauna rarely seen anywhere else. This is where the Prince of Wales, at age 27, came on a hunting expedition in 1922. Then the Chitwan Valley was completely wild, and the only way to get there was by elephant. This was no problem for the Prince. It was the day of the Raj and they could literally move mountains for their royal guests. The prince arrived in Nepal with an entourage of 100. After ten thousand Nepali tribesmen had cleared the site for the royal camp, several hundred elephants were used to beat for and ring tigers and rhino. Across India, before Nepal, the prince had covered 11,000 miles, supported by three trains. One engine pulled just the box cars packed with his polo ponies and horses. At the border, the royal party mounted the horses, since there were no roads. Our passage there required a bit of doing, too.

After landing in a field, near a thatched-roof village, we were met by a caravan of Land Rovers which transported us to a crocodile infested river where we paddled across to more Land Rovers which took us over rutty roads deep into the jungle toward Tiger Tops. Along the way, graceful spotted deer stopped in their tracks as if playing "Freeze!" and gave us the once-over with their big soulful eyes. A whole tree full of langur monkeys seemed to be showing off with acrobatic feats specifically for us interlopers.

"Do you think we will see a tiger?" our Indian driver was asked. He was not too hopeful. When the Chitwan Valley was used as the hunting preserve of Nepal's rulers, the Rana Prime Ministers organized great hunts, with Viceroys of India or European royalty invited as guests. Tigers and rhinos were so plentiful that nearly every one of the nobles bagged large numbers of them, just for the sport of it. Many a palace had its Royal Bengal Tiger rug.

"Fifty years ago, we had over 40,000 tigers in the Indian subcontinent" our driver revealed. "Now the tiger population was decreased to a little over 3,000. There are maybe 300 in all of Nepal — and only 40 are roaming about in the park."

We peered ever more intently from left to right, even in trees above, hoping to see a big striped cat. Suddenly a form rippled the high grass. "Look," someone whispered, "it's a wild boar!" But we saw no tigers before arriving at our camp. "Remember," our guide consoled, "the tiger is a shy, cautious, retiring animal. It hunts by night — you know 'tiger, tiger burning bright, in the forests of the night.' During daylight the tiger lies in thick cover where it is not likely to be disturbed by humans. They are not like lions who roam in packs. The tiger is a solitary animal. Males and females stay far apart except at breeding time. Even then their association is brief. Cubs remain with their mother until nearly two years old. Since the tiger is a lone hunter, it's difficult to locate in any one area. A male tiger may have a territory of up to 40 square miles."

So, we were warned that the tiger is a difficult animal to see in its natural state. Even though Tiger Tops uses baits to improve the odds, tigers are sighted only at intervals of a few days. We just hoped that tomorrow would be our "day of the tiger."

However, that night was our warm welcome to Tiger Tops. Three charming British beauties in scruffy camp clothes greeted us and pointed out the treehouses where we would be lodged. Actually they were treetop hotels mounted on high poles about two stories above ground and in the open, away from trees that might lodge a leaping leopard or a "tiger, tiger" in the night.

Since we were already clad in our tiger-tracking garb (khakis, cap and camera), we lost no time in starting our tiger hunt in the jungle. As staff and guests lined up on both sides of the path, a chain of over a dozen Asiatic Elephants loped towards us, each carrying a passenger bench and his mahout, or driver, who sat squarely in the middle of the beast's forehead, steering from the ears. To mount our mammoth steed, we had to climb about two stories of steps to a small boarding platform and be helped down onto our seat. We rode two sideways, one as a "tail gunner." The elephant stood patiently still while all this was going on. Our Babar was being very, very good. We grew increasingly grateful that it was so well-trained as we headed toward a very slippery bank, wading deep into a river where we encountered our first slithering sword-nosed crocodile. We hoped our elephant could swim, and we were oh-so-grateful that we were high above the water, well out of snipping distance from that razor-tooth croc-snout. Our Asiatic elephant was not as large as the wild elephants we had seen in Kenya. The African bush elephant weighs over six tons compared with the Asian elephants' five tons. Since our elephant was about nine feet high at the shoulder, we seemed comparatively safe from the crocodiles — but what would happen if we encountered a crouching tiger lying in the high grass on the banks beyond? Soon we were in high jungle. No longer in a long line tail-to-tail, we had swerved away from the procession and were dashing full speed through walls of elephant grass, 20 feet high. How else could we penetrate such encumbrances except with these remarkable bulldozing animals? We barged into the brush so silently that we didn't disturb a shaggy black bear, quiet as a dark shadow under a tree. Up went the binoculars to reveal an ugly animal with a long muzzle and short hind legs, weighing about 300 pounds. It even had a varsity "V" on its chest. As it rumbled back deeper into the bush we learned that it was a sloth bear, and despite its clumsy appearance, could be very agile.

Soon we became very adept in spotting game. A herd of wild oxen grazing on a hillside, sambar, civet cats, wild dogs, an Indian porcupine, long antlered Chital deer, and exotic birds all preened and preyed within our view. Riding so high on an elephant gives you a high-and-mighty complex — you are a Master of the Universe, a Marco Polo, Hannibal and Sabu in one — that is, until you suddenly come into a clearing in the mass of grass and stare head-on into the furious face of a Great Indian one-horned rhinoceros guarding her baby. No rocket-powered tank could charge the enemy with such speed and force as that rhino heading straight toward our surprised elephant.

"Uh oh — this is it," flashed through our minds. "So, this is how it will all end we thought. Sideswiped, trampled and gored by a rhino — Nearer-my-God-to-Thee in Nepal!" Not even I could imagine that.

But our elephant swerved just in time, its trunk flashing like a whip through the air, letting out a bloodcurdling trumpet bellow — and that mad-mama of a rhino grazed right past us, baby at her heels, and disappeared as we lumbered onward.

Fortunately, I had my camera at the ready, and recorded the whole scene in a snap. But would we have been so lucky if that rhino had been a tiger?

We'll never know, for on our short stop at Tiger Tops, the tigers were a no-show.

PS. On Earth Day it was reported that poachers have almost completely wiped out the rhino population of Africa, estimating that only 50 of these magnificent beasts are left. Since our face-to-face encounter, we feel a very close bond with that animal, and want to do everything we can to keep those mama rhinos and babies on Earth.

Can you believe that their mass slaughter is just for their horn? In parts of the Orient it is believed that ground-up rhino horn is a great aphrodisiac. (Is that where the expression "horny" springs from?) Also in Yemen, which has the biggest rhino-horn market of any country, it is considered ultra macho and high-status to wear a dagger sporting a carved rhino-horn handle.

George Plimpton has pointed out that a rhino's horn is about as effective as the human fingernail, since it's composed of keratin, a protein found in hair and fingernails. It isn't like a bull's horn that grows out of the animal's head. Plimpton claims that the Asian who wants to improve his sexual prowess would do just as well by nibbling his fingernails — and leave those poor rhinos alone.

FOLLOWING THE PATH OF SOMERSET MAUGHAM

There was a young lady from Guam
Who spread her charms
Charm by charm
She cut quite a swath
Following the path
Of William Somerset Maugham

(With apologies to Ogden Nash)

Following the path of Somerset Maugham isn't such a bad idea. During his career he traveled to some fascinating places, met equally fascinating people, and wrote stories about them. Everywhere we went on our travels, it seemed Mr. Maugham had also once been there. Even in as remote a spot on this earth as Arequipa, Peru.

We had seen his villa at Cap d'Antibes when we visited my cousin the barone Dorothy de Graffenried-Villars at her villa, which had once belonged to Sara and Gerald Murphy, of "living well is the best revenge" fame.

Living well takes talent as well as money, and Maugham had plenty of both. He stopped at the most elegant places, dined in the most fashionable restaurants, collected only-the-best art and antiques, shopped for "quality" whether in Capetown or Calcutta.

Southeast Asia seemed to be Maugham's favorite territory. He would camp out in a suite at Singapore's Raffles

Hotel, order a Martini from the barman, and like that "young lady from Guam" start spreading his charm in such a magnetic way that he attracted the most interesting characters there. Over drinks with exiled Brits, he brought out lurid stories of their life in the charged atmosphere of remote colonial stations. Bette Davis and Herbert Marshall starred in a film, THE LETTER based on a real life happening told to him, in confidence, at Raffles.

At The Oriental Hotel in Bangkok, he wrote THE GENTLEMAN IN THE PARLOR and PRINCESS SEPTEMBER from material he had gathered at The Strand Hotel in Rangoon while returning down the Irawaddy River from Mandalay.

In 1998, we, too, took off on the road to Mandalay, deciding to plot our trip to Southeast Asia and follow the path of Somerset Maugham in Singapore, Bangkok and Rangoon.

We began in Hollywood, where he was often an honored guest. Tyrone Power made THE RAZOR'S EDGE; both Joan Crawford and Rita Hayworth starred as Sadie Thompson in movie versions of his short story MISS THOMPSON.

We stopped at The Bel-Air, to us the most idyllic hotel in America. It is so special that Tyrone Power honeymooned there TWICE. It's where Audrey Hepburn stayed while filming MY FAIR LADY. Grace Kelly always resided in a poolside room there while making her movies. Garbo came here when she "vanted to be alone." Celebrities choose it because it is so private no one knows they are there.

What makes The Bel-Air especially desirable is its exclusive location and sublime landscaping on eleven secluded acres right in the heart of Los Angeles' mega-bucks estates neighborhood.

It doesn't seem like a hotel at all. No big lobby. No elevators to wait for. No long corridors. Here you amble to your quarters through a bower of flowers blooming in all of their glory, along paths with Silverbells and Cockleshells all in a row. You pass intimate courtyards with bubbling fountains and terra cotta Ali Baba jars aburst with magenta blossoms. In the distance, down a greensward, swans sail serenely across a mirror-like pond. Here and there, fanciful gazebos grace garden nooks. Brilliant bougainvillaea blossoms cascade over Mediterranean-tile roofs. Low, Spanish-pink rambling buildings, some with California-mission archways, give the place a colonial cloister peacefulness.

At The Bel-Air we felt tucked discretely away in an enchanted Eden.

Yet , we couldn't lap up all this class without at least peaking at Hollywood crass on the "other side of town." So went off on THE GRAVE LINE TOUR of Hollywood.

It was a tour with a different twist, carefully researched and wittily produced.

As we strolled down Hollywood Boulevard past Grauman's Chinese Theater, stepping over Judy Garland's slipper prints and Rin Tin Tin's paw prints cemented in the sidewalk, our hearse arrived, right on time to take us for our "viewing."

Our tour "funeral director," dressed in swank undertaker striped trousers and "mourning" coat, welcomed us with a somber souvenir: a copy of Marilyn Monroe's Certificate of Death.

As we settled into different sections of the long, grey hearse, a radio moaned funereal organ music, as an unctuous voice whispered: "Dearly beloveds...we welcome you on slab...on board...of Grave Line Tours. You are about to view the remains of scores of spooky and kooky attractions which were dug up exclusively for this tour. Every site which you will be escorted to points where best views are possible, so those of you with cameras must aim and shoot quickly for we must keep a dignified funeral pace in traffic. Now, sit back and rest in peace."

We then headed out into star Hollywood, with the voice of "dear, departed" Bette Davis interrupting our tour guides narration with "FASTEN YOUR SEAT BELTS! IT'S GOING TO BE A BUMPY NIGHT" (right off the soundtrack of ALL ABOUT EVE.)

We passed the apartment house where Janis Joplin overdosed, and the digs of Dracula-star Bela Lugosi, always "good to the last bite."

DIAMONDS ARE A GIRL'S BEST FRIEND music broke into the gloom as we had pointed out to us where Marilyn Monroe once lived with Joe DiMaggio; then past the cottage at Beverly Hills Hotel in which she trysted with Yves Montand; to the house said to welcome John F. Kennedy often; and also we made a detour to glimpse the hideaway where her nude calendar photos were snapped. Sacred sites, all.

Too, we saw where John Belushi "checked out" at Chateau Marmont, and Jayne Mansfield's "piles of pink" mansion in Beverly Hills where she made "a last dip" in her heart-shaped swimming pool.

"Tarzan" Johnny Weismuller did his laps at his house which was completely surrounded by a moat in a jungle-like setting. Naturally, he always felt at home stroking in the underbrush.

We were asked to bow respectfully at the mailbox of President Ronald Reagan and Nancy. "Note the house number here," alerted our spokesman. "It is 668. Originally, it was 666, but that is the DEVIL's number. They say superstitious Nancy Reagan had it changed. You must admit, it takes a lot of clout to change your post address number."

At each stop we paid silent tribute to the "star site," and were given a briefing of each star's rise and demise. We skipped down "the yellow brick road of memories" and were reminded of film favorites long forgotten: freckled-faced Alfalfa, who was shot over a $50 gambling debt on January 21, 1959; and his fellow OUR GANG member, Darla Hood... both buried in Hollywood Memorial Park.

Grave Line Tour even provided us with a map to guide us to plots of such long-gone greats as Rudolph Valentino; Douglas Fairbanks, Sr.; Mae West; Errol Flynn; Jean Harlow; Humphrey Bogart; plus my friend of Georgia Caravan days, Clark Gable.   All gone, but not forgotten.

Where else could we have done this, but Hollywood?

From there we flew to Maugham's other haunts in Singapore, Bangkok and took an Orient Express cruise "on the road to Mandalay."

ON THE ROAD TO MANDALAY

Y ou really MUST go on the Road to Mandalay cruise, it's like nothing else on earth...magical, dreamlike, truly out-of-this world."

This was gushed to us again and again by world travelers who had "been there, done that," so knew what they were talking about, insisting that we would be floored by it.

And were we ever! Even our first sight of Rangoon "knocked our socks off." Literally. For from the moment we arrived at our first shrine, we had to go barefoot. Socks off. Feet on cold marble; 14 acres of it, housing a Shangri La-like timeless world of dazzling golden pagodas— 68 of them along with hundreds of pavilions and prayer-halls surrounding the mightiest of all, Shwedagon Pagoda, a lofty golden spire rising 100 meters towards heaven. Paved with 80-TONS of solid gold, topped by a jewel-encrusted weather vane and a golden orb inlaid with more than 4,000 diamonds, it is almost overpowering. Walking clockwise around it is regarded by Buddhists as a form of prayer, and thousands of Burmese pilgrims are there doing so almost every hour of every day, men, women, children, all wearing brilliant native sarongs, called longyi. One is immediately swept into this holy environment joining these stately, sleek souls walking with perfect grace paying homage to countless Buddha images of bronze, wood and stucco. Glass mosaics, metal flowers, creatures of mythology cover almost every surface. Bells, large and small, hang everywhere. Everything and everyone circling the Shwedagon seems to be smiling.

Rangoon is where our fellow cruise passengers gathered before flying north to board our elegant river cruiser "Road To Mandalay." Operated by Orient Express Hotels, Trains and Cruises, this luxury river cruise ship has been created from a former Rhine "ultra-shallow-draft" passenger vessel, MS Nederland. Making this happen is another travel miracle by former Pennsylvanian, Yale '55 graduate James Sherwood, who made a fortune heading Sea Containers, then revived the world's most celebrated train, the Venice Simplon-Orient Express. Determined to restore the golden age of travel, he tracked down dozens of classic 1920 Pullman and Wagons-Lits carriages from all over Europe, had them lovingly restored to their former glory (some from an almost hopelessly dilapidated condition) and put it back on the tracks for passengers to luxuriate while entraining from London, Paris, Venice, Rome and Prague.

Now his travel empire includes such grand places as Venice's Cipriani Hotel; New York's "21"; Villa San Michele in Florence, with its facade attributed to Michelangelo; top hostelries in Madeira, Cape Town, Bora Bora, Charleston, Rio and Sydney plus the Eastern & Oriental Express train from Singapore to Bangkok.

Each new venture was chosen for its unique character and location. In order to explore places steeped in the romantic mystery that inspired Kipling's "on the road to Mandalay, where flying fishes play," Sherwood has provided a moving 5-star hotel of a ship gliding down the majestic Irrawaddy River, Burma's equivalent of the Nile. This river, known in Kipling's day as "the road to Mandalay," inspired the ship's name ROAD TO MANDALAY. More than $5-million was spent on renovations, consisting of reducing the number of air-conditioned cabins from 98 to 72, each luxuriously contemporary blending with traditional Burmese. Our twin beds combined teak and cane. The desk lamp was Burmese black lacquer; on our fabric covered walls were pictures of hill station buildings in old Tangoo. We had built-in closets, a bathroom with marble counter tops; bedside telephone and a TV-video unit that rises from a central chest at the push of a button. All this with two picture windows for better viewing the timeless riverscape and pagodas slip slowly past. It couldn't have been more attractive or comfortable.

Passengers on ROAD TO MANDALAY's maiden voyage included such guests as Princess Michael of Kent; Prince and Princess Michael of Greece; Viscount and Viscountess Norwich; Sir Francis and Lady Dashwood; the Duke of Albercorn; and WINGS OF THE DOVE star Helena Bonham Carter.

Hearing all this, we wondered who we would have as cruise-mates, so at Bangkok airport we looked to see if any departing passengers carried luggage with MANDALAY tags prominently displayed. Luckily, a chic lady with a British accent spied our tags, introduced herself and asked: "Where are you from?"

When we answered "Philadelphia," she replied, "Ha! Phil-a-del-phi-a! Henry McIlhenny! I visited Henry there. Loved it."

"Where did you know Henry?" we inquired, pleased that we, too, had visited Henry for a party or two.

"We have a horse farm near his castle in Ireland. He loves gardens and is particularly fond of my mother's gardens in France."

This gave us a clue of the caliber of our cruise-cast to follow.

We had another sampling when we dined at Rangoon's

grand Strand Hotel that night, when a bevy of bluebloods sashayed into the dining room like a covey of peacocks, obvious British lords and ladies on holiday. We later learned they were Lord and Lady Eden's party, all eight joined our ship in Pagan.

They did add color to our cruise. Fellow Americans included a jolly group from Columbus, Ohio; lovers from Dallas; a Chilean dignitary from the United Nations; CEOs of international corporations; French, Italians, Swiss, and "the last Brit out of Burma before it changed its name to Myanmar."

It was like being on an international houseparty...lounging around the pool; cocktailing on Mandalay Rum Sours as the pianist plunked out Cole Porter tunes in the lounge; getting costumes together for the night of our big longyi party, where we all came attired in just-purchased sarongs. Our cruiser made an ideal floating base to explore Burmese treasures just beginning to re-emerge after years of almost complete isolation from tourism. Places like Pagan: land of the towering temples, a ruin-scattered Ankor Wat-type plain. During the era of the builder kings, between 1057 until overrun by Kublai Khan forces in 1287, Pagan (now called Bagan) was covered by some 13,000 temples, pagodas, and other religious structures. To reach its core, visitors rode in horse-drawn buggies with canvas tops colorfully adorned in fancy embroidery.

Pagan in many respects was the most remarkable religious city in the world. Certainly Jerusalem, old Benares or Rome never had the multitude of temples or the lavishness of Pagan. Today, however, Burma's former capital is a deserted, medieval, haunted landscape of crumbling red brick shrines, some high as an 18-storey modern building. Being off the tourist path, we had never been told of Pagan the way we heard, again and again, the Taj Mahal, Pyramids or Great

Wall of China. Yet 1000-year old Pagan is one of Asia's most astonishing spectacles, stretching over 16 square miles. Among the pagodas and stupas ox-carts pull produce from fields of cotton, corn and sesame. Now there is a drive on to restore the ancient monuments and open old Pagan to tourism.

Lacquerware is the big attraction for shoppers in the village at Pagan. Bowls, service plates, trays, decorative boxes are eagerly sought after in the many small workshops scattered about not far from the banks of the Irrawaddy. In fact, visiting such villages, seeing their marvelous craftsmen at work, up close and personal, was a highlight of our journey on the road to Mandalay. We would arrive at these villages in early morn when lines of Buddhist monks in deep-red robes were lining up with their begging bowls soliciting house-to-house for a breakfast of rice. Some of the houses were charming works of art in teak or woven bamboo.

Every village seemed to have its specialty. Weaving and embroidery is a time-honored craft, as well as work in silver, gold and brass. We particularly admired the Burmese puppets, marvels in style, dress and connecting parts. Each marionette usually has 20 strings, some as many as 60, which allow an uncanny display of dance movements. After-dinner entertainments on our cruise were provided by some of these exotic puppeteers. Also, we would sometimes have demonstrations by basket weavers, cigar makers, woodcarvers, musicians and dancers who moved their fingers, wrists, knees, ankles, elbows, even toes, effortlessly in stylized directions, each little movement having a meaning all its own. All in stunning costume.

Even the Irrawaddy River presents a constantly changing dramatic water parade of boats gliding by on their daily rounds...large teakwood barges with intricately carved prows; bamboo rafts with a thatched hut on deck amidst cargo of clay jars; tiny sailboats and canoes big enough for only one paddler but carrying a family of three; double-decker ferries jammed with people waving as they passed. Scenes on the riverside seemed right out of Asia's past...bullocks coming down to slurp water; steep banks covered with brilliant-hued river-washed laundry stretched out to dry; sunsets turning pagoda-dotted hills to molten gold.

Being on a 7-day cruise gave us time for exotic side trips to ancient Sagaing, Ava and Mingun. Orient Express buses marked English, German, French, Italian awaited at the main dock, so passengers always had a guide speaking their language. On one occasion, a private Mercedes took us, with a Swiss couple, to Mount Popa, the Buddhist Olympus, home of the nats gods. To reach its summit, required climbing 770 steps, bare footed. We decided to sit halfway up, surrounded by monkeys, and watch hundreds of pilgrims from multitudes of tribes pass by us heading up the steep slope to kneel before the spirit gods above. Each tribe sported a different costume. One group wore huge turbans patterned in an orange-and-black plaid. They reminded us of Princeton alums on their pee-rade.

On another excursion, to the medieval town of Mingun, we rode in oxcarts, parading in a line past a village of art stalls the grandiose Mingun Pagoda. It was to be the world's largest, 499 ft. high, but an earthquake in 1838 halted the construction half-way. Now its a massive mount of brick. Standing 328 feet, from its summit, on a clear day, one can see Mandalay. Winding steps, leading to the top, had red-robed monks holding bright orange parasols greeting climbers at different levels.

Next to Mingun Pagoda stands a pavilion housing the world's largest uncracked bell. King Bodawpaya had it cast in 1790 to be dedicated in his huge Mingon Pagoda. Weighing 87 tons, more than 12 ft. high, it makes our Liberty

Bell look small. Besides, they let us BONG it with a wooden mallet. Super sound!

Somerset Maugham, passing through Mandalay in the 1920s, found little to admire on its modern, crowded streets, but, like us, he loved the name, saying "it does not matter: Mandalay has its name; the falling cadence of the lovely word has gathered about itself the chiaroscuro of romance."

To us old travelers, the greatest thing about Mandalay was going there...on the ROAD TO MANDALAY.

Our next joyous journey was to Maugham's home town, London.

GREAT TIMES IN GREAT BRITAIN

What's it like living it up in London's lap of luxury?

We found out recently, spending a long languorous weekend there at The Lanesborough, that ultra-posh hotel from those who gave us L.A.'s Bel-Air and The Mansion On Turtle Creek deep in the heart of Dallas.

Friends who had experienced The Lanesborough before us had raved: "They sent the head butler in the hotel's Bentley to fetch us at the airport. He was the most perfectly attired gentleman waiting at Heathrow, striped trousers, morning coat...the works. Jeeves never looked so good. And...when we arrived at the hotel, the staff greeted us by name. Our very own butler, in livery, welcomed us to our rooms with a pot of tea waiting, with cakes. He pointed out such amenities as our personal fax machine, direct dial telephone, channel cable TV, video cassette player, compact disc player, safe the size of a brief case, computer hook-ups..."

It all sounded so grand that we feared we might feel intimidated. But no. Just the opposite. At the gracious Lanesborough we felt, always, at home. Our name was printed "in residence" on hotel stationery, even calling cards. Our favorite brands had been stocked in our well-equipped bar. Our butler unpacked and pressed our travel-rumpled clothes, and told us he was at our call 24 hours.

"We understand you would like to attend the Maggie Smith

matinee on Saturday. We checked with the box office and reserved two good seats for you. Would you prefer being transported to the theatre in the hotel car or by taxi?" he asked, making us feel assured that all our needs would be "no problem."

Managed by Rosewood Hotels, The Lanesborough is a historically authentic renovation of a landmark Regency-era building. Originally built in 1719 as an elegant private residence by the late Viscount Lanesborough, it later served, from 1734 to 1980, as St. George's Hospital. When Rosewood Hotels and Resorts was commissioned to turn it into a London showplace, many of England's most respected historical organizations helped supervise Rosewood's meticulous restoration of both exterior and interior. Custom furniture makers, textile artisans, teams of internationally-renowned interior designers went to work to faithfully recreate a 19th century residence fit for a duke.

London's Royal Fine Arts Commission, Georgian Society, Victorian Society and English Heritage all played a part in the operation. Furniture, fabrics, paintings and draperies were copied from actual examples of the 1820s and 1830s. When designers found an antique chandelier they liked, they would take it apart and have many copies cast of it. Every detail seemed inspired.

Most fun of all, to us, is the hotel's Conservatory, recalling that fantastical Oriental whimsy of the Royal Pavilion in Brighton. Under a vast arched, glazed ceiling, The Conservatory abounds in Gothic settees, Chinese Chippendale faux-bamboo chairs, potted palms, chinoiserie, glass Japanese lanterns and chandeliers created with inverted glass tasseled parasols. The overall effect is an open garden patio. We liked it so much that we would have breakfast and meet friends for afternoon tea here, then sup there after the theatre and dance among the potted palms to

241

Confrey Phillips and his music.

Confrey also played piano a la Bobby Short in The Lanesborough's cozy Library and Withdrawing Room, all booklined, handsomely paneled and inspired by the library Robert Adams had designed for Syon House.

Of course, we didn't go to London to spend four days in a hotel. The City itself has always been the lure. There's something royal about London; you can't top it when it comes to tradition and style, from Buckingham Palace's changing of the guard to those black Daimler limos carrying bespoke-suited diplomats to Bond Street. Certainly no other city has such a concentration of quality shops noted for taste and superb workmanship. So top on our list of touring town was to revisit on a whirlwind window shopping spree. To Jermyn Street's Paxton & Whitfield, for cheese; Von Posch, where the countess sells rare porcelains; Turnbull & Asser for shirts; Floris, purveyors of scent. And, around the corner on Piccadilly, Fortnam and Mason, the ultimate grocery, specialty store for pleasant tea-room lunch, and a quick look next door at umbrellas and country clothes in the windows of Swaine Adeney Brigg. From umbrellas to books at Hatchard's, where we spied Jackie Collins signing her newest hot novel. Since The Lanesborough is in Knightsbridge, we could visit Harrod's, Burberry's and Liberty's legendary emporiums by just walking a few blocks away.

Too, we were curious to see Spencer House, ancestral town mansion of Princess Diana's family, the only great 18th-century private palace to survive intact. Begun in 1756 by John, First Earl of Spencer, it has been recently restored to its original splendor under the sponsorship of Lord Rothschild. We also did not want to miss dining at Mosimann's, the exclusive dining club created by the celebrated Swiss chef Anton Mosimann. Formerly Chef des Cuisines at London's grand

Dorchester Hotel, Mosimann has transformed a picturesque neighborhood church in swank Belgravia, to a dining club that had the exciting clientele of Manhattan's old "21".

Naturally we want not-to-miss London theatre's newest whether it be from Andrew Lloyd Webber, Royal Shakespeare at the Barbican or wild farce. But shopping and theatre had to be squeezed in before Sunday, for on the Sabbath, all shops are closed. Consequently, we saved Sunday to stroll through those elegant residential parks, checking out Adams or Henry Holland architecture; admiring lacquered front doors with handsome brass knockers; window boxes aburst with blooms. At Annabel's, that very exclusive gambling club on Berkeley Square, you pass an entrance with iron grillwork erected in the days of Beau Nash, with notches to hold torches carried by porters when their passengers alighted from sedan chairs.

Walking in Berkeley Square and Belgravia at night reminds us of ON THE STREET WHERE YOU LIVE in MY FAIR LADY.

We usually make a return visit to St. James's Street, with its shoemakers, hatmakers and Regency gentlemen's clubs: Boodle's and Brooks's. James Bond author Ian Fleming regularly lunched at Boodle's and Winston Churchill liked to plop himself in its Adams-style bow window, puffing at his cigar, watching passers-by outside watching him. Boodle's has oodles of horse paintings depicting Grand National winners owned by members. Club walls flaunt a splendid Stubbs, a rare Sartorius, 18th-century caricatures and a stag hunt painted by Hondius, circa 1671.

Across from Boodle's, and very grand, sits stately Brook's Club, especially dear to us for its Great Subscription Room on the first floor, and The Dilettanti Society portraits (1741-1749) of those bad Brooks's boys who were also fellow revelers in the scandalous Hellfire Club. Here you see Sir Francis

Dashwood, of Hellfire Club fame, posed as a Franciscan monk, a costume probably worn as one of the Mad Monks of Medenham orgies which played such an important part in our comic novel RED HOT & BLUE: AN X-RATED HISTORY OF THE AMERICAN REVOLUTION.

Sunday in London is also a great day for visiting the Cabinet War Rooms Museum, underground headquarters of Churchill and those who directed World War II as bombs burst above on London town. As you wander through its dimly lit tunnels, with sound effects that chill your spine, you cast a silent prayer that such wars will never happen again.

At a party on Cheyne Walk it was suggested that we board a river taxi on the Thames, stopping off to see Michael Caine's new penthouse in the chic marina-condos overlooking Chelsea Harbor. By boat is a super way to view London's newest architectural wonders, gliding under its famous bridges, on towards Greenwich, where the Queen's House on the Thames is open to the public.

All this was great fun, but we found ourselves ready to return to our creature comforts at The Lanesborough.

We still are.

BATHING IN THE BEAUTY OF BATH

When we think of Bath, England's most elegant Regency city, we see Fielding's Tom Jones bowing to Sarah, Duchess of Marlborough who is waving from her sedan chair being handcarried by footmen in powdered wigs and knee breeches. We envision Beau Nash in his velvet, brocade and satin, greeting elaborately tailored, neatly bewigged gentlemen swaggering long gold tipped canes and fashionable ladies flirting behind their fluttering fancy fans.

It is very easy to conjure up all this while visiting Bath, still very Georgian, with its wide streets and terraces of graceful 18th Century Palladian houses built with honey-colored stone.

No other city just reeks of Pickwick, Pepys, Pitt, Pope and the Pump Room. In fact, the Pump Room today is still where one goes to see-and-be-seen and start the day on Sally Lunn buns and hot chocolate, as a string ensemble softly drones morning music. It is a perfect place to begin your Bath browse, for it is on this spot where Bath began in 54 A.D. Then Roman legions found wallowing in the local mud and mineral waters most therapeutic. Hence the steaming underground pools became sort of a Roman officer's club, and future generations have found "taking the waters" here the fashionable thing to do. It is fascinating to explore these restored Roman baths today and see where the Romans built their first pools, pump-rooms, villas, libraries and theatres over the hot spring which still make Bath a medical center and archeological gem.

You discover how they piped hot water under mosaic pavements to heat their ornate swimming pools and massage rooms. Bath is built on layers of civilizations, beginning with the Druids before Stonehenge; then Roman; Saxon; Norman' Medieval, with its Gothic Bath Abbey, built in 1499, and still the social center of town. Abbey services have been a must for all those who wanted to be in the social swim, where the elite meet to greet, exchange invitations, make assignations. Beau Nash, Bath's master of the revels, would ring those Abbey bells on the arrival of a distinguished visitor. Tourists today are particularly fascinated by the Abbey's great west window of seven lights framed with carved angels climbing Jacob's ladder. The Abbey church has such an abundance of stained glass that, lighted at night, it is called "The Lantern of the West," since the city lies in England's West Country hills.

One of Bath's great delights, too, is shopping...the best outside London. Antiquarian bookshops abound, along with stores featuring antique linens and lace; rare wines; good sporting paintings; Regency treasures; British crafts and folk art. There is also THE BOGGLE JUGGLING SHOP where all five-club jugglers out there come and have a go. At THE BOGGLE SHOP you are likely to run into stilt walkers, clowns, face painters and maybe a unicyclist or two.

We found that one of the most memorable ways to bask on the elegant aura of Bath was staying at Lucknam Park, a magnificent Georgian country house hotel-spa six miles from Bath, set in extensive parkland of 280 acres. A focus of fine society gatherings and gracious living for over 250 years, it now has its own state-of-the-art modern spa, marvelous for de-stressing and re-charging the old bod without having to resort to all that mud and rotten-egg sulphur smell those Roman legions had to put up with.

Even the front driveway leading to Lucknam Park's grand manor house is impressive...a mile-long avenue lined with ancient beechtrees. At Lucknam's, we were to stay, a la lord of the manor, for several days making it home base for branching out to explore Dr. Doolittle-like thatchroof villages; stately homes such as Bowood House and Longleat, where the Marquess of Bath now resides. From here, too, we would return again and again to "browse Bath."

Lucknam Park itself is fun to explore. Some suites are set in out-buildings once used for storing brew, ice or coaches. Bedrooms, each different and luxuriously low-key, are softly opulent, with cheery British chintz, Regency antiques and generous space, all serviced by splendidly-trained maids.

We would have high tea, beautifully butlered, before a sparkling fire in Lucknam's paneled, book-walled library. Our early morning walks took us past an octagonal dovecote in a formal garden, and out to horses gamboling across acres diamonded with dew.

There was no need to go out evenings, for *everyone*, even from neighboring estates, came here to dine at the Michelin-starred restaurant in Lucknam Park's charmingly-refurbished conservatory. Local lords and ladies, too, would join us in the bubbling waters of Lucknam's Leisure Spa within a walled garden, built in the theme of a Roman villa.

Like the Romans of yore, we loved bathing in the beauty of Bath.

GOLFER'S HEAVEN IN SCOTLAND

For golfers, a visit to Scotland and St. Andrews is like going to heaven. Maybe better, for you don't have to die to do it.

Even if one doesn't play golf, it's heavenly flying British Airways and staying at the St. Andrews Old Course Hotel, now golf's ultimate hostelry. A top-star consortium created it, bringing in fabled international hotelier Robert D. Zimmer as design, development and management consultant. We experienced the Zimmer touch of luxury at Hotel Bel-Air and The Mansion on Turtle Creek, so promise of his newest jewel, this elegant resort and European spa adjoining golfdom's most hallowed course, lured us like bears to honey.

Staying there was like being an honored guest at a great Scottish estate. Careful attention had been given to comfort. Marble baths; mixed English florals in colorful hues; fine paintings and porcelains enhancing the rooms...and a panoramic angel-from-a-cloud vista. From our balconied perch, we had an unobstructed view of the most famous golf links in the world, stretching endlessly toward a broad bay of the North Sea. In the distance we could see medieval St. Andrews' towers and spires silhouetted as the sun rose. At night the Royal and Ancient Golf Club stood lighted, a dramatic, glamorous centerpiece guarding its precious Old Course.

It is believed that the game of golf began in St. Andrews 500 years ago. Records show that by the time Columbus had sailed the ocean blue, Scottish kings were prohibiting golf since the game took men away from military duties. Then, one of those kings, James IV, became a golfer himself and from then on golf became everybody's passion at St. Andrews and the Old Course just evolved, a creation of Father Time and Mother Nature.

On first sight, those accustomed to lush golf courses designed by Jack Nicklaus, Arnold Palmer, Robert Trent Jones and such, are rather awed to find what looks like miles of pocked meadow. Treeless. Flat. No waterfalls or flowering shrubs.

As we walked the course we could imagine Mary Queen of Scots gliding across the fairway, club in hand, her long skirt ruffled by a strong wind from the North Sea Bay. Then, our thoughts did a fast-forward to Bobby Jones, knickers and all, striding to victory in the 1930 British Open, first leg of his Grand Slam. St. Andrews loved Bobby, gave him Freedom of the City, named Old Course's 10th hole for him. Jones loved St. Andrews, too, saying before he died, "If I had ever been set down in one place and told I was to play there and nowhere else for the rest of my life, I should have chosen the Old Course."

Gene Sarazen called it "undoubtedly the finest golf course in the world," adding, "I wish that everyone who plays golf could play St. Andrews once!" All the great golfers have made a point of doing so.

When we approached the first tee, a foursome from Australia sank to the ground and salaamed. "At last, we made it!" these golf-pilgrims chorused before teeing up in front of the Royal and Ancient clubhouse. As they drove their balls, that opening hole looked so easy; 370 yards, Par 4, with a wide, clear, innocently welcoming fairway. However, out there, out of sight, a small stream, Swilcan Burnbrook, snakes smack in front of the green. Too, a narrow public road, Granny's Clark Wynd, cuts across halfway out. Plus, there's the sudden switch of strong crosswinds from the sea. The more you get into the Old Course, the more hellish it is than paradisiacal.

For instance, on the 352-yard third hole you have to shoot into space, since there is no target to drive at. On the right is a Maginot Line of bunkers, some so deep it's hard for you to crawl out, much less whack the ball out, too. Then. on the other side, a series of ridges looms up, and in between, very uneven ground can send your bouncing ball every which way.

On every hole, spiny, low, many-branched shrubs, thickets, heather, bracken, wire-grass, all can grab golf balls like man-eating plants. No wonder they suggest you start with two dozen balls.

Since every visiting golfer wants to play the Old Course, demand exceeds available playing time, so a daily lottery is held to determine who can play and when. We found it best to leave all the arrangements to the stewards at the hotel. As Scotland's beloved poet Robert Burns has noted, "the best-laid schemes o' mice and men gang aft agley (can go awry)", so we were prepared not to make the Old Course and just be happy that we had 30 other courses available, three within walking distance from the hotel.

Besides, St. Andrews offers much more than the world's best golf. Non-golfing wives or "significant others" love shopping for tres-cher cashmere; antique-ing; taking escorted side trips from the hotel to stately homes, fishing villages, castle towns; walking the wide stretch of North Sea beach nearby where St. Andrews students were filmed jogging in CHARIOTS OF FIRE. Here is one of the world's great ancient towns to explore on foot. Not only does it have the oldest university in Scotland, it offers an historic cathedral, a romantic castle and History with a capital H.

Since its beginnings in the fourth century A.D., St. Andrews' past has been tumultuous. According to legend, the monk St. Rule was shipwrecked at the site while carrying the bones of apostle St. Andrew from Greece to an unknown destination. Evidently he liked the area, so he stayed and established a religious community. By the eighth century, religious pilgrims were pouring in to pay respects to the bones and site of the supposed shipwreck.

In the Middle Ages, St. Andrews served as headquarters of Scotland's Roman Catholic Church. A magnificent Gothic cathedral was built on its headland. Then along came that reforming zealot John Knox during the Reformation. Preaching his anti-Catholic message, he so incited the towns-people that the mob rushed to the cathedral and started "tearing it doon." The cathedral's roof was destroyed, stones carried away and it stands today, a ruin. St. Andrews' role as a political and religious center was finished.

However, it remained as a seat of learning. St. Andrews University, founded in 1411, is the Scottish equivalent of Oxford. To this day it maintains standards of excellence in medicine, divinity, the classics and languages. Rudyard Kipling was rector here from 1922-25.

By 1840 this medieval university town became a seaside resort, a favorite of intellectuals — writers like Thomas Carlyle and Anthony Trollope. Europe's top artists painted it, and some exquisite paintings of that era now grace the walls of the hotel.

Golf had been played on the Old Course around 1400. It started "point to point" with players striving to reach a certain point, then return, with the fewest number of strokes. Gradually, Old Course golfers learned how to control the ball in the winds, to take advantage of the downhill contours and to avoid natural bunkers and sand traps.

In 1754, the "Society of St. Andrews Golfers" was formed by 22 noblemen and gentlemen. Eighty years later, King William IV agreed to be patron of the Club, awarding its current title: The Royal and Ancient Golf Club of St. Andrews (the R&A.) A palatial clubhouse was built behind the first tee, eventually becoming a virtual shrine to the game. The R & A soon became recognized as golf's rule-making body. Today, the R & A clubhouse has its own museum, library of rare golf literature and trophy room, where a vault is lined with silver and gold medals that date back to the club's founding.

Its 1,800 members are from six continents. No more than 1,050 may live in Britain and Ireland; of the remaining, a privileged 275 can be U.S. residents. Presently, this one golf club and the United States Golf Association's 5,000 clubs jointly make golf's worldwide rules.

Everywhere, this old gray town on the east coast of Scotland is recognized as the cradle of golf. Mecca. Thousands of devotees make a pilgrimage to St. Andrews annually, and find it captivating...with its narrow wynds or lanes; golf club-makers' shops; parks; rare book stalls; seals at play in the mouth of River Eden; University students adorned in red "graduation" gowns parading down by the harbor. We enjoyed eating at Peat Inn, outside town, and at The Grange, a golfer's restaurant high on a hill with a 360-degree panoramic view. Most memorable of all meals, however, were enjoyed at the hotel, presented by former Gleneagles chef Billy Campbell. Here we had a choice of two restaurants, the formal Old Course and the informal Road Hole grill on the fourth floor. The latter is named after the 17th hole, which it overlooks, and which many consider "the most famous hole in golf." International chef and food consultant Anton Mosimann, of London, has worked along side

Chef Billy to create the unique food concepts utilizing the finest of Scotland's fresh produce, seafood and game. After a round of golf, only a chip away from the Road Hole itself, we enjoyed unwinding in the hotel's pub, Jigger Inn, a remodeled local train station.

The hotel's general manager, Peter Crome, formerly of London's legendary Savoy, has ensured that this "new" Old Course Hotel and spa is a destination in its own right.

All this...and heaven, too.

ELEGANT IRELAND

NGELA'S ASHES? MY LEFT FOOT! Let's not have a crying game for poor Ireland. On a trip to Dublin, we found the Old Sod is blooming, picking up from where she left off during the days of the Restoration, Sheridan and Goldsmith.

In the 18th century, Dublin was considered one of the most elegant cities in Europe. Irish gentry build handsome Georgian brick mansions lining posh streets and squares. Families of the elite resided on Merrion Square, in homes reflecting the epitome of Georgian tastes. Irish craftsmen found great scope in the decorative arts...extraordinary and elaborate plasterwork; spectacular carved doorcases and mantelpieces; fanlit doorways in brilliant colors, embellished by such brass touches as fanciful doorknockers, boot scrapers and mailshoots.

Merrion Street was the grand address. In the 1700s Lord Monck, Lord Mornington and the Duke of Wellington lived here. A century later Oscar Wilde resided at #1 Merrion Square, a large house where his father had his surgery and his mother entertained leaders of the capital's intellectual life at her weekly salon. ("Come home with me," Oscar said to a Trinity College classmate. "My mother and I have formed a society for the suppression of virtue.")

Desmond Guiness had told us about this world in a lecture, IRISH HOUSES AND CASTLES, several years ago at University Hospital's annual Antique Show in the Armory. Friends who had visited Henry McIlhenny's castle Glenveagh in Northern Ireland, and horse lovers, too, insisted that nothing quite compared with "elegant Irish." Then, when we heard that we could experience it at Dublin's new five-star "boutique" hotel, The Merrion, we were lured to that fair city, now experiencing economic boom, to see why all the raves.

The Merrion Hotel is set in four adjoining red brick Georgian townhouses on Upper Merrion Street in the heart of Dublin opposite palatial Government House. All of these are superb examples of Irish Georgian architecture, especially No. 24, originally known as Mornington House and built in the 1760s for Lord Mornington, the first Duke of Wellington's father. Here, six magnificent rooms on the ground and first floors have been joined and carefully restored. Designed to be used separately or in combination, the salons vary in size and color. Rooms are decorated in suitable grand style retaining those outstanding features for which Georgian Dublin is so famous. Each of the three grand salons are interconnected through the use of color, fabrics and specially commissioned carpets with an 18th century pattern.

In addition, antique pieces of furniture and a most stunning collection of 20th century Irish paintings, give guests a feeling of being in a grand, relaxed, private house where drinks and chat are enjoyed by a cheery fire, or in a romantic classical garden created by Ireland's eminent garden-designer, Jim Reynolds.

The Merrion also had on-site the nation's only two-star Michelin, Restaurant Patrick Guilbaud. With its airy white walls hung with contemporary art, Restaurant Patrick Guilbaud occupies the ground floor of No. 21, and has continually won most every major food award in the world.

From The Merrion, it was only a walk around the corner to famed Dublin pubs, such as Doheny & Nesbitt. Grafton Street shops; National Gallery of Ireland and Trinity College's Book of Kels were not far away. We enjoyed strolling the city, chuckling at Dubliners' irreverent wit. A statue of Molly Malone selling her cockleshells was referred to as "Tart With A Cart." The new Oscar Wilde sculpture with the poet sprawled spread-eagle on a huge rock they named "Fag On The Craig." A fountain depicting the goddess of Dublin's Liffey River has a nickname: "Floozy In The Jacuzzi."

Of course, no visit to Dublin is complete without catching a performance at either the Abbey or Gate theaters. The Abbey was founded by W.B. Yeats, J.M. Synge and Augusta Gregory a century ago, and has produced such legendary playwrights as Sean O'Casey and today's Brian Friel.

Since our main interest was to see grand houses and gardens, we couldn't have done better than traveling 12 miles south of Dublin to POWERSCOURT, one of the most beautiful estates in Ireland. Situated in the mountains of Wicklow, POWERSCOURT was built in 1300 for the Power family, hence its name. In the 18th century, Ireland's Age of Elegance, the 4th Viscount Powerscourt, Sir Richard Wingfield, commissioned the creation of a magnificent mansion, parkland and terraced gardens. A century later, the 6th Viscount Powerscourt instructed his architect, Daniel Robertson, to draw up schemes for the gardens. Robertson designed an Italianate garden nearest to the house, adorned with an amazing collection of statuary, ironwork and fountains. Suffering from gout, Robertson directed operations from a wheelbarrow, fortified by a bottle of sherry. When the sherry was finished, work ceased for the day!

On another day, we motored to Jim Reynolds' place, BUT-

TERSTREAM, described by HOUSE & GARDEN as the most imaginative garden in Ireland. Jim created it himself, single handed, and has enhanced it continuously since the early 1970s.

BUTTERSTREAM comprises a series of carefully integrated compartments with unexpected surprises at every turn. Here, a Gothic bridge leads over a babbling brook to an all-white garden. There, an ancient tower turns out to be a folly adding drama to a Petit Trianon-type formal garden. Hedges of beech frame a Roman Villa design garden house facing a lily pond. Yew is trained obelisk shaped. A garden drama in many acts!

Plantsmen, including Prince Charles, consider it to be among the British Isles best. Open daily from April 1 - September 30, BUTTERSTREAM is about an hour's drive from Dublin, and well worth a side trip just to visit with Jim Reynolds in person.

RETURN TO PORTUGAL

We found Portugal even more exciting the second time around. While checking out of The Ritz in Lisbon, we met J. Carter Brown, fresh from Washington's National Gallery of Art, in the lobby. Minutes later, as we waited for our car under the hotel marquee, V.I.P. police and Chinese plain clothesmen were assembling for the imminent arrival of China's Prime Minister, Li Cheng.

Outside the city, all along the Algarve coast, building, building and more building seemed to be going on everywhere—international headquarters, hotels, convention centers and golf courses. It appeared that sleepy little Portugal was about to cast off its peasant shawl and make the Big Time.

That's why we were glad to return and revisit areas once home to Magellan, Vasco da Gama and Columbus. Yes, Columbus. Reading Nancy Rubin's fascinating biography about Queen Isabella, we learned that as a young man, Columbus lived and wed in Lisbon, then the premier European city of navigation, mapmaking and sea exploration. Standing on the ramparts of medieval St. George's Castle—high atop one of Lisbon's seven hills—we looked down on the docks that these explorers had sailed from five centuries ago to open up the new worlds, trade routes and avenues of expanding knowledge. Portugal was at the cen-

259

ter then, too, and parts of Lisbon appear unchanged since the Middle Ages. Especially its "casbah," Alfama, a labyrinth of alleys, corkscrew winding cobble-stone streets climbing up, up, up like mile-long staircases to St. George's Castle—a fortress that has survived attacks by the Visigoths, Moors, Crusaders, Spaniards, Napoleon, earthquakes and fire. For centuries, families of seamen and fisher folk have inhabited this beehive of tenements. Clotheslines fly from iron-grill balconies like flags on Tall Ship mizzenmasts. Streets are so narrow that people have to duck into doorways when a car squeaks past. Guarding over it all is an old grandma of Lisbon churches, Saint Vincent, named for the city's patron saint.

Speeding down from the Alfama, over Lisbon's sprawling hills, the city-scape looks like a mega-Moorish mosaic of whitewash buildings with red-tile roofs sparkling in the sun. Small wonder it has been called the White City.

Said to have been founded by Ulysses, redeemed from the Moors for Christianity by the Crusaders in 1249, Lisbon has a past like no other European city. It has been occupied by Phoenicians, Greeks, Carthaginians, Romans, Visigoths and finally conquered in 1147 by Portugal's first king, Alfonso Henriques. Consequently, the whole country offers a feast of fascinating architecture. Lisbon park, Avenida da Liberdade, is a Portuguesean Rue de la Paix, with fin de siecle Baroque buildings and kiosks, plus statues of heroes standing majestically among the palms.

Because styles change with each new ruler, some parts of town appear Gothic, some Moorish and some chic Moderne—like the Rossio area with its swank boutiques. Among the city's great charms are promontories with sweeping vistas, and 1920ish streetcars clanging through the crowds. Reminding one of THE LITTLE ENGINE THAT COULD, these trolleys are painted like billboards promoting products from Scotch whiskey to Pepsodent toothpaste.

Unforgettable, too, Portugal's palaces, especially those around Sintra, a half hour from Lisbon. Pena Palace, cresting a peak overlooking the town like a Mad King Ludwig creation, presided over by a multi-story sculpture of a growling naked giant, spread-eagle with fish-fin footsies. Inside and outside is nightmare of motifs...Ali Babaian, Victorian, Wagnerian...you name it. Much saner, more like Versailles, is the palace of Queluz—which might well serve as a setting for Marie Antoinette or the film IMPROMPTU.

We loved a hotel with exquisite interiors, gardens, pool courts, stables and dining rooms...Hotel Palacio de Seteais (pronounced shuhteash, in Portuguese language the "s" is a whisper...ssh). Even though The Seteais is THE place to stay in Portugal, the place to play is in Portugal's southermost province, the Algarve, with over 150 miles of superb sandy beaches...totally unpolluted. Here's where you find brightly painted fishing boats, miles of cork trees, almond orchards, and squat whitewashed Moorish houses topped with open-lattice chimney pots—no two alike. Most fun are the farmers' markets, where you see untouristy Portugal at its most colorful.

We especially liked Loule's market and the 16th and 17th century architecture. The Algarve is particularly famous for its fresh fish and variety of seafood, washed down with local wines or cool champagne Vinho Verde (green wine).

Each day in the Algarve, we would either play golf, or visit a different town: Silves, a walled city with a 13th-century fortress and cathedral; Monchique, an ancient spa resort set high in the mountains; Faro, where Columbus first saw Portugal; Vila Real de Santo Antonio, a show case of town planning across the bridge from Spain, now a mass shopping center.

The Algarve is especially famous for its azuelos, blue and

white tile murals that cover walls of churches and palaces. The big problem is picking from those easy to pack and taking them with you on the plane, since its not smart to mail them.

No visit to the Algarve is complete without a visit to Cape Sao Vincente, where Europe is closest to Nantucket. Here is the Continent's southwestern most point, with a famous light house and spectacular cliffs rising up from the sea. Here, if you suffer from vertigo, you'll sweat ice cubes watching the fishermen cast their lines from the edge of cliffs—a 295 foot straight drop to the sea-foaming rocks below.

Highlights of this point: Sagres (shaw-grash) where Prince Henry the Navigator established his famous School of Navigation. It's also the home of Algarve's lobster fishing industry. En route to this end of a peninsula, we saw windmills, shepherds tending their flock, sandy coves with ice cream cone dunes, buildings aburst with brilliantly decorated native tiles, peasants riding packed burros to market, and here and there an ancient castle on a hill. Our car radio had someone singing fado, the Portuguese blues. Now, every time we hear fado, we get the blues for a return visit to Portugal.

WATERWAYS OF HOLLAND

One summer we visited water-world.

Not the movie.

The real thing: Holland...The Netherlands...where Dutch pioneers created a wonderful, livable waterworld by reclaiming land from the sea.

Unlike Kevin Kostner, they did it the old fashion way: by building windmills, drainage canals, dikes.

Now they have a country that is so low that it is the only place in the world where birds fly BELOW sea level and boats sail ABOVE the land!

"Nether" means lying-below-the-earth's surface, so cruising the waterways of The Netherlands we would look UP to the land.

What we saw was a constant, soothing pastoral scene, a landscape green as Easter-basket grass, with grazing dappled cows and puffs of sheep gazing at us inquisitively as we glided by.

From our boat we felt Holland's close intimacy with sea and town. Giethorn, a reclaimed-from-the-sea town, has canals instead of streets. Only means of transportation here is by boat, mostly punts.

It's an enchanted village of thatch-roof houses set on tiny garden islands reached only by their own bridges, or along their own streams.

265

Swans sail silently by, sometimes passing a flotilla of baby ducks with mama along the way.

Since there are no trucks in Giethorn, even cows and sheep are transported to market in wide, wooden flat bottom boats pushed along by a boatman with a long pole. Sixteen sheep lined up back to back in two rows of eight might be boated from field to field via what looks like a large rowboat.

Village after village, like Giethorn, had an elusive quality of timelessness.

In some of Northern Holland's medieval towns we saw buildings that were there when our Pilgrim forefathers left in 1620 sailed on the Mayflower from Plymouth, England and landed in America.

They had come here seeking religious freedom. We had come there, 375 years later, for pure, unadulterated pleasure. Certainly, no other form of travel provides freedom-from-care faster than a deluxe cruise. At least we found this so once we boarded our 100-passenger ship OLYMPIA in Amsterdam, docked only a short distance from museums of van Goghs and Rembrandts. Designed for canal cruising, our liner could anchor so close to town that we could walk down the gangplank directly to shore, and in Amsterdam, seemingly back into the Golden Age of Holland.

During Holland's Golden Age, in the 17th century, Amsterdam was booming commercially. Holland trade ruled the seas. Merchants grew rich, built palatial homes, bought fine art. Floating down Amsterdam canals one night we passed block after block of palatial homes, standing state-ly as if in a royal receiving line on both banks.

On four neighboring canals we saw a greater concentra-tion of grand 16th, 17th, 18th-century buildings than in any other European capital city. Even names of their canals were grand: The Gentlemen's Canal (immortalizing the city's regents); The Emperor's Canal (a tribute to Holy Roman

Empire Emperor Maximilian); The Prince's Canal (acknowledging the ruling Dutch Princes of Orange).

In passing we could glimpse into handsomely furnished parlors, softly lighted by stunning chandeliers. Obviously, aristocracy and style is alive and well and living in Amsterdam.

This was evident, again, at tea in the riverside conservatory of Amsterdam's most elegant hotel, The Amstel. A limo of a launch arrived at the Hotel's private dock carrying a bride, splendid in white satin, with her formally attired wedding party.

Of course, Amsterdam has its seamy side, too.

Since it doesn't get dark until 10 p.m., it seems safe and fun, to stroll at night. Even in Amsterdam's famed redlight district, The Seamen's Quarter.

Here, ladies-of-the-evening are displayed in store windows framed by glowing tubes of red neon. Clad only in scanty bras and panties, they come in all shades, colors and nationalities, and pose, without any come-on gestures, like wax mannequins. All are "government inspected." Even sex-for-sale is sanitary on the Zuider Zee!

Of course, our interests were on a much higher level. We visited museums (Amsterdam has 62); we browsed for Dutch antiques and old books; and we roamed the waterfront marveling at Holland's boating scene.

At last count, 2,000 houseboats, alone, bobbed on Amsterdam's waterline. We were told that Holland has more pleasure-craft per person than any country. With its network of rivers, canals and coastal waters, it is truly a sailor's paradise. Nothing delights a Dutchman more than sighting a ship under sail, especially if it is a traditional wooden sailing vessel which once formed the backbone of Holland's merchant fleet.

We encountered a harbor-full of such boats at one port of

call: Hoorn.

A quaint old fishing port, Hoorn seems like a Nantucket-with-wooden shoes. Jammed with boaters on holiday, this old port invited us right away to come-on-in-and-join the fun. Sitting on a wall at its entrance are three bronze figures, of small boys attired as if they were looking out at sea in days when Hoorn had been a very rich trading port of Dutch East India Company.

Hoofing-it around Hoorn, we noticed on streets lined with brick patrician residences, that some buildings LEANED towards us!

"Oh," a town guide explained, "Many Hoorn houses are built that way so rain would run off roofs into the gutter, thus protecting the bricks."

In 1616, when tiny Hoorn sent her ships around the world, one native son was first to round South America's southern tip. He named it Cape Hoorn (later Horn) for his hometown.

Horn was just one jewel in Holland's necklace of towns along its north coast...ports with marvelous names like Urk, Spijk Sneek and Enkhuizen, whose glory preceded Amsterdam on the tide of trade from the Indies. In the 17th century, Enkhuizen's herring fleet numbered 400 vessels. Its carillon had been pealing arrival of ships since 1540. We visited a Bottle Ship Museum there housed in a building containing an original sluice gate used to close off Enkhuizen's inner harbor from the Zuider Zee in 1351.

Depicting centuries of shipping, Jan Visser's museum has world's largest collection of ships-in-bottles, with dioramas detailed by old-time sailors to fit into bottles of any size. This was their handicraft while on long lonely voyages.

Mr. Visser welcomed us cordially, and demonstrated how sailors made their artifacts, some so small they could be inserted in a flashlight bulb. Visser's museum now comprises 500 specimens including models from Windjammers, steam navigation, fisheries, whaling and life-boat service.

From port-to-port we discovered other museums that we never knew existed, like Deventer's Toy and Tin Museum, with its great collection of antique bicycles.

Cycling is a way of life in The Netherlands, with its 9,000 miles of safe, scenic paths, and 14-million bicycles. At Otterloo's 12,000-acres national park, Hoge Veluwe, we saw 800 white bikes ready and rent-free for visitors touring the surrounding woodlands.

We were at Hoge Veluwe to explore one of Europe's greatest museums of modern art: the Kroeller-Mueller Collection. It has 278 works of Van Gogh! Plus canvasses by Picasso, Braque, Mondrian and other masters of that ilk.

Before Claes Oldenburg installed his 45-ft. CLOTHESPIN sculpture in Philadelphia, he had planted a tree-high BLUE TROWEL in Kroeller-Mueller's stunning 27-acre sculpture park. Here we wandered among works by such legendary artists as Henry Moore, Rodin, Barbara Hepworth and Jean Dubuffet.

In nearby Arnhem, of Bridge-Too-Far fame, we attended a gala dinner party at 12th-century Doorwerth Castle. A former stronghold of Middle Ages' robber barons, we had to cross its moat to enter. As we crossed the drawbridge, a troop of trumpeters, attired in loden splendor, fanfared our arrival.

This was our only "dressy" evening of the journey. Our fellow cruise passengers were "old tennis shoe" sorts, relaxed and congenial. Main Line mixed with Mid-west. Palm Beach paled with Palmyra.

Many ended up new-best-friends after our wild adventures in the real WATERWORLD...Holland.

ENCHANTING ITALY

Capri. Ravello. Positano. Sorrento.
The very sounds of these seductive sites on Italy's southern coast roll off lips like love songs.

Sensuous and alluring, these sanctuaries for that sybaritic way of life on the savagely beautiful Sorrento Peninsula.

Sirens are said to have lured Ulysses to these shores. In Homer's ODYSSEY, reportedly Ulysses had himself bound to his ship's mast to keep from jumping overboard and joining them. Roman emperors romped and ruled from Capri, perhaps the first beach resort known to man.

Garbo and Stokowski romanced high above it in lemon-blossom-scented gardens around Ravello. From its perch 1,100 feet above the Tyrranian Sea, Ravello commands one of the most peaceful, spectacular, breath-gasping views in the world...mountains, sea, sky, terraced fields of olives and grapes sweeping down into a panorama of the coastline.

In Ravello, Wagner wrote THE MAGIC FLUTE. Byron, Longfellow, D.H. Lawrence, Ibsen, Dumas, waxed poetic about "their" Ravello. John Huston came here to film BEAT THE DEVIL with Capote, Bogart and Morley. Gore Vidal's Ravello villa RONINAIA ("Swallows Nest"), with six acres of cypress-bordered gardens, seems suspended in air from the side of a cliff. From its prow one catches far-off vistas of ancient Roman watchtowers, tiny hidden beaches tucked snugly into towering rocks...private islands once owned by Lorca, Massine, Diajelev, Nureyev...villas of Sophia Loren and Franco Zeffirelli.

What finally lit our fire and set us off to Sorrento like a Roman rocket was this notice in Elderhostel's International Catalog. Headlined MYTHS, MARVELS, SIRENS AND SONG, it read:

"With the ancient Greek archeological sites of Paestum and Cuma, the Roman sites of Pompeii and Herculaneum, and the celebrated Archeological Museum of Naples close by, Sorrento is ideally suited for an especially rewarding study of ancient civilization. All of these sites and monuments are included in the course-related trips (except Herculaneum, which may be easily visited independently) and constitute the principal focus of the educational program. The curriculum also includes lectures on modern Italian history and contemporary Italian society, which encompasses topics such as education, religion and the role of women. Other lectures treat the subject of Neopolitan music from the classical and operatic traditions to popular song. Periodically, when available, guest lecturers are also invited to speak on their areas of specialization. Trips to Capri and over the panoramic Amalfi Drive are also included in the program. Arrangements are made for participants to take optional trips on the scheduled free day to Mt. Vesuvius, the Benedictine Abbey of Monte Cassino, Caserta, Ravello and Positano. Information will be provided for participants wishing to attend performances at the San Carlo Opera House in Naples."

Our "study" of ancient civilizations, and visits to the actual sites, were fascinating. Let's face it, Pompeii is one impressive archeological dig. Downright porno. Sin city until

271

Vesuvius erupted nearby and covered it all. Some of the, pardon, erections were off limits to ladies until recently. Professors from Hartford's Trinity College and the University of Naples gave us the low-down on a place one day, and the next morning we would visit it with a top-notch guide.

We explored the Greek ruins of Paestum and Cuma, the oldest archeological site in Italy. Founded in 8 B.C. by a group of Greek colonists, Cuma harbors the Grotto of the Sibella, which Virgil told us about in the AENEID.

One day we bused to Naples' National Archeological Museum, built in 1585. It houses Pompeii's amazing mosaics and those magnificent Brontosaurus-size statues from Rome's Baths of Caracalla. Here, too, is "the girl with the beautiful bottom," a Greek statue called Aphrodite Callipyge...a woman admiring her bare-derriere as reflected in a pool.

At our Elderhostel hotel in a garden right in the midst of charming Sorrento, we could walk to town tavernas, shops and, best of all...the cemetery! Surely, the most delightful garden-of-the-planted-departed ever conceived. Every day, as far as one could see, fresh flowers on every grave. At night, eternal flames glowed under glass photos of the gone-but-never-forgotten loved ones. Never did we think we could fall in love with a cemetery. Talk about fatal attraction. Yet, we'd make the trip back just to see it (but not for a permanent visit).

Topping everything, literally, was the Amalfi Drive, one of nature's most remarkable spectacles and man's greatest road-construction feats. Its two lanes zig-zag across peaks, through tunnels, across viaducts, edging perilously close to cliffside guardrails. Thank God we had hired an English-speaking chauffeur, for those Italian drivers are the best in the world.

Freed from fear-at-the-steering-wheel, we could seep in scenery like none other anywhere. On both sides of the road: a necklace of ancient fishing villages washed by the sea; hillside homes chiseled into rock cliffs; Saracen watchtowers built in the 6th or 9th century for protection against Saracen marauders; grottoes, waterfalls, bougainvillaea, night-blooming jasmine; tier on tier of terraced hill towns.

On our return, we thought of that old bromide: "Now That You've Read The Book, See The Movie."

Well, we saw the movie ENCHANTED APRIL and now we've seen, first hand, enchanted and enchanting Italy.

SPLENDIDO PORTOFINO!

Now we know why Portofino has long been the playground of such jet setters as David Niven, Rex Harrison, Bogart, Bacall, Di and Dodi (whose yacht anchored there the week before they returned to Paris). Portofino is paradisio for the yachting crowd; playground for The Beautiful People.

At first sight, its everything we imagined The Riviera to be: yachts bobbing nonchalantly in shimmering aquamarine waters; svelt Swedish blondes bidding bye bye to their yachtsmen hosts, before heading for Hermes; Bellinis; bikinis; CEOs with wives in tow, ordering truffles on the dining terrace; houses in shades of strawberry, lemon, tangerine hugging the half-moon harbor, each with a facade of trompe l'oeil embellishments; Agelli villas perched on a lush mountain of pines, poplars and palms, embracing one of the most idyllic havens on water: Portofino, Italy's fashionable fishing village, a natural reserve of rare eclat.

Topping it all is handsomely refurbished Hotel Splendido, originally an ancient villa poised high above the spectacular bay. Set on the hillside in four acres of romantic tropical gardens, it is luxuriously Ligurian-Mediterranean. Its gardens run wild down the slopes beneath the hotel to the sea. Bushes of lavender and wild herbs grow thickly under old olive trees. Masses of bougainvillaea blanket a necklace of front balconies a block long.

We arrived there, not by yacht, but by train, Orient Express-style, in a first class compartment passing views of wine farms and Cararra marble quarries en route. Alighting at Santa Margherita Rail Station, 4 miles from The Splendido, we taxied to the hotel along one of the most stunning coastal roads in all of Italy.

The Splendido certainly lived up to its name...splendid in every way, yet delightfully informal and relaxing. The front desk staff, masterminded by Fausto, a legendary concierge who has been there 30 years, gave us a warm welcome. Right away we felt we belonged.

We started our stay lunching on the handsome roofed dining terrace, stretching across the entire hotel front, with its views of gardens and swimming pool that seemingly floats over the bay. The Terrace turned out to be center of social activity breakfast, lunch and dinner. Wonderful people-watching. Very cosmopolitan: Swiss, Milanese, Belgian, Dutch, Swedish, French, German and American, enlivened by a smattering of handsome honeymooners.

Fellow passengers on our train informed us that we were headed for a walkers mecca. Portofino's promontory is a renowned nature reserve. No roads, only well-marked walking paths. They lead through olive groves, vineyards, up into forests along steep slopes high above the Ligurian Sea.

Serious hikers take a 2-hour excursion boat to Cinque Terre (Five Lands)and walk from village to village on cliffs with breathtaking views of wild landscape. The five villages which give this region its name, originated as fish towns in the Middle Ages. Built on rugged alpine ridges inland from the harbors, they were inaccessible by land for centuries.

We preferred taking jasmine-scented strolls for gentle souls surrounding our hotel. On cool mornings we would walk to the summit of Monte di Portofino, which towers

275

2,000 feet over the Ligurian Coast, or down the footpaths dotted with blooming heather, to town, with its smart shops and portside cafes.

After dark the yachting crowd would gather at Ristorante da Puny, right on the square, where tables are set up under trees on the outdoor terrace. Nearby is the bar where the likes of Onassis, Sinatra, Ava Garner and John Wayne used to hang out. Legend has it that when Rex Harrison was drinking there one day with the Duke of Windsor, he excused himself to get a package of cigarettes, and never came back. On the way he ran into Kay Kendall and they eloped!

One day we took a boat to San Fruttuoso, a twenty minute journey along a coast of jagged rock formations, some topped with an ancient light house. We arrived at a tiny cove with a pebbled beach fronting Benedictine Abbey, said to have been built in the 11th Century. Scuba-divers' boats were on hand for snorkelers, and a glass bottom skiff awaited to take us to view the underwater statue "Christ of the Abyss," 40 feet under the waves. The medieval monastery has tombs of the powerful seafaring Doria family (as in ANDREA DORIA) and its octagonal tower was built as a lookout to warn of approaching pirates. Behind the abbey, about a mile away, a shore battery was installed on top of the cliffs during the Second World War. It's certainly peaceful there now!

In the eleventh century, too, Portofino sailors participated in the Crusades and brought back relics of Saint George taken from Palestine. They now rest in the crypt of Portofino's Church of San Georgio, still a place of pilgrimage for local sailors. The eve of Saint George's Day, April 24, is celebrated on the town square with a towering bonfire made from a pile of dried old boats, and on the nearest Sunday, a procession of sailors and townsfolk head for the heights to San Giorgio's ancient cemetery, paying homage with fireworks and music.

Sightseeing is fun, but nothing compares with enjoying all Hotel Splendido has to offer. Pasta, pasta, pasta e basta; salads of zucchini blossoms stuffed with mozzarella, anchovies and deep-fried; perfect carpaccio, lightly grilled; best basil in the world is grown in this region!

Why return to the real world when you have the "Pearl of the Riviera" in the palm of your hand?

VENICE FROM A PALAZZO

Once we fantasized what it would be like to live in a magnificent Venetian palace on the Grand Canal, a la Henry James or Peggy Guggenheim.

On our recent visit to this city that calls herself La Serenissima, our fantasy became fact when we were ensconced in a top floor suite of a palazzo built by a Venetian nobleman, Doge Vendramin, in the 15th-century. Overlooking the Grand Canal, St. Mark's Square and the Doges Palace, Palazzo Vendramin has been luxuriously renovated and opened as an elegant addition to legendary Hotel Cipriani on the island of Giudecca, 5 minutes by The Cipriani's private boat from the center of Venice.

With its own private entrance, Palazzo Vendramin provides the sort of splendorous security desired by a Princess Di. Its airy rooms are Fortuny-inspired, with fine oil paintings, rare Venetian furniture and mirrors. Walls are playfully painted by a master of trompe l'oeil who transformed the tiny elevator to our floor into, seemingly, a cozy library of rare books.

Palazzo Vendramin suites are each served by a private butler. It was especially nice having ours, Umberto, on hand to serve tea and cocktails to our invited guests, and bring hot morning coffee as we breakfasted by our entrancing windows watching water buses, tugs, cruise liners, gondolas and private launches glide and dart in a marine minuet below.

A wise traveler once told us: "The next best thing to being rich is traveling as though you were."

At least once in one's life, it is worth the extra expense to experience staying in the best rooms, with the best views and best food of the most romantic city in the world: VENICE!

It's a city afloat, risen out of the sea, reflecting both East and West, Renaissance, Rome and Byzantium and spirits of those who have labored and loved along its canals for over a thousand years. When wit Robert Benchley first saw it, he cabled New York: "Streets full of water; please advise."

Here, Byron wrote DON JUAN; Casanova romanced; Wagner composed his opera TRISTIAN AND ISOLDE. Venice lagoons mirror thousand-year old palazzos where the greats-of-time have lived. Shakespeare, Marco Polo, Canoletto, Browning, George Sand, Lizst, Veronese, Sargent, Dickens, Shelley, and Monet have all succumbed to the charms of Venice, and left its kiss remembered in their immortal works.

Few evenings go by without a concert featuring Venice's own Vivaldi and Monteverdi, played by musicians in costumes of the time when these composers were at work as choir director or conductor of San Marco Church's orchestra.

On our first visit years ago, with visions of Hemingway's ACROSS THE RIVER AND INTO THE TREES in our heads, we headed straight to Harry's Bar, but on the way were stopped in our tracks beholding the most perfect city square of antiquity, Piazza San Marco, before pigeons and people took over.

We would never forget first seeing those huge, bold, bronze horses of St. Marks, proud spoils from the sacking of Constantinople, or looking up to The Winged Lion of Venice poised on the moors-topped clock tower. This winged lion symbol of Venice and its empire appeared all over. In

Carpaccio's THE LION OF ST. MARK which hangs in Doges Palace; carved over The Arsenales entrance doors; crowning one of the two marble columns which stand at the Watergate welcoming all arrivals to the Square so suggestive of grand occasions to follow.

Grand occasions are sure to follow once one enters this city of serendipities. Exploring "real" Venice by foot is a magical adventure. Walking streets tucked out of the way along small canals that twist through neighborhoods with laundry flying like flags overhead; crossing hump-backed bridges that lead to surprising shops and secret gardens behind walls of once-elegant mansions.

One of the pleasures of our recent sojourn was walking Venice with Tudy Sammartini, author of SECRET GARDENS OF VENICE, and seeing her family's noted garden. Through its iron-wrought gates we faced the splendid palazzo where Henry James wrote WINGS OF THE DOVE.

Stopping by the "secret garden" of whimsical painter/ appliqué artist Liselotte Hohs, we discovered that her adjoining studio had once been occupied by Modigliani and later by English painter Graham Sutherland. Hidden behind high walls, the Hohs garden and art-packed atelier has long been a popular gathering spot for visiting cognoscenti and celebrities. The garden is noted for its 18th-century garden sculpture representing The Four Seasons.

Through Lisslotte Hohs, we learned about the genius of Fortuny, Venice's late great designer of fabled textiles, fashion, stage lighting and theatrical sets. She is said to have THE great collection of Fortuny, which she continued to collect after he died.

Though there is water water everywhere, Venice has only ONE swimming pool and that one, 660-sq. meters big, is at The Cipriani, Venice's grand resort/hotel on the Grand Canal. Select Venetians belong to its exclusive Seagull Club and do their laps there daily. Several grand dames we know keep trim strolling across town to take the Cipriani private launch at St. Mark's Square landing; take the private launch direct to the club; swim; shower; then meet friends for lunch buffet on the poolside terrace. Hotel guests, of course, see the pool as their own, but feel the swank club members add to the ambiance.

All transportation is on the water. Venice's main street is the Grand Canal. Instead of cars parked in front of neighborhood houses you have boats. Venice is built on a cluster of 116 islands connected by a web of 176 canals (over 30 miles of waterways) and 400 bridges.

So, boatsport is big with the boys. Many of them start early at rowing clubs. In May, the first Sunday after Feast of the Ascension, masses compete in The Vogalonga, open to anyone with the muscles to row the 25-mile course. Like other local festivals, its a celebration of Venice's mastery of the sea. The Voga is designed to promote and maintain Venetian pride in their lagoons.

Boatsmen also gather for the Festa del Redentore commemorating the end of the 16-century plague.

Families decorate their boats with loops of lanterns, liters of wine, basket-loads of food, forming a bridge across the Guidecca Canal. On Guidecca island stands Palladio's masterpiece Church of the Redeemer, erected in 1577 in gratitude for the ending of the plague. The Festa goes on tipsily into the night with lots of fireworks and funiculi-fanicula.

Venice's biggest fest, Regata Storica (Historical Regatta), takes place on the first Sunday in September. Here people come from all over the world to watch a spectacle of crews costumed as Renaissance doges and noblemen in a brilliant parade of decorated boats and barges. Climax of the day is a fiercely competitive race, the Regata Sportiva, between different classes of gondolas. Crowds of partying guests cheer all from festooned balconies of the palazzi.

There's another great thanksgiving celebration held November 21: the Festa della Salute. Throngs parade across a pontoon bridge spanning the Grand Canal from Gritti Palace to picnic at St. Maria della Salute, an island of a church which rises from the water like a mountainous domed wedding cake. All marble and marvelous with monumental steps, statues of saints, columns, arches, scrolls, swirls and banisters, it ,too, commemorates the ending of the plague.

We especially enjoy taking an excursion water bus to Torcello, the island where Ernest Hemingway and his wife Mary went in 1948 for a month of writing, duck shooting and exploring the charms of this ancient colony and its inn. We love dining in the Locanda's delightful garden, and ambling around in Torcello's old churches: cathedral of Santa Maria dell'Assunta and the Church of Santa Fosca, next to it. Here you feel how ancient this place is. Settled in 639, Torcello once was richest colony in Venice. Hemingway, in ACROSS THE RIVER AND INTO THE TREES, described it as a kind of dream oasis.

That's also how we remember our Palazzo Vendramin; its gardens in the moonlight; the luminescence of nighttime Venice and boatlights reflected in the Grand Canal below our palace windows...a kind of dream oasis.

Shopping with the legendary Liselotte, at vegetable stands, wine-shops, bakeries, paper-makers in her neighborhood, she pointed out the house where neighbor Erika Jong had written her brilliant novel of Venice, SERENISSIMA.

Another serendipitous pleasure of our stroll was visiting San Trovaso boatyard, where gondolas are hand-built, some fitted with sofas, cushioned chairs and oriental rugs.

A special treat was lunching on the garden porch of Peggy Guggenheim's Palazzo Venier dei'Leoni. The original owner kept lions in the garden, hence the name. Now it houses sculpture of Giacometti, Henry Moore, Jean Arp and Max Ernst. Two inscriptions behind the gazebo indicate where the late Peggy's ashes and her seven Lhasa terriers are buried.

The people-friendly restaurant and garden are part of the museum of modern art assembled by "The Appasionata of Avant-Garde," American-heiress Peggy Guggenheim.

Knowing about appasionata Peggy's flamboyant Bohemian lifestyle and love affairs, visitors of all kinds have swarmed around the Palazzo since she opened her Collection to the public in 1951. Curious students, artists and writers flock to see her equestrian bronze statue by Marino Marini standing on the gondola landing up front. Peggy had it cast so that the rider's erect phallus could be respectfully detached when religious personages came by. The horse, too, is said to have different-sized parts.

1998 was Peggy Guggenheim's centenary year. From October through January 1999, the museum staged a special exhibition of her personal objects, works of art, documents and never-before shown signed-guest books, some illustrated and annotated by artists, intellectuals, socialites and other personages who constituted Peggy's circle.

Summing it all up, Peggy's greatest work of art was her own creation...a never-to-be-forgotten free-spirited life.

AEGEAN ISLANDS BY CATAMARAN

Z orba the Greek, yes.
But The Virgin Mary?
Come on!

We never knew that our mother of God had ended up dying in Ephesus...or that Antony and Cleopatra cruised the Aegean Sea on one of their love boats then had sand shipped in from Egypt to make one of their tryst shores more comfy.

There were a lot of surprises about ancient history that kept popping up on our recent adventure cruising Aegean Islands with 13 other hearty souls on a Greek catamaran yacht, M/Y DOUBLE FORCE.

Fortunately, our vessel was just the right size, well equipped and experienced to maneuver in and, out of coves, bays, fjords, deserted islands...over submerged ancient ruins in clear shallow waters. It was like being on our own private Odyssey without having to put up with Ari, Jackie or Homer. One day we would anchor off a tiny island that had once contained a Greek, then Roman, city where we would find ruins of a gate erected in the 2nd century A.D.; a Roman aqueduct; necropolis; and city streets abandoned in the early 13th century. We found this aged maritime metropolis, with its three harbors, high mountain, pine plantation, completely deserted...all ours to explore.

On another shore, we found where St. Nicholas (our Santa Claus) sprang from, and on the way stopped at Myra, with

its amazing collection of tombs cut out of cliffs and remarkable Roman theater still standing nearby.

One glorious clear morn we anchored off Patmos, a mountainous island with an abundance of small coves. Crowning
its mountaintop stands fortress-mighty Monastery of St.
John. Leading up to it, a mass of gleaming white cubical
houses stack one atop another like so many stairsteps.
Interspersed among them are tiny churches and sea captains'
mansions, all separated from each other by narrow lanes and
squares opening onto breathtaking views of the deep blue
Aegean. Massive grey stone walls rise all around the
monastery, with battlements protecting its chapels and
shrine where St. John was inspired to write his Book of
Revelations in 95 A.D. Tradition has it that John took The
Virgin Mary to Ephesus after the Crucifixion. While there,
Romans banished him, because of his beliefs. At Patmos, he
took refuge secluded in a mountaintop cave. During his soli-
tude, came visions of the Apocalypse, which he dictated to a
scribe. On this site, in 11 A.D., Greek Orthodox priests built
the monastery, with a main church and five small chapels.
One houses a priceless library filled with stunning Byzantine
icons, 9th century embroideries, ancient scrolls and pages
from a manuscript of the Gospel according to St. Mark. Also,
miniatures from the Book of Job and ship pendants of emer-
ald and diamonds donated by Catherine The Great.

An Audrey Hepburn-handsome guide garbed in flowing
white Grecian chiffon led us to St. John's cave, where we
were welcomed by a bearded monk in a long black tunic with
matching square-shaped top hat. Later, passing Gothic arches and belltowers, we heard monks chanting mass, then crept
silently into their chapel decorated with frescoes on a gold
background illustrating the life of St. John, and his apocalyp-
tic visions. It was all worth a very steep climb.

At sundown, we ascended another steep hill for dinner

overlooking the sea in a family-run taverna right out of ZORBA THE GREEK, its handsome Olympic-manly dancers perfect for Central Casting. It was all candlelight, moonlight, and NEVER ON SUNDAY bouzouki music, over long tables flowing with ouzo (that potent anise flavored drink that gets cloudy when iced and sends drinkers into Cloud Nine after so many sips.) Our waiters, donned in flowing Cossack-style coats, dashed to a stage, and began that graceful swaying dance Greek men perform: The ZEBEKIKO. All to tunes of Mikis Theodorakis and Manos Hadjidakis. Their performance climaxed in lively prancing, leg-swinging, leaping that even Baryshnikov would envy.

Everyone agreed that Patmos is truly "the quintessential Aegean town." That is, until we cruised into Symi, serene unspoiled island of sponge sellers. Its brilliant-hued houses sport neoclassical pediments and decorative doorways. On Symi's waterfront we met free-spirited exiles and fishermen doing-their-thing far from "the uptight world."

We found another free-spirit island, apparently settled by beachcombers among deserted sarcophagi. We promised natives not to reveal their hidden bay, but we can tell you it's all simply enchanting. A beachfront bar, built from ship-wreck flotsam washed ashore, uses an upturned rowboat as its roof. Hippy maitre'd, bearded, barefoot, ragged-jeaned, one-earring shining under a purple-satin pirate-fashion headgear looked every bit "ho-ho-ho-and-a-bottle-of-rum." A rickety-sign warning "No ghost allowed!" had been erected since this establishment had been erected next to a pile of pillar-tombs. With submerged ruins all around, village gardens winding through a necropolis and plateaus of rug merchants, this place is a far, far cry from that Colossus island, Rhodes.

On first sight from the sea, Rhodes appears to be one huge crenelated-walled castle. You feel you're sailing into a medieval stronghold manned by Crusaders to keep out invaders. Once you dock, however, you find today's Rhodesians welcome all with open arms, open shops, open museums and open tavernas. Its Old City stands much the way it was when occupied by Knights of St. John during The Crusades. Here Pindar wrote a victory hymn dedicated to Rhode's boxing champ of the 454 B.C. Olympic Games. He also penned: "Forth from the watery deep, blossomed the island Rodos, child of the love-goddess Aphrodite to be bride of the Sun."

Now, over Rhodes' ancient stone walls, roses still blossom aplenty. And there are plenty of love-goddess Aphrodites offering up themselves to Rhodes sun...and sons. Swank resort beaches blossom with bikinied Nordic vacationers year round.

However, main concern among our yacht-mates was not Rhode's dazzling daughters, but its holidaying DONKEYS.

Donkeys are de rigeur for ascending Rhodes' #1 tourist draw, Acropolis of Lindos, which is almost impossible to climb on your own. Horror struck upon arrival at its giant cliff when we were told "Monday is our donkey's day off... and this is Monday!"

So if you plan to visit Rhodes' acropolis, just remember Greek movie star Melina Mercouri's motto NEVER ON SUN-DAY has been changed there, by donkey edict, to "Never On MONDAY!"

Also, if visiting islands of the Aegean, choose to cruise.

PALATIAL ISTANBUL

Until Ciragan Palace arose Phoenix-like recently on the Bosphorus, we thought nothing in Istanbul could top Topkapi.

Topkapi is a palace turned into a museum.

Ciragan is a palace modernized into a grand hotel. Now, one can STAY at Ciragan Palace, Sultan-style.

When friends came back from a Union League cruise in Turkey, they raved so about their Ciragan Palace visit that we soon mounted our magic carpet (rather Swissair, which flies to Istanbul direct from Philadelphia) to give it a try ourselves.

Believe us...it's an adventure in opulence.

Istanbul has intrigued us as a place to explore even before Agatha Christie wrote her MURDER ON THE ORIENT EXPRESS from Pera Palas Hotel there. The Pera was once a palace, too, but not near as sumptuous as Ciragan Palace (pronounced "Chiraan"), last regal residence of Ottoman Sultans. Built of wood in late 16th century, then rebuilt in marble for Sultan Abdulaziz in 1857, it had all the glamour associated with such Eastern potentates as Solomon, Cleopatra and Tutenkhamun, all who conjure untold wealth. Pre-eminent among those whose great power created great beauty were the Sultans of Turkey. When it came to lavish collections of jewels, artifacts, architecture, precious metals, fabrics and porcelains, Sultans set the mold.

Their lifestyle had reached fabled proportions as early as the sixth century when Constantine the Great chose Byzantium as capital of the Christian world. At his Seraglio Point complex, now occupied by the Blue Mosque, gilt lions guarded his throne and guilt birds tweet-tweeted in trees around it. When visiting dignitaries approached, the lions roared, the birds twittered, and the emperor's throne (reported to have belonged to Solomon) was raised, apparently miraculously, by mechanical contraptions.

Sulleyman The Magnificent's palace was of course magnificent, too. His Mosque, even more so. Intended to be Sultan Sulleyman's statement of Ottoman Empire political splendor, combined with Islam's religious power, it dominated a hill overlooking the Golden Horn. He built a palace nearby for a Grand Vizier, whose concubine squandered his money by covering walls of its 200 rooms with furs.

Dolmabahce Palace, erected by Sultan Abdul Mecit in 1853, and still furnished "knocked our sox off" with its staggering proportions. It contains 285 rooms, 43 major salons, and scores of handloomed Turkish and Persian carpets. Entering its Grand Salon, you are bedazzled by Baccarat and Bohemian crystal everywhere...quintuple chandeliers, quadruple CRYSTAL fireplaces, a swooping three-story staircase with CRYSTAL balusters, and, as its centerpiece four-and-a half TON Waterford crystal chandelier, gift from England's Queen Victoria. Our guide said it is undoubtedly the largest in the world.

We were awfully lucky having an Istanbul aristocrat guiding us. Her clients had included the likes of Oscar de la Renta and the Kissingers, so she led us into some glorious private places. One we particularly admired was an 18th-century yali, a jewel box of a house, painted in the traditional dark red pigment, astboya, a colour reserved for the most privileged of Ottoman Sultans' Turkish subjects. It had belonged to a distinguished Turkish diplomat, once ambassador in London, then to NATO. His impeccable taste, acerbic wit, and erudite art-of-living were bywords in Europe and America, thus this yali is infused with his personality. (Our guide explained that a yali is a summer house close enough to spit into the Bosphorus.) His had an unsurpassable view, looking from the Asia banks of the Bosphorus to embrace the skyline of Europe Istanbul with its mosques, domes and minarets. The Bosphorus, known as the Canal of Constantinople, is said to surpass the Grand Canal of Venice in beauty. Bosphorus' dramatic and constant-changing watertraffic...ferries, caiques, fishing boats, freighters, gulets, cruise ships...also reminded us of Hong Kong harbor, sans its jostle of junks.

Cruising on the Bosphorus is a delightful way to glimpse Istanbul at its grandest, especially arriving by boat to Ciragan Palace's royal Watergate, all gold, marbled, filagreed and soaring several stories high. Beyond it: terraces, gardens and a waterfront swimming pool. Overlooking it all, we dined on Ottoman cuisine in The Ciraganis stylish Tugra Restaurant, while musicians strummed serene Turkish tunes.

Of course Istanbul itself is magical, the only city in the world built on two continents. Everywhere you turn you are faced with living history. When they talk about 1800 here, they are referring to 1800 BC! Istanbul began somewhere in the 7th Century BC as Byzantium. Two thousand years later, Ottoman Sultans built an empire so powerful it stretched from Egypt to Vienna.

Their mosques are a must-see, starting with Saint Sophia, built without regard for expense in 532 as patriarchal church of the Eastern Roman Empire by Emperor Justinian, later converted to a mosque and museum. Its dome is so huge it seems suspended from Heaven, and of course, that was the intent. The Blue Mosque, with it 21,000 blue Iznik tiles, 6 minarets and 260 windows, arises nearby. But due to the film starring Melina Mercouri, Peter Ustinov and Robert Morley, TOPKAPI, the palace with that name is where tourists head first. They just have to see the dagger encrusted with diamonds and emeralds big as jawbreakers. It's on display in Topkapi Palace's Treasury, along with hundreds of other jeweled items.

Near Topkapi, Basilica Cistern, a huge underground reservoir, brought back memories of PHANTOM OF THE OPERA. You half expected to see The Phantom paddling through its darkened basement lake, his way lit by torches, with strains of Beethoven echoing throughout its mass of marble pillars.

Another tourist mecca for those who shop-til-they-drop, The Grand Bazaar, a covered market of 4,400 shops on 50 streets under one roof. Streets reflect names of ancient guilds such as Makers of Saddle Girths or Makers of Fezzes. In another covered bazaar, Egyptian Spice Market, you could buy everything from henna to aphrodisiacs. We bought a pound of pistachios.

However, most delightful discovery of all that we encountered, was an entire block of charming Turkish-style wooden houses, restored as small hotels, furnished with antiques, and operated in the tradition of European pensions. Having a memorable lunch by a bubbling fountain in its shady garden restaurant, we heard that this enchanting oasis is all due to one man, Mr. Celik Gulersoy, director general of Turkey's Touring and Automobile Association. He wanted the world to know what Old Istanbul was like, so he set out to save blocks of large old mansions set in spacious gardens, with breathtaking views of Topkapi, Saint Sophia, The Blue Mosque and Basilica Cistern. President Mitterand visited its small hotel, Yesil Ev (for "Green House"). We wished that

Philadelphia had a Celik Gulersoy to lovingly and sensitively restore that row of houses facing Fairmont Park.

For mid pleasures and palaces, wherever we may roam, our thoughts always return to home-sweet-home.

BOTSWANA & THE CROCODILES

Somewhere over the rainbows...BOTSWANA!

Not one rainbow, but several arced over us in the spray of Africa's mammoth Victoria Falls, gateway to one of Africa's last surviving wild areas: Botswana.

On our "Wings Over The Kalahari" adventure we had run through the gamut of Africa's natural phantasmagoria: wild waterways; jungles of giraffes; mountain-high sand dunes looming over the world's oldest desert; a sea that's really a mirage; gorges 400-ft. deep, gouged by thundering mile-wide Victoria Falls, wonder-of-the-world discovered in 1855 by Scottish explorer David Livingstone in his search for source of the Nile.

We had landed there on our journey to "unspoiled Africa" in neighboring Botswana, farsighted protector of its precious wilderness and wild animals.

Reportedly, 17% of Botswana had been set aside as game parks...well-maintained; untouched; untarred; unfenced; protected from poachers..."a last African Eden."

Unfortunately, we did NOT find Victoria Falls "un-touristed," or uncivilized. This sightseer mecca bulged with souvenir stands, even a Bungee Jump. However, we still found remnants of British-colonial grandeur at its Victoria Falls Hotel, and seeing the falls was well worth the trip, even if we had to pay for a pricey "fly-over" by helicopter to view it all.

We had already been from A to Z: arid Namibia then into watery Z-land: Zimbabwe, Zambezi River and Zambia. Next, their neighbor Botswana was our choice for a safari. Here wildlife roams free over primeval landscape. Its elephant population, numbering more than 30,000, is considered Africa's largest concentration still surviving within confines of a proclaimed national park. During Africa's harsh dry season, herds migrate to congregate along Botswana's enduring Chobe River in Chobe National Park. (On our first safari in Kenya, we had to go far into the bush for game-viewing; at our Chobe Lodge, game came to us!) Up and down the river, thousands of elephants, hippo, buffalo lined the banks. We would encounter square-lipped rhino, wild dogs, wildebeest, zebra, bushbuck, sable, roan antelope and crocodile. Never before had we seen such diversity in profusion.

Since there is no poaching, we would find elephants in our backyard tame as moo-cows. Looking out of our Chobe Lodge window, we'd see lovable little warthogs grazing on our front lawn. (At home, it would be squirrels.)

Chobe Lodge is one of Africa's most luxurious safari resorts. Elizabeth Taylor and Richard Burton had one of their weddings here, honeymooning in a suite with its own private pool. (Plus its 45 luxury en-suite rooms, Chobe Lodge provides four suites, each with its own swimming pool. One morning we heard a cry from one of them: "Darling, quick come look, there's an elephant at our swimming pool!" "Oh, damn, and I can't find my contact lenses!")

At Chobe, we'd make dawn game runs with professional guides in 4-wheel drive vehicles. At sunset we'd take a cruise on an African river barge, cocktailing among the crocodiles. During the day we'd skim across the waters in speedy "mosquito" boats dodging hippo bobbing about like

Two-ton Tillies at a fat farm. When semi-submerged hippos suddenly splash up, yawning at you with wide-open mouths big as car trunks, it is not very comforting to hear from your boatman: "De hippo is most dangerous animal in dis river. Dat's why we have dese fast boats...to getaway quick, or dey sink us!"

On our game-runs we made up a game of our own, "Celebrity Look Alikes." Amazing how wild animals can become cartoons of real people. Sample: haughty, long-legged, sauntering giraffe we tagged "Charles De Gaulle." Cape buffalo with its ox-yoke hairdo and droopy lips, "Lillian Hellman." An ostrich peering down at us from its elongated neck looked like Edna Mae Oliver without her lorgnette. An ape full-face, resembled George Burns sans his cigar.

Since Botswana has 450 varieties of birds, naturally bird-ers among us had a field day. You'd hear them shout names like "Blackeyed Bulbul"; "White Bellied Sunbird"; "Wire-tailed Swallow!" "Boubou!" "Brubau!"

When they seemed stumped by a bird they didn't recognize we would supply them with what we considered suitable *noms-des-plumage*: "full-breasted Parton," say, or the "bobbed Bobbitt."

The big treat for our fresh-water anglers was casting in Chobe's deep waters for "Africa's fighting marlin," tigerfish. A guide told us, "There is something special about tigerfishing at night. All your senses are on full alert. Your imagination runs wild. A fish swirling in the shallows sounds like a crocodile. In fact, that sound could be a crocodile. Once angling in pitch-black dark we thought we saw tiny green Christmas lights twinkling on the shore. But they weren't Christmas tree bulbs...they were crocodile eyes a-gleaming."

We found it quite unnerving one night returning from a sunset picnic when our vehicle broke down deep in the jun-

295

gle and a bull elephant suddenly met us head-on, blocking the road with a, "this is my turf" stare.

Fortunately our guide radioed for help. As we waited, dead silence surrounded us. Suddenly, it was shattered by a scream, then shrieks, roars, trumpets, grunts, growls, snorts, chitters, bellows...a whole mad staccato of jungle noises. When our rescue truck finally appeared, our elephant and spooky sounds all disappeared.

After that, we limited our late-night wildlife forays to the Lodge bar, where there were enough human animals stalking around, eyeing their prey, to keep things lively.

Spectacular sunsets, however, had us out on the river, where water and sky seemed aflame in a translucent glow. In this golden dusk, we'd toss bait into the water, luring a white-faced fish eagle to swoop down and go-fetch from its high perch. We'd make bets on how many seconds it took from take-off to pick-up.

Seeing thousands of animals together, untamed, unslaved by commercial man, is like seeing God's original order of things for the first time. Striped zebra; green crocodile; gray elephant; ebony buffalo; tawny lion living along with squat, ugly, lovable warthog; scruffy, sneaky hateful hyena; tall, aloof giraffe; bare-bottom baboon; separate, but together, only joining other species as a group when taking communion at the big waterhole of Botswana.

All exist in harmony on the same turf, without mixing. You never see a cheetah pal-ing around with a lion, even though they are both cats. Elephants live in a community of their own, protecting each other *en famille*. Vegetarians roam with vegetarians; meat-eaters mingle with their own carnivorous ilk, only straying when hungry for more exotic flesh, such as venison on the hoof. Ostriches never breed with emu. There's no combo giraffe-elephant. We couldn't image what pattern might be begottten by the mating of leopard and zebra. A leobra?

Being amid them made us wonder, muse, be amazed even more by the Great Designer's ingenuity, creativity, sensitivity, intent. In this peaceable kingdom, things only went off-kilter when one got greedy, poaching from the other.

One day, Land-Roving into Botswana wilds, we came upon a freshly shot kudu. When you see such a regal animal lying bleeding, coat still sleek, open eyes glassed by death, killed only for its graceful corkscrew curved horns, you become sickened with rage and revolt.

In order to protect its wildlife from such poaching, Botswana sought to win its indigenous people's trust and cooperation. Locals living among wild animals were per-suaded that by preserving animals, with government help by controlling culling of over-abundant game, they'd benefit from tourism, serving as gameminders, gamespotters, and guides.

Its program has been a resounding success, attracting safari seekers from all over the world.

And it's why we now say, "If you want a superb game-viewing adventure, you wanna Botswana."

SUPER DUPER SPA-ING

In the world of grand luxe to the International set, Brenner's Park-Hotel and Spa managing director Richard Schmitz is their "heavenly host." When it comes to personal attention, Brenner's set the standard for "world class."

A special breed flocks to this watering hole year after year...all thoroughbreds. Your fellow guests here might be Paloma Picasso or Prince Philip. Americans from the Laurence Rockefellers to Brooke Astor come to this old-world grand hotel to recharge their batteries. Tired muscles, aching backs, worrisome wrinkles, bulging midriffs and stressed nerves seem to EASE away at Brenner's. For unlike some American spas that send their clients through a sort of luxurious boot camp exercise regime as if preparing them for Olympic competition, the emphasis at Brenner's is on relaxation. A stay here is like one long marvelous massage.

Plus, it is equally enjoyed by powerful men. Over 2,000 years ago, Emperor Caracalla and his Roman generals soaked in Baden-Baden's natural mineral hot springs after an exhausting battle. So did Napoleon III and Eisenhower. Today, CEOs of Ford, General Motors, Chrysler, Mercedes and Porsche, with their spouses, beat it to Brenner's for a healthy holiday, for here they can have a physical checkup, exercise at leisure and enjoy the good life all under one roof.

You can stroll from an early morning exercise class in the Pompeian swimming pool to a private massage room or a daily treatment at the Lancaster-Beauty Farm. Or, if you prefer, go out to the links for a round of golf, or the stables for a canter through the surrounding fabled Black Forest. It's a walker's paradise. Where else can you feel safe walking through moonlit gardens to the world's most elegant casino, through old-town streets of swank shops or to a choice of Michelin-starred restaurants?

So, when we wanted to "experience a spa," we took ourselves to the most celebrated of them all, Baden-Baden. Easily accessible by air, we had a choice of airports—Strasbourg, Stuttgart or Frankfurt—where we would be met by the hotel's Mercedes limousine, and driven through Hansel-and-Gretel-ish landscapes to the most tranquil palace anywhere, Brenner's Park-Hotel and Spa. It's called a "parkhotel" for it sits in the midst of its own private green park.

There's nothing quite like being welcomed by name on your first visit, and at Brenner's, from the moment you sign in, "everybody knows your name." You not only are put at home, you are made to feel "master of the house." And what a house it is! Unpretentious beauty, quiet, genteel luxury abounds, for every corner is made pleasing, soothing to the eye. The grand "conversation salon" is all sunshine and crystal, antiques and handsome paintings, in colors as refreshing as sherbet. A priceless Persian carpet, gift of the Shah to the Brenner family in gratitude for sublime visits, stretches royally across the floor.

Our fourth-floor suite, with its iron-grilled balcony overlooking the rippling flower-bordered stream, was as spacious as a Park Avenue apartment, offering touches that fairly lure you to relax: bed pillows plump and white and soft as clouds; heated towel racks; and a tub deep and long enough to immerse full length in waters that are a balm to the tired-old body. Your floor butler is just across the hall, to whisk ice or breakfast to your room at your beck and call. Your own floor maids seem to know the exact right time to put your quarters in order, freshen the flowers, replace the fruit, and turn down the covers, leaving a tiny chocolate surprise in a pretty pink box on the pillow.

It was suggested that we have our breakfast served in our room with a view of the sunrise over the Vosges mountains in the distance. Then we would don our hooded full-length terry robes and amble down the halls for a half-hour exercise wake-up in the Pompeii-style swimming pool, with its frescoed walls and window-wall that brings the park beyond in full view. Our instructor, limber as Baryshnikov and Boris Becker, jovially puts us through our aquatic exercises under water, promising, "Less strain on the muscles." If special exercises are in order, one could then proceed a few paces to a state-of-the-art exercise room equipped with just the right machine for your need.

First off, after jet-travel, my wife headed for the Lancaster Beauty Farm, only a hall away. Here she set her beauty regime for the week, one day a new coiffeur, another a facial or massage, all attended by charming Audrey Hepburn-ish specialists. Hair, skin, and fingernails never looked better, and the pedicure was "divine."

The management insisted that even I try a facial, which to my innocent mind meant lipstick and eyeshadow. "Oh no," laughed my attendant as she ran her smooth, soft fingers over my puffy eyes and chinny-chin-chins. "For men, this is a skin treatment. Your face and feet need attention, and we set you on a course to keep your exterior looking and feeling marvelous."

Next, I had a full medical checkup in the separate Schwarzwald Clinic, which is also attached to the hotel. If I had an ulcer, or needed constant medical attention, I could room here and have the comforts and services of a hotel. The clinic has nine specialists on call, including a noted Swiss plastic surgeon. Here the doctors and nurses make the whole procedure as painless as if they were entertaining you at a cocktail party.

One morning I had the privilege of pouring over the hotel's guest books, filled with the signatures of the world's rich and famous, from Victoria to the Mountbattens. On the facing pages dated July, August, September 1953, I found such signers as Phildelphians Jessie and George Widener, the Duke and Duchess of Windsor, Prince Ruspoli, di Gasperi, tin-king Antonio Patino and copper-king Gulbenkian, which gives you an idea of the kind of clientele this place has been catering to all these years.

Four generations of Detroit's Ford family have been coming back to Brenner's. For years, members of the Anheuser Busch clan have returned to join European nobles at the posh six days of horse racing at the 122-year old race track in Iffezheim.

Knowing of all this subdued grandeur, we approached our stay somewhat intimidated. Especially when we heard that a MUST in Baden-Baden is to take baths at the famed Roman-Irish bathing palace, the Friedrichsbad, totally nude...and that sometimes it is "co-ed." If we had builds like Arnold Schwarzenegger and wife, perhaps we wouldn't feel so shy, or embarrassed. But bobbing around naked in public?

As it turned out, Friedrichsbad allowed mixed bathing only at special times. There's a lady's and a men's bath. We each went through the entire 15 stages of the bath; steaming, soaking, rubadub-dubbing; wearing only the key to our lockers attached to a wrist band.

The thermal pools are literally fit for a king: tile, marble cathedral-high dome decorated with mosaic murals; encircled by nude maidens...stone, of course...carved by sculptors in the height of Belle Epoque.

As for my bathing companions, they were all tubbies-in-the-tubby. Obviously, German beer had been their life-long over-indulgence. I felt I was bobbing about in a pool of hippos!

THE HOTEL IN THE BULL RING

D id we dream all this? Or did we really go to Zacatecas?

We had certainly dreamed of going there after hearing about its astonishing "hotel of the bull ring."

"It is without a question the most unique five-star luxury hotel in the world" we were told by a renowned Mexican architect who had just returned from there. "Like a phoenix, it has arisen from what was Mexico's oldest bullring, right in the heart of our splendiferously old silver city of Zacatecas."

Zacatecas? We had never heard of such a place.

"Like San Miguel de Allende and Guaunajuato, Zacatecas sprang from lavish silver mines. Discovered by Spanish explorers in the mid-1500s, this town became one of the richest in New Spain, and certainly one of the most beautiful. Tucked away about 8 hours north of Mexico City, it has been off the tourist track" our friend continued. "But no longer! Its magnificent new 'hotel of the bullring' has worldly wanderers flocking to it like hummingbirds to honeysuckle."

Recently, we headed there, too, driving through scenic cattle country and charming colonial towns en route. Just outside of Zacatecas, we saw a site that had us gasping, as if a flying saucer had just landed in our path. Rising out of a field, like stalagmites in a moonscape, stood silos— Guadeloupe rockets pointed skyward. This was not your usual hacienda, or advance guard to a city. However, as we were to discover, Zacatecas was not your usual city. Unlike so many other picturesque places whose beauty had been raped in the name of progress, city fathers here had preserved their treasure intact. Instead of tearing down to replace with "modern ugly," over the past 25 years they have conserved Zacatecas' aged colonial charm with tender-loving-care, keeping its style and unity much the same as it was in the 17th century. Zacatecas architecture is quietly elegant, pretty-pink terra cotta rather than cold marble or limestone block.

Here there's still a close relationship between town and country, for Spanish elite who owned rich silver mines, also owned masses of land surrounding the city, their outlying haciendas supplying Zacatecas with its meat, hides, grain and bulls to match brave matadors in their proud bullring. Even today in mid-town, rancheros in sombreros are leading burros past shops bursting with bridles, boleros, lassos and Spanish boots for charros.

Zacatecas streets, with their steep slopes, sharp turns, and sudden vistas recall California's San Francisco, only 18th-century Spanish rather than Gold-rush tarah-rah-boom-te-ay.

Before we had even arrived at "the hotel of the bullring," our reason for coming to this miles-from-nowhere place, we had fallen in love with the town. Especially enthralling are aged convents now converted into awesome museums, and a Cathedral with a wonder-of-the-world facade. Never, ever, have we seen anything so exuberantly carved, miraculously baroque with masses of angels playing instruments, saints blessing with bibles, all entwined with God's bounty: swirls, curleycues of blossoms, shells, fruits, feathers. You see why Zacatecan stone cutters are the most renowned in all of Mexico.

And you see why town fathers refused to have their townscape changed with a modern high-rise hotel. Rather than displace their bullfight coliseum, architects for Quinta Real, Zacatecas' hotel of choice, came up with a brilliant solution, transforming it into a hotel. Now, what was once the V.I.P. box where senoritas might be presented the bull's ear by an admiring matador, has become a multi-level grand dining room. On ground level surrounding the bullring, smart shops have taken over from stables. Where bulls were once released, Bullshots and Margaritas are served in romantic candlelit coves with guitarists serenading in the background. The hotel's 46 suites are decorated with quietly elegant Mexican flair, reminiscent of Beverly Hills' best.

Charming as Hotel Quinta Real is for dining and relaxing, one of its great attractions is its location, only a short stroll to parks, museums and mid-town shops manned by local silversmiths and craftfolk. At every turn, there's a new "discovery," say a garden of calla lilies, or, a unique antique fountain. Even traffic-pace seems unchanged by time, moving to a slow rhythm. One is hardly aware of automobiles. Most surprising of all, however, are museums with collections of unsurpassed quality. Obviously those sons of the silver grandees had an "eye" for art and history, with the money and "eye" to roam the world and collect. One of them, Rafael Coronel, gathered together the largest collection of masks in the world: 5,000 in all...rooms of them depicting every imaginable creature: supernatural animals, Moors, Christians, Devils, Conquistadores. Only half of them are on display, yet they cover nine enormous chambers in what was once the enormous Convent of San Francisco.

Coronel also collected rare Diego Rivieras, pre-Hispanic pots, and enchanting folk art, all on display in the converted convent's cloisters, cells and sacristies. Two favorite rooms of the public feature charming marionettes rescued from a 19th-century puppet company that had been disbanded. Full casts of marionettes are presented in constructed scenes on lighted stages, all costumed, choreographed and in settings just as they must have appeared at the turn of the last century. Certainly, this is one of the best museums of folk art in the world.

Equally grand is the collection and works of Zacatecan painter, Pedro Coronel, Rafael's brother. Housed in a royal seminary building built in 1616, Museo Pedro Coronel offers an array of the very best example of universal art...Meso-American, Tibetan, Chinese, Greek, African, Egyptian and, most surprising, super paintings by Picasso, Miro, Roualt, Dale, Braque, Cocteau and Motherwell.

As it turns out, Zacatecas has so many extraordinary art museums, we could have spent days browsing in them. At the Temple and Convent of Guadeloupe, about 20 minutes from our hotel, we were awe-struck by what must be one of the largest collections of colonial religious art in the Western hemisphere. This is where missionaries got their training to evangelize New Spain's "heathen territory" (now Texas, New Mexico, Arizona and California).

In halls so high horses can gallop through, paintings of saints are hung that are so colossal in size, they dwarf the viewer. One of Saint Christopher balancing a cherubim on his shoulder was so tall we only came to his toe.

Of course all this Catholic grandeur was made possible thanks to the silver and gold produced by the mines. We were told, therefore, not to leave the area without taking a cart into Zacatecas's silver mine. Amazingly enough, it seemed to be located in the heart of town, sort of like the subway on Times Square. After going to its depths we then rose to the heights atop La Bufa, a hill commanding a condor's-eye view of the city.

From La Bufa, the town stretched below us like a tossed salad of steeples, steps, swoops, domes, arches and aqueducts (and not a billboard or neon sign in sight). This must have been very much how it looked when Pancho Villa battled here during the Mexican Revolution. It is certainly a cityscape we'll never forget.

But...silos shaped like rockets ready to take off? A hotel rising out of a bullring? A palace of colossal-size saints? Corridors lined with thousands of bizarre masks? A silver mine in a city?

Surely this was a dream.

Or...did we *really* go to Zacatecas?

ROYAL TOUR OF SWEDEN

When we scouted Stockholm, we looked for the stores where Garbo bought her big-sized shoes; for the opera house where young Ingrid Bergman made her stage debut; and the studios where Ingmar Bergman made FANNY & ALEXANDER.

Our friend Annika, the Swedish Tourist Board's vivacious travel consultant, thought our movie buff's tour a delightful idea, adding as a fillip: "And if you go to Uppsala where FANNY & ALEXANDER was set, why not time your visit with our King and Queen's? They will be there to celebrate that university city's 700th birthday, so you'll see all sorts of costumes and festivities. Besides, you'll begin your trip where our country began, ancestral home of those Swedish settlers from your part of Pennsylvania. They landed in Chester, you know."

Uppsala, indeed was a find. Vikings and pagan kings romped here 1500 years ago. At Old Uppsala, wild festivals every seven years featured bloody sacrifices to pacify Thor, god of war; Frey, god of peace; and Odin, god of wisdom, poetry and agriculture. Odin prevailed, and Uppsala became Scandia's seat of learning and Christianity. An archbishop was ordained here in 1164; a cathedral consecrated in 1435. Talk about OLD towns! Uppsala Cathedral, by the way, is the biggest church in all the Nordic countries, and

Uppsala University is 500 years old. Sweden's present King, Carl XVI studied here, so students turned out in droves to welcome him back to his old, very old, alma mater.

King Carl and his lovely Queen Silvia arrived by boat and were greeted by students bizarrely dressed as Visigoths—horned helmets, furs, shields and all.

Carl and Silvia are dearly beloved, and their marriage seems right out of a movie starring Audrey Hepburn and Gregory Peck. She was born in Heidelberg, Germany, and they met when she was assistant head of protocol at the 1976 Winter Olympic Games at Innsbruck. Twenty-nine and beautiful, she had graduated from the Munich School of Interpreting with a diploma in Spanish. She spoke fluent Portuguese, English, Spanish, German and Swedish, hence was assigned as interpreter to the young bachelor King Carl while he was on tap for the Olympics.

Carl, who might be played on the screen by a devilish aristocratic David Niven-type that doted on skiing and car racing, had ascended the throne at age 27. He succeeded his grandfather, Gustave Adolf VI, four days after the 90-year-old king died. Until then, Carl had roamed the world as sort of a student-prince-in-training. Athletic, boyishly handsome, he was quite a catch for a commoner.

They were married at his 608-room Stockholm Palace. Now, they are living happily-ever-after at the charming, smaller, Drottningholm Palace on the shores of Lake Malaren with their two pretty princesses and little prince.

The King's press secretary Elisabeth Tarras-Wahlberg, who had attended Mount Holyoke College in the United States, arranged for us to visit their palaces, and also accompany them on their rounds during the Uppsala celebration. As we were having tea with the royals in the shadow of Uppsala Castle, we gazed at the tower where Queen Christina solemnly abdicated in 1654. How well we remembered

Garbo's last closeup in QUEEN CHRISTINA, looking sto-
ically ahead like the figurehead of a Viking ship. She had just
given up her lover, Ramon Navarro, and her throne to
become a nun. Now, here we were with another Swedish
queen, and we have a teacup memento to prove it.

Since many of the citizenry were attired in period costumes, some driving wagons pulled by Percheron horses, it
was like FANNY & ALEXANDER re-visited. So, on the very
first day of our film-freak fling in Sweden, we had visited the
locales of two favorite Swedish-based movies...then we were
off to Garbo's hometown, Stockholm.

Before leaving from home, friends who knew Stockholm
made suggestions on where we should dine.

"You mustn't miss having dinner at Operakallaren, the
grand restaurant of Sweden," Pete Kriendler of "21" insisted.

"Café Opera is where swinging Swedes swing night and
day," restaurateur and writer George Lang revealed.

Dick Welge, the dining-guide-map king, liked both Bistro
Ruby and Gourmatique, in Old City, and "that restaurant run
by a mad Englishman, Min Lilla Tradgard, which means 'My
Little Garden.'"

Our Stockholm friend, designer Bjorn Peterrson, suggested K-B, a cozy restaurant popular with artists and writers.

All warned: "Bring money! Stockholm makes Paris seem
like a thrift tour."

Since we prefer intimate inns in prime locations, like
Mayfair Regent and The Mark in New York, we stayed at
Hotel Diplomat, right on the harbor, only a block away from
where Greta Garbo, Signe Hasso, Mai Zetterling, Viveca
Lindfors and dear Ingrid Bergman trained at the Royal
Dramatic School. Other than the Palace, the Royal Dramatic
Theater had the most impressive facade of any building at
the top of a block-long stoop of steps. Two giant gilded stat-
ues, male and female figures representing the Muses, stood

on either side of the entrance. On the stage inside, Liv Ullmann was starring in a play by Strindberg, Sweden's leading playwright.

Before touring the town, however, we headed for Stockholm's Film Institute, studios that produced Ingmar Bergman movies and such award-winners as MY LIFE AS A DOG. The only stars we recognized here were in the cafe commissary named "Laurel and Hardy." Cartoons of Stan and Ollie dominated the decor.

Our two most memorable stops in Stockholm were visits to The Royal Palace, where receptions for Nobel Prize winners are held, and Skansen, a short ferry-ride away. Here it is great fun to see the Swedes on family outings, visiting a zoo featuring animals of the north country: reindeer, white fox and polar bear. Folk museums feature actual ancient Swedish farmhouses and, also, live folk dancers in period costumes.

Highlight of Skansen, however, is Vasa Museum, where the mighty Viking warship is dramatically exhibited. Oldest battleship in the world, it is an important archeological treasure in Scandian history. Kirk Douglass and his cast from THE VIKINGS would love it.

One of Stockholm's special surprises was its City Hall. When we were told not to miss a tour of the City Hall, we couldn't imagine why that could be interesting. We tried it anyway, and it was sensational...great murals and artifacts summing up the history of the city. Now, we recommend it as a first stop on touring the city of Stockholm.

When we returned to these shores from our film-freak fling in Garboland, we quizzed our traveling partner: "What did you like the most?"

"Oh," came a quick reply, "Scandinavian Airways serving their rolls *hot*... and those divine chocolates that came with *breakfast* on the plane."

312

LAND OF GOOD HOPE

They were all there. Castro. Arafat. Prince Philip, Duke of Edinburgh. Al. Tipper. Hillary Rodham Clinton, too. Jubilation time!

Nelson Mandela had been sworn in as president of a new, free South Africa.

It was as if an ominous dark cloud had quietly lifted with a bright, smiling African sun emerging over all the land.

Suddenly the Cape of Good Hope was truly a land of hope. Of promise. Opportunity at last for black and colored. A fresh clean start of togetherness with whites, aiming to make South Africa an example of a successfully-created new kind of nation for our forthcoming 21st century.

We had not experienced such an exuberant mood all over since V-J Day. We just happened to be there, in swank, ultra-modern Sandton Sun Hotel outside Johannesburg soon after Mandela's swearing-in ceremonies at Pretoria, nearby. We were on our first stop, beginning a safari into Namibia's Kalahari Desert, then on to Victoria Falls, and Chobe Lodge, where we were to cruise among the crocodiles and hippos in Botswana. Being right on the spot at the very birth of a new nation had not been on the itinerary when we planned this jaunt six months previously. Then we didn't dream that we would be staying on the very floor with the President of China and his delegation, all scurrying around looking like recent graduates of Wharton of Harvard Business Schools, attired in their conservative black Brooks Brotherish business suits. Twice we shared an elevator with chairmen of Chinese banks and a handsomely groomed Chinese lady, Givenchy-chic.

We were especially interested in what the local press carried about our American representatives, among 182 official delegations present for the ceremonies. Quote: "Diplomats grumbled about the U.S. delegation's absurdly long motorcade. It had apparently held up the departure of other delegations after the breakfast in the Presidency, and more guests than expected had arrived," reported Johannesburg's May 15 SUNDAY TIMES. "They also arrived in the wrong order as distinguished guests were still jamming themselves into every available space while President Mandela mounted the steps of the podium to take office."

At receptions in our hotel, people joked about Washington's "condescending attitude." One columnist commented, "In contrast to the armor-plated, jaw-jutting limousine-laden security which accompanied the American contingent to the inauguration of President Mandela, Britain's Prince Philip arrived in town rather more modestly, by scheduled South African Airlines flight from Cape Town, accompanied by just one detective."

Two weeks later, we were on an SAA scheduled flight to Cape Town, and were there at the opening of South Africa's first democratically-elected Parliament. As outriders led Mandela's motorcade through the entrance of the National Assembly near our hotel; cheers of joy and songs of praise rang through the streets of Cape Town. Overhead, six Air Force Impalas conducted a flypast trailing smoke depicting the six colors of the new, transitional flag. Inside Parliament, most of the 400 MPs and 90 Senators repeatedly applauded President Mandela during his hour-long speech exhorting citizens of the new South Africa: "Let us all get down to work." He received a thunderous standing ovation.

All during that week, we had a special treat breakfasting with members of delegations staying at our elegantly appointed Mount Nelson Hotel. French officials were there preparing for the arrival of President Mitterrand. Dignified diplomats, tribal chiefs resplendent in brilliant colored African dress, casually-attired media moguls made a fascinating parade to and from the Oasis Room's bountiful breakfast buffet. Certainly one of the happiest there was the hotel's general manager, Nick Seewer. Once again, the Mount Nelson would be welcoming elegant travelers from all over the world. Considered South Africa's greatest hotel, the Mount Nelson's extraordinary charm and vivacity has made it an international destination in the grand tradition since it opened in 1899. Among its guests: Winston Churchill, Agatha Christie, Cecil Rhodes, H.G. Wells, Arthur Conan Doyle, Lord Kitchener and Rudyard Kipling. We noticed that recent visitors signing a guest book were Monty Python's John Cleese and South Africa's distinguished writer/explorer Sir Laurens van der Post.

As a city hotel, the Mount Nelson's charm, like Cape Town itself, is utterly individual. The hotel has somehow retained the atmosphere of a country retreat...gracious, classically stylish, standing in gardens as beautiful as they were a century ago. When it first opened, tourists arrived by luxury steamship, in the Union and Castle lines, to spend the northern winter in the milder climes of the southern tip of Africa. With its gold fields and diamond mines, South Africa was an Eldorado of opportunity and Cape Town the gateway to this promised land. Considered, with Rio de Janeiro, as one of the seven natural wonders of the world cities, Cape Town offers views and scenery beyond imagination...and still unspoiled. Sir Francis Drake described it as "the fairest cape in the whole circumference of the earth," and we certainly found it so.

From the top of its massive flat-topped bare granite Table Mountain, "on a clear day you can see forever." Below wide stretches of white beach curve along the lapping surf of two oceans, the Atlantic and Indian, all within the space of a few miles. Driving across its steep granite ridges towards the Cape of Good Hope, where the Atlantic and Indian oceans meet, we thought "It's Italy's Amalfi Drive, California's Big Sur, the Riviera's Corniche, Antibe's beach glamour all with the added plus of extraordinary flora and fauna." Everywhere, a surprise...baboons running across the road with their babies on their backs...a cove of tuxedoed penguins waddling across the sand...delightful rest stops with quality food and crafts to buy. We were particularly charmed by Cape Dutch and Victorian architecture all through Cape Town and its surrounding wine estates at Constantia and Stellenboesch. In fact, it is the wine estates, with their recently-converted restaurants and inns that will be drawing well-to-do sophisticated travelers to the new South Africa, and soon. Having a splendid luncheon at one of them, Boschendal was once owned by the de Villiers family, French Huguenot wine growers who fled from France to escape religious persecution around 1715. Their impressive Boschendal Manor House, with its handsome Cape antiques and paintings, is now a national monument, lovingly restored to its former splendor by the Rhodes Heritage Trust.

Cecil Rhodes purchased the Boschendal property in 1896 and established a deciduous fruit-growing industry, still known as Rhodes Fruit Farms. After imperialist Rhodes died in 1902 Boschendal was controlled by De Beers. Today, De Beers and the Anglo-American Corporation have made it into a favorite destination for lunching as well as testing and purchasing wines in a majestic setting.

Seeing how delighted we were with Boschendal, it was suggested that we stay over and visit another Anglo-American treasure, the 7413-acre winery, gardens and fruit plantation, Vergelegen, situated at the foot of Hottentot's Holland Mountains in Somerset West. Vergelegen has been a gardener's paradise since the 1700s, and is considered South Africa's most stunning showplace. Few visitors who come to this estate fail to marvel at five magnificent camphor trees planted by the owner in 1700. They now grace the front of Vergelegen's splendidly-restored homestead.

Such restorations, re-conversions and refurbishing seem to be going on all across the Cape. One of the most popular new additions in Cape Town is The Waterfront, an exciting complex of shops, inns, cafes reminiscent of Baltimore's Inner Harbor. It's where the action is for all ages and all colors, night and day.

Of course, all is not magnificent plantations, gardens, playgrounds and luxurious resorts in South Africa. One can visit shack-towns and ghettos aplenty. Yet, somehow, we feel all that will change in the new South Africa, where there is high hope in the land of Good Hope.

HUGH BEST, native of Rome, Georgia, attended Darlington School For Boys; Washington & Lee; University of Georgia; Columbia. He has served on the staffs of HOUSE BEAUTI-FUL; HOLIDAY; N.W. AYER ADVERTISING AGENCY, and in every capacity as a writer in "the pen trade," including Publicity, Public Relations, TV, Radio, Stage, Novels, Short Story, Direct Mail, Speeches, Song Lyrics, Advertising Copy, Commercials, History, Billboards, Art, Sales Presentations, Newspaper Features and Travel Articles.

He is author of the Bicentennial best-seller RED HOT & BLUE: AN X-RATED HISTORY OF THE AMERICAN REV-OLUTION; SPIRIT OF A CENTURY; WONDERFUL WED-DINGS (AND SOME NOT-SO); DEBRETT'S TEXAS PEER-AGE; and THUNDERBIRD COUNTRY CLUB.

Hugh and his wife Barbara have spent their entire married life as residents of Philadelphia's Main Line.